Plea Bargaining:
Critical Issues and Common Practices

William F. McDonald

Associate Professor of Sociology
Deputy Director of the Institute of
Criminal Law and Procedure,
Georgetown University

WITHDRAWN

July 1985

GALLAUDET COLLEGE LIBRARY
WASHINGTON, D. C.

U.S. Department of Justice
National Institute of Justice

For sale by the Superintendent of Documents, U.S. Government Printing Office
Washington, D.C. 20402

National Institute of Justice
James K. Stewart
Director

This project was supported by Contract Number 1-0260-J-OJARS, awarded to Institute of Criminal Law and Procedure, Georgetown University by the National Institute of Justice, U. S. Department of Justice, under the Omnibus Crime Control and Safe Streets Act of 1968, as amended. Points of view or opinions stated in this document are those of the authors and do not necessarily represent the official position or policies of the U. S. Department of Justice.

The National Institute of Justice reserves the right to reproduce, publish, translate, or otherwise use and to authorize others to publish and use all or any part of the copyrighted material contained in this publication.

Copyright © 1982 by William F. McDonald

345.072
M32p
1985

013201

Acknowledgments

This project was supported by Contract Number 1-0260-J-OJARS and Grant Number 77-NI-990-49 awarded to the Institute of Criminal Law and Procedure, Georgetown University Law Center, by the National Institute of Justice, U.S. Department of Justice, under the Omnibus Crime Control and Safe Streets Act of 1968, as amended. Points of view or opinions stated in this document are those of the author and do not necessarily represent the official position or policies of the U.S. Department of Justice, Georgetown University, or any other person or organization involved in this study.

This reanalysis and report is based primarily on the work done in Phase II of the project on Plea Bargaining in the United States, done for the National Institute of Justice (Grant Number 77-NI-99-0049). The following people participated in one or more of the design, data gathering, and data processing components of Phase II of that project: William F. McDonald, Henry H. Rossman, Vicki Kullberg, John Baker, Howard Daudistel, Samuel Foster, Jeanne Kleyn, Janet Connolly, Marilyn Budish, J.A. Cramer, and H.S. Miller. Samuel Dash, Director of the Institute of Criminal Law and Procedure, provided guidance and general supervision of the original project and the reanalysis.

In addition, the project benefited from the advice of Richard Schwartz, Marvin Aspen, Norman Lefstein, Joan Jacoby, Abraham Blumberg, Joseph Campbell, and Robert Morgenthau. Mary Ann DeRosa provided tireless clerical support during the original project. The Georgetown University Law Center Faculty Support Services has provided high quality typing and reproduction services. Dean David McCarthy and Associate Dean John Kramer have backed the project and assured its satisfactory completion.

Also of special note is the continued support, encouragement and advice of the project monitors at the National Institute of Justice, Cheryl Martorana and Linda McKay. In addition we gratefully acknowledge the assistance of numerous prosecutors, defense attorneys, judges, other court officials, police officers, and defendants who cooperated with this project. While we appreciate the support and advice of all those who have helped make this report possible, we absolve them of any errors in it and of responsibility for its conclusions. The writing, analysis, and conclusions of this reanalysis are solely the responsibility of the author.

Abstract

This analysis of critical issues in the plea bargaining controversy is based on data obtained in six jurisdictions including structured observations of 711 in-court acceptances of guilty pleas; structured interviews with a total of over 200 judges, prosecutors, defense counsel, defendants, and police officers; a plea bargaining decision simulation and quasi-experiment administered to 138 prosecutors and 105 defense attorneys; and a statistical analysis of case file data from 3,397 robbery and burglary cases. The findings suggest that plea bargaining cannot be abolished but can be changed. The policy choices are: how much of a concession should be given to defendants; which criminal justice official should give it; and what procedures are necessary to safeguard against the institutional weaknesses of the plea bargaining system.

Eliminating or severely restricting plea bargaining among prosecutors appears to force judges to increase the size of the sentencing discount used to induce pleas—from 14 percent in a jurisdiction where prosecutors regularly make charge concessions to 138 percent and 334 percent in jurisdictions where prosecutorial bargaining is restricted or eliminated. In jurisdictions where prosecutors' offices have established explicit policies fortified with centralized managerial control over the decisionmaking of their assistants, plea bargaining is freer of some of its controversial characteristics including inaccurate charging; manipulation of charges solely for purposes of plea bargaining; obtaining convictions in cases where the evidentiary strength is weaker than it could be; and failure to make a record of the plea agreement.

The practice of plea bargaining is neither as bad as its critics fear nor as good as its reformers hope. The decisions of prosecutors and defense counsel regarding whether to plea bargain a case and on what terms is not as haphazard as it may appear. There is considerable agreement among and between the two types of attorneys as to what factors are important and how much weight to attach to them in deciding the appropriate disposition of cases. Prosecutors systematically take into account the seriousness of the criminal and the crime as well as the evidentiary strength of the case. Defense counsel consider these same factors but also look for characteristics of their clients or the case upon which to base a special appeal for an even more lenient disposition. When presented with the same hypothetical cases prosecutors and defense counsel were in remarkable agreement in their estimates of the probability of conviction in those versions of the cases where the evidentiary strength of the case was strong. But in the weaker version there were significant differences among and between them.

Also, contrary to expectations, prosecutors given the weak version of the cases were not more likely than those given the strong version to recommend it be plea bargained (rather than dismissed or taken to trial). Thus, the description of the "plastic, exploding" character of plea offers when cases are weak and the "half-a-loaf" hypothesis were not supported by the findings. Similarly, the existence and significance of other reported practices are questioned by the present study. Prosecutors do not appear to engage in elaborate frauds or substantially deceptive practices in order to bluff defendants into pleading guilty. Defense attorneys do not engage in "court busting." The "overcharging" of prosecutors does not involve unethical or unlawful conduct. The problem lies with the concept of "overcharging" itself. Existing national standards for the charging decision require inconsistent purposes of the charging decision which can be regarded as "overcharging." Much of what is referred to as "overcharging" involves cases in which there are accurate charges with supportable evidence, but as a matter of local policy these cases involve types of crimes or criminals who are regularly disposed of with less serious charges.

One major reform of plea bargaining has been to increase the judge's responsibility for assuring the fairness of the process. Before accepting guilty pleas judges are to inquire as to whether the pleas are intelligent, voluntary, and accurate. Our observations indicate that this reform has resulted in a much lengthier and more careful plea acceptance process than once occurred. Defendants entering pleas are usually informed by the judge of at least one of their constitutional rights (70 percent); of the nature of the charges (69 percent); and may be told of the maximum possible sentence (48 percent). They were usually (65 percent) asked if any threat or pressures had caused them to plead guilty. Usually (71 percent) the specific terms of any plea agreement were entered into the record; and usually a factual basis for the plea was established by asking the defendant if he committed the offense.

This increase in judicial supervision of the guilty plea process is undoubtedly a salutary development. But there is *less* here than meets the eye. Pleas that are "voluntary" under these standards are not free from pressures or inducements. Virtually all defendants still plead guilty to obtain the inducements offered by the state. In establishing the factual basis for pleas, judges do not examine the strength of the state's case. In responding to the plea acceptance inquiries of judges, defendants say what their counsel have told them to say in order to get the promised bargain. Also, despite the required judicial inquiries, pleas are rarely rejected (2 percent).

Table of Contents

Chapter One
The Plea Bargaining Controversy

Introduction

Plea bargaining has been a controversial issue in the administration of criminal justice for at least a half century and seems destined to remain a perennial source of misunderstanding, public anxiety and scholarly disagreement. This fate is not for want of research or scholarly interest in the topic. In the United States there have been three main periods of intense research on plea bargaining: the 1920's and 30's; the 1950's and 60's, and the 1970's. Each era has identified shortcomings, dangers, and abuses associated with plea bargaining, and each has had its share of critics condemning the practice. But at the same time there has also been a continuing recognition that plea bargaining can serve useful and just purposes. Thus, rather than supporting the abolition of plea bargaining, some commentators have recommended reforms designed to minimize or eliminate dangers and abuses associated with it but leave the essence of the plea bargaining system intact.

The controversy over plea bargaining is complex. It involves both matters of fact about how plea bargaining actually does or could work and matters of policy regarding whether plea bargaining should be allowed to operate and, if so, according to what set of blueprints. For instance, while there are differences of opinion as to whether plea bargaining should be allowed to exist, there are also disagreements over the related question of whether it is even possible to eliminate plea bargaining. Among people willing to accept the plea bargaining system with modifications there are disagreements over what modifications are appropriate; who should do the plea bargaining; what considerations should be given; and under what circumstances and with what procedural protections it should be done. Among researchers there are disagreements over how plea bargaining actually operates; for example, whether defendants are in fact punished for going to trial rather than pleading guilty. There is even disagreement at the most fundamental level of all, language. The very definition of key terms in the plea bargaining controversy is in dispute. Two key terms, namely "plea bargaining" itself and "overcharging," are subject to a number of different uses and interpretations.

Given the complexity of the controversy, no single study is likely to address all the issues involved or even be definitive on a sample of issues. Rather, at this stage in the development of the literature, authors must content themselves with the nonillustrious task of retracing old paths. With the help of new and sometimes more robust data, they must reexamine the terrain long since identified with the names of the trailblazers in the field. Their joy must be the muted satisfaction of confirming or challenging established truths; revising some beliefs; extending others; and occasionally adding new insights, clarifications and perspectives.

This report, "Plea Bargaining: Critical Issues and Common Practices," is such a work. It does not address or even enumerate all the issues related to plea bargaining. Rather, we have selected issues which revolve around the question of abolishing or reforming plea bargaining. This focus, of course, did not automatically specify a list of issues. Additional choices were made on the basis of both practical constraints arising from the available data and resources for this study, and the author's judgment regarding the relative importance of certain topics.

Our report is based on a secondary analysis of the data collected by the plea bargaining study of the Institute of Criminal Law and Procedure of Georgetown University, primarily upon Phase II of that study.[1] The Georgetown researchers collected qualitative and quantitative data on many aspects of plea bargaining from many perspectives. Our choice of issues was necessarily limited by theirs, and theirs was influenced by the abolitionist and reformist arguments. Without taking a position on whether plea bargaining should (or could) be abolished, the Georgetown researchers set out to determine whether the foundation for the abolishment argument was as solid as it appeared in the literature and in the mind of the general public.

Were prosecutors "giving away city hall"? Was the safety of the community routinely compromised by plea bargaining? Were these perceptions of the general public well founded or were prosecutors and other criminal justice officials more rational in their decisionmaking than it appeared? Were the reports in the literature about "court busting" by defense attorneys and "bluffing" by prosecutors accurate? Were defendants being punished more severely for going to trial than if they had pleaded guilty? Had the "no plea bargaining" experiments really worked? Was it possible to adequately reform plea bargaining short of abolishing it? Did the major reforms and experimental programs regarding plea bargaining actually change the plea bargaining systems where they had been implemented? Was plea bargaining different in significant ways in jurisdictions where it was regulated by guidelines in the prosecutor's office? Was it different in jurisdictions where there was thorough initial case screening? Was it different where judges had been given an extended role in supervising the taking of guilty pleas?

Plea bargaining is a complex topic involving numerous issues with threads leading off to still other issues. There is no rank order of importance among the many questions which arise, nor is there any single critical issue that, if settled, would quiet all of the anxieties about plea bargaining. Consequently any selection of issues to be addressed is necessarily arbitrary. Some issues can be addressed quickly and simply while others require lengthier analyses. Differences in the length of the analyses are irrelevant to the significance of the issue. Because of the differences in the complexity of the issues as well as the

amount and nature of the data available to examine them, it is not practical to divide this report into separate chapters for each issue. The report has been divided into six chapters as follows:

Chapter One presents a summary of the major findings; discusses the history of the controversy over plea bargaining; defines plea bargaining; and explains the methodology of the study and gives some background on the study sites.

Chapter Two focuses on several issues related to the charging process and its relationship to plea bargaining. These include early scrutiny of cases, questionable charging practices referred to as "overcharging," and the effect of increased formalization and centralized policy control within prosecutors' offices. The belief that if discretion is restricted at one stage of the process it will be compensated for in other ways is also discussed.

Chapter Three follows up the matter of charging further by focusing on the specific allegation that a common feature of plea bargaining is prosecutorial bluffing.

Chapter Four examines how the plea bargaining decisions of prosecutors and defense attorneys are reached. It analyzes what factors are influential in that decisionmaking process; whether the process differs by type of attorney; and whether it is as arbitrary as some descriptions make it appear.

Chapter Five analyzes the question of whether defendants who plead guilty are given less severe sentences than those who are convicted after trial. This sentence differential is examined both objectively and subjectively. Also, the chapter addresses the question of what happens to the differential when the prosecutor's office restricts its charge bargaining or eliminates plea bargaining altogether.

Finally, Chapter Six examines what some reformers believed would be a major solution to a critical weakness in the plea bargaining system. It analyzes the extent to which the increased degree of judicial supervision of the guilty plea process has offset the danger of false conviction.

Historical review

The crime commissions of the 1920's and 30's (e.g., Pound and Frankfurter, 1922; Missouri Association for Criminal Justice, 1926; Illinois Crime Survey, 1929; and U.S. National Commission on Law Observance and Enforcement, 1931) documented the existence and central place of plea bargaining. They established that most justice was not the product of trial by jury but rather was

[1] Phase I of that study was supported by Grant Number 75–NI–99–0129 from the National Institute of Law Enforcement and Criminal Justice (now National Institute of Justice) to the Institute of Criminal Law and Procedure, Georgetown University. The report of that part of the study is contained in Miller, McDonald, and Cramer, *Plea Bargaining in the United States,* 1978. Phase II of that study was supported by Grant Number 77–N–99–0049. While a report of this research was submitted to the National Institute of Justice in February 1980, that report was not published. A copy is on file with the Georgetown Institute of Criminal Law and Procedure.

the result of decisions to plea bargain, dismiss, or not accept cases. They found that of every one hundred arrests only 8 percent to 37 percent resulted in convictions; and of all convictions only 14 percent to 50 percent were the result of trials (U.S. National Commission on Law Observance and Enforcement, 1931). Most convictions were the result of defendants pleading guilty, and it was believed that in most of these cases there had been some consideration given to the defendant in exchange for his guilty plea. One important consideration appeared to be sentence leniency. The commissions had analyzed sentencing practices and found substantial differentials in sentences between defendants convicted at trial and those who pleaded guilty to the same offense. The pleaders got lighter sentences.[2]

It was also established that a crucial component of this new system of justice by guilty plea had developed during the nineteenth century. New York statistics (Moley, 1929:164) showed the transformation of the jury trial system into the guilty plea system. In 1839, 22 percent of the convictions for the entire State of New York were the result of guilty pleas. By 1869 this increased to 70 percent; and by 1920 it was 88 percent.

Having described the guilty plea system, however, the commissions did not recommend its elimination. They were surprised at the statistical insignificance of the jury trial as the means for dispensing American justice. They were concerned about the enormous potential for abuse of power, and about inefficiencies, political influence, and the competence of prosecutors. In this regard they were as concerned about the numerous cases that were rejected or dismissed as they were about the guilty plea cases. They wanted greater accountability in the system and recommended that reasons be given as to why these various discretionary decisions were made in individual cases.[3]

In keeping with their systemwide approach to the understanding of the administration of justice, they recognized the connection between the initial screening (charging) process and the pattern of case dispositions (including dismissals, pleas and trials). They realized that the volume of cases being referred to the urban courts had far exceeded the courts' capacities and that dismissals and guilty pleas were ways of disposing of the excess caseloads. Rather than recommend the elimination of the guilty plea system, they recommended that the initial screening process be improved. Prosecutors should review cases shortly after arrest and only accept those cases where evidentiary strength was much more than the minimal legal standard necessary for arrest, namely, probable cause.

The guilty plea system was criticized by some of these early writers, as Alschuler (1979) has shown. The Illinois Crime Survey (1929:318) argued that plea negotiation "gives notice to the criminal population of Chicago that the criminal law and the instrumentalities for its enforcement do not really mean business. This, it would seem, is a pretty direct encouragement to crime." Dean Justin Miller (1927:72) wrote:

> "There can be no doubt that [our low visibility system of administering criminal justice] is dangerous, both to the rights of individuals and to orderly, stable government . . . . The necessity for making a good record . . . may well result in prosecutors overlooking the rights, privileges and immunities of the poor, ignorant fellow who . . . is induced to confess crime and plead guilty through the hope of reward or fear of extreme punishment."

But on the other hand, while it was being pointed out that many cases were "compromised" through laziness, politics, or ignorance, it was also noted that there are a number of "valid" reasons for the prosecutor to "compromise" certain cases. Dean Miller himself (1927), as well as Professors Jerome Hall (1935) and Newman Baker (1933), contributed to the list of justifications for plea bargaining. These include the following:

(a) the inadequacy of the prosecutor's office's resources to handle caseloads;

(b) the public burden of jury and witness duties;

(c) overloaded court dockets;

(d) weakness in the state's case which could result in acquittal (hence, a "half-a-loaf is better than none at all");

(e) mitigating circumstances present in certain cases but unrecognized in the statutes.

The second era of empirical interest in plea bargaining occurred in the 1950's and 60's. During this period a split emerged between reformers and abolitionists. Some writers described the plea bargaining system and its relative merits but withheld judging it. Other writers made similar assessments but concluded that the system was useful and necessary although in need of reform. Still others concentrated on the weaknesses and supported abolition.

---

[2] For details of these analyses see Chapter 5, Differential Sentencing, *infra.*

[3] The importance attached to this solution to the problem of discretion can be seen in a study done by Weintraub and Tough (1941). One of their main findings was that reasons for discretionary decisions were not being recorded in the case files.

In his classic study, Donald Newman (1966) described in detail the operation of the guilty plea systems in three states. His analysis is relatively detached and impartial. He describes the process; points out its advantages and disadvantages; identifies certain weaknesses; and notes that even with these remedied there would still remain the fundamental question of "whether bargaining for guilty pleas is a proper form of criminal justice administration" (1966:236). He does not offer an opinion on this question. But others did.

Writing for President Johnson's Crime Commission (President's Commission on Law Enforcement and Administration of Justice, 1967b:117) Enker described plea bargaining as serving many useful ends. He also enumerated some of the costs of the system, but on balance he felt the benefits outweigh the costs. He and the Johnson Commission did not recommend abolition but reform.

> . . . I have suggested that plea bargaining serves several useful ends: It eases the administrative burden of crowded court dockets; it preserves the meaningfulness of the trial process for those cases in which there is a real basis for disputes; it furnishes defendants a vehicle to mitigate the system's harshness, whether the harshness stems from callous infliction of excessive punishment or from the occasional inequities inherent in a system of law based upon general rules; and it affords the defense participation in and control over an unreviewable process that often gives the appearance of fiat and arbitrariness. These are not insignificant accomplishments.
>
> But we have also seen that the system pays a price for these accomplishments. It bears a risk, the extent of which is unknown, that innocent defendants may plead guilty; negotiation becomes directed to the issue of how many years a plea is worth rather than to any meaningful sentencing goals; factual information relating to the individual characteristics and needs of the particular defendant are often never developed; and a sense of purposelessness and lack of control pervades the entire process. This is a high price.

Enker (1967:119) sees the problems with the plea bargaining system as not inherent in or limited to the negotiation system itself. Rather they are the result of problems in the context in which it arises, namely, the broader sentencing process.

> The absence of "legal standards to govern the exercise of individualized correction," both procedural and substantive, the subjectivism and unreviewability of most sentencing decisions, and the failure to articulate goals beyond the most general and unhelpful are not only attributes of plea bargaining but

are endemic to the entire peno-correctional process. It is precisely because of this ambiguity in the total process that it lends itself to the kind of manipulation described above.

> The ultimate answers to the problems [of plea bargaining] cannot come from mere tinkering with the process of negotiation but must be sought in improvement of the total process.

Similarly the Johnson Commission (1967a:135) issued a separate list of useful functions and potential abuses of the plea negotiation system and also concluded that overall the system should be maintained although reformed.

> Plea negotiations can be conducted fairly and openly, can be consistent with sound law enforcement policy, and can bring a worthwhile flexibility to the disposition of offenders. [But in many jurisdictions] it is desirable for judges and prosecutors to reexamine existing practices.
>
> Negotiations should be more careful and thorough, broader, and preferably held early in the proceedings.
>
> [Plea discussions should be between prosecutors and defense counsel and] should thoroughly assess the facts underlying the prosecutor's case, consider information on the offender's background and correctional needs, and explore all available correctional alternatives as well as review the charge to which the plea will be entered.
>
> [The negotiated plea agreement] should be openly acknowledged and fully presented to the judge for review before the plea is entered.
>
> The judge's function is to insure the appropriateness of the correctional disposition reached by the parties and to guard against any tendency of the prosecutor to overcharge or to be excessively lenient.
>
> The judge should satisfy himself and insure that the record indicates that there is a factual basis for the plea, that the defendant understands the charge and the consequences of his plea, and where there has been an agreement on sentence that the agreed disposition appears within the reasonable range of sentencing appropriateness.

Echoing an idea that had been advanced in the 1920's the Commission (1967a:133) also noted that the problem of overcrowded court dockets could be partially relieved by improved early screening procedures by prosecutors.

In the year following the Johnson Crime Commission's endorsement of the plea negotiation system, Professor Alschuler (1968:52) published his influential study of plea bargaining. His "admittedly unorthodox position

[was] that plea bargaining should be abolished." The justification for his position was to be a comprehensive analysis of the guilty plea system and its alternatives. He cautioned readers that his justification was so lengthy that only a portion of it was contained in his initial 62-page law review article. Thus there is some risk of oversimplifying his objections in any attempt to summarize them. Nevertheless, some sense of his argument needs to be given.

He presents a list of the "horrors of the guilty-plea system" (1968:64). Included among them are the practices of bluffing and overcharging by prosecutors as well as their willingness to magnify pressures to plead guilty if an acquittal appears likely. Also, there is the danger of false conviction against which the safeguards of the plea negotiation system are in his view inadequate. The primary source of weakness is the fact that the strength of the state's case significantly affects the plea bargaining decision. When cases are weak the main protection against false conviction is the personal opinion of the prosecutor that the defendant committed the crime. But he notes (1968:59) that in such circumstances prosecutors "seem to exhibit a remarkable disregard for the danger of false conviction." As for the flexibility of the system which Enker and others regarded as beneficial, Alschuler (1968:71) writes:

> The flexibility of today's guilty-plea system would be duplicated if our society abandoned traditional legal restrictions and gave its judges the powers of Solomon . . . [A] lawless system of courtroom justice would have most of the advantages that Professor Enker perceives in the guilty-plea system and fewer of its faults."

In the 1970's the split between the reformers and the abolitionists continued with the latter gaining momentum. The National Advisory Commission on Criminal Justice Standards and Goals (1973) recommended that plea bargaining be abolished no later than 1978. Several jurisdictions announced "no plea bargaining" policies were being inaugurated. But at the same time reforms were being introduced either by prosecutorial policy, new case law requirements, or experiments supported by the National Institute of Justice. Also during this period there was a burst of additional studies of plea bargaining. Some evaluated the new experimental policies. Others probed more deeply into the actual operation of plea bargaining. In June 1978 a Special National Workshop on plea bargaining was convened at French Lick, Indiana, by the National Institute of Justice.[4] Scholars and

practitioners assembled to assess the state of the knowledge about plea bargaining. They found that despite a half century of research and commentary, the controversy over plea bargaining persisted. The split between the reformers and the abolitionists continued, but it was evident that academics had become more sympathetic to plea bargaining than had been the case.

In introducing the papers from the French Lick conference, Feeley (1978:204) notes that none of them provides definite answers. They probe the questions more deeply. In this controversial topic, there are no definitive answers. Rather there has been a slow accumulation of evidence about how the system operates and how it responds to new policies. The present study does not purport to be definitive but rather only to contribute new insights into our understanding of plea bargaining.

Plea bargaining defined

Two of the more controversial aspects of plea bargaining are its name and its definition. At one time the practice of negotiating for guilty pleas was referred to as "compromising" or "settling" cases. When we began, it was called "plea bargaining." Today the fashion is to refer to it as "plea negotiation." Some practitioners, especially prosecutors, prefer not to use this rubric because it sounds bad and is misleading. The public gets morally outraged at the thought of "bargaining" with criminals, and negotiated agreements are not necessarily "bargains." We shall use the phrases "plea bargaining" or "plea negotiation" interchangeably.

Of course it is not the name but the essence of the practice that is important. Discussions about plea negotiations with some American practitioners and with foreign justice officials often require one to avoid the use of labels like "plea bargaining" altogether and instead talk in terms of the essence of the practice. Otherwise, one may be led to believe that no "plea bargaining" by any name occurs in the jurisdictions at issue. Some officials maintain that the law in action is identical to the law on the books.

In our search for an adequate definition of plea bargaining we began with Newman's (1966:60). He wrote:

> The negotiated plea implies a preconviction bargain between state and accused whereby the defendant trades a plea of guilty for a reduction in charge, a promise of sentencing leniency, or some other concession from full, maximum implementation of the conviction and sentencing authority of the court. However, it should be noted that in any waiver of trial even without overt negotiation there may be an implicit bargain in the form of a reasonable expecta-

---

[4] The papers of this conference have been published in 13 *Law and Society Review* (1978).

tion of sentencing leniency on the part of the offender and an established practice by the court of showing differential leniency to defendants who plead guilty in contrast to those who demand trial.

We modified Newman's definition only slightly. In our view a negotiated plea occurs when a defendant enters a guilty plea with the reasonable expectation of receiving some consideration from the state. This definition has certain advantages. It is cast in general terms which allow for most—but not all—of the various ways in which plea bargaining is done to be subsumed within it. The presence or absence of plea bargaining does not depend upon whether various nonessential conditions obtain, such as differences in the nature of the consideration given; differences in which official does the negotiating; or differences in the degree of explicitness or specificity of the consideration. The usual consideration will be some form of differential sentencing (i.e., leniency in exchange for the plea), but other considerations might be given. The only limit on the nature of the consideration given is the imaginations of the people involved.

The primary disadvantage of our definition is that it is cast in terms of guilty pleas. This is overly restrictive. In some jurisdictions at home and abroad (see Goldstein and Marcus, 1977) some trials are more like guilty pleas than trials.[5] Defendants learn that if they agree not to contest the trial they will receive more lenient sentences than they might if they challenge the cases against them. These cases get counted as trials and help maintain the appearance of a trial system, but they involve the essential feature of the guilty plea system, namely, defendants are induced to minimize the state's burden in convicting them by being offered some benefit from the state in exchange.

In sum, then, the test of whether there has been a "plea bargain" is whether a defendant has reasonable grounds to believe that he or she will receive some perceived benefit from the state by pleading guilty or not contesting the case against him or her. A defendant's belief could be reasonable even if there has been no overt negotiation and even if an official "no plea bargaining" policy was in effect. If a general belief in differential sentencing (or other considerations) had existed in the recent past in that jurisdiction or in other jurisdictions with which the defendant was familiar and that belief persisted despite changes in local policy, a defendant might be justified in concluding that he or she would benefit from his or her plea (either from the local judge or from the parole board or governor). The point at

which defendant's belief becomes unreasonable cannot be easily defined. Thus our definition is somewhat open-ended in this respect, but this reflects the reality it attempts to define. Moreover, it underscores the point that it is the perception of the defendant which influences his or her decisions. Consequently, jurisdictions which have relied on guilty pleas in the past or are part of a larger system which continues to rely on them cannot suddenly claim to have eliminated plea bargaining by changing policies.

Methodology

This study is a secondary analysis of data gathered by the Georgetown Plea Bargaining Study. That original study used four methods: semi-structured interviews; structured observations; a statistical analysis of data from court case files; and a decision-simulation technique which incorporated a quasi-experimental design. Data from each of those sources have been used in this current report. All of the instruments used in the original study are available in a separate report entitled, *The Study of Plea Bargaining in Local Jurisdictions: A Self Study Manual* (Institute of Criminal Law and Procedure, 1978).

The original study had two phases. During the first phase 30 jurisdictions were visited for brief open-ended interviews with prosecutors, judges, and defense attorneys. That study developed a classification of plea bargaining systems and a clarification of basic issues in need of in-depth analysis (Miller, McDonald and Cramer, 1978). The second phase of the study conducted in-depth analyses in six jurisdictions. The sites were chosen to represent a continuum in terms of the degree of formalization of the prosecutor's office. By formalization was meant the degree to which the prosecutor's office had implemented and enforced formal written policies governing decisionmaking regarding plea bargaining (or other) decisions and/or the degree to which the executive level prosecutors reviewed and controlled the decisions of their assistants. This factor was used as a primary basis for selection because of its potential policy significance. Reformers have suggested that the control of prosecutorial decisionmaking through office policy is desirable and could bring consistency and control to the plea bargaining process (see, e.g., Katz et al., 1972).

No quantitative measure of the degree of formalization was used. Rather selections for five of the six sites were made on the basis of field visits to potential sites in which executive level and assistant prosecutors were asked about the existing office policies and the office's review and control of decisions. The sixth site, El Paso County, Texas, was selected because of its "no plea bar-

---

[5] For a description of these trials in Baltimore County, see Chapter 6 *infra*.

gaining" policy under which both the prosecutor's office and the judges refused to plea bargain. Because this policy basically eliminated the usual plea bargaining discretion and because the office had controlled its initial screening through policy, the El Paso prosecutor's office was placed at the high end of our continuum of formalization.

We believe that the rank order of jurisdictions which resulted from our assessment is accurate. If it is in error, it involves at most a reversal of the ordering of contiguous pairs of jurisdictions. The ranking in terms of decreasing degree of formalization is as follows: El Paso County,

Texas; New Orleans, Louisiana; Seattle (King County), Washington; Tucson (Pima County), Arizona; Delaware County, Pennsylvania; Norfolk (independent city), Virginia.

In addition to formalization, other factors influenced the final selection of the five sites (other than El Paso). These included: cooperation from the prosecutor's office; regional differences among sites; and jurisdictions able to produce a combination of 700 or more robbery and burglary cases that went to guilty plea or trial per year. Selected features of the six sites which were chosen are presented in Table 1.1.

Table 1.1 Selected Characteristics of the Six Study Jurisdictions—1976

	Jurisdiction					
	El Paso	New Orleans	Seattle (King Co.)	Tucson	Delaware County	Norfolk
Population	359,000	562,000	1,157,000	500,000	600,000	285,500
Square miles	1,058	305	2,131	9,240	184	52
Estimated annual Indictments/Informations filed	808	5,063	4,500	2,309	3,000	2,800
No. felony judges	2.5	10	8	7	4	3
No. prosecutors	13	63	69	39	30	15
% Conviction robbery & burglary by guilty plea	85%	81%	86%	87%	80%	78%
No. felony trials per year	229	1,069	4,567	270	491	648
Two tier court?	Yes	Yes	Yes	Yes	Yes	Yes
Type of defense counsel & estimated % of defendants covered	Assigned 80% Retained 20%	Public 65% Assigned 10% Retained 25%	Public 64% Assigned 16% Retained 20%	Public 70% Assigned 3% Retained 27%	Public 65% Retained 35%	Assigned 75% Retained 25%
Any prosecutorial restrictions on plea bargaining	Yes, plea bargaining prohibited.	Yes, limited charge bargaining.	Yes, for high impact cases.	Yes, for career criminals.	Yes, but minimal.	Yes, but minimal.

The selection of persons to be interviewed on site was designed to assure a thorough understanding of plea bargaining in that jurisdiction. The sampling was purposeful and jurisdiction-specific. Within each site interviews were conducted with a target of ten prosecutors, ten judges, ten defense attorneys, and ten defendants, and from two to five police officers. The prosecutors interviewed were selected from among the executive and line staffs and the staffs of special programs such as screening units. The judicial officers interviewed included both judges of courts of general jurisdiction and ones from the lower courts. The defense attorneys included both assigned counsel and public defenders. The defendants were all interviewed after their convictions and were usually serving time at a state facility. The police officers interviewed were patrol-level or middle command-level officers.

The structured observations focused on the taking of guilty pleas in court. The target sample size was 100 cases per jurisdiction. In each jurisdiction, a target of 20 plea-takings were to be done in the lower (misdemeanor) courts. In all jurisdictions, an attempt was made to divide the 100 observations among different judges up to a maximum of five judges. In the end, a total of 711 plea-takings were observed.

The individual case file data were obtained from court and/or prosecutors' records. The sample consists of burglary and robbery cases which were disposed of by either a guilty plea or a trial during the 18-month to 2-year period prior to June 1977. In each jurisdiction the sampling plan called for the selection of up to 750 cases. In the end, data were collected on 3,397 cases. Burglary and robbery cases were chosen because of their statistical frequency and because they pose a range of seriousness of offense and can be the subject of "overcharging."

The plea bargaining decision simulation technique is explained in Chapter 4. Briefly, it involves presenting decisionmakers with two hypothetical cases that they must dispose of by plea bargaining or other means. The methodology allows for an analysis of the information used in reaching this decision and for the impact of two variables which were manipulated, namely case strength and the prior criminal record of the defendant. These simulations were administered to 138 prosecutors and 105 defense attorneys, of which 46 percent were from the five jurisdictions studied in depth. (El Paso was excluded due to the ban on plea bargaining there.) The other respondents were obtained at national professional meetings and at jurisdictions convenient to the District of Columbia.

Chapter Two
Charge Bargaining and the Case Screening Process

Introduction

Plea negotiations involving charge reductions or dismissals have been the focal point of much of the criticism of plea bargaining and the target of "no plea bargaining" policies instituted by prosecutors in Alaska (Rubinstein and White, 1980); New Orleans, La.; El Paso, Tex.; Blackhawk County, Iowa (Iowa Law Review, 1975); Maricopa County (Phoenix), Ariz. (Berger, 1976); Oakland County, Mich. (Church, 1976); and Multnomah County (Portland), Oreg. (Parnas and Atkins, 1978). Behind the criticisms of charge bargaining lies a set of interrelated but distinct issues which often get indiscriminately lumped together as complaints about "overcharging." It is difficult to assess the meaning, much less the validity, of some of these criticisms and suggested reforms because of the ambiguities of language, the lack of unequivocal standards of proper charging, and the diversity in the ways in which the charging process is organized. Although the term "overcharging" is widely used and regularly described in pejorative language, it has no universally accepted definition. Commentators and practitioners use it in various ways and, naturally, reach problematic conclusions.

Standards for proper charging that go beyond the constitutional minimum requirements have been promulgated by national groups. But they are not unequivocal. Some assign incompatible goals to the charging process. None provides a clear methodology for determining whether their standards are being met. Most fail to identify which decision they regard as *the* charging decision. This compounds the confusion in the literature on the charging decision because there are four different decisions located at different points in the justice process that are variously referred to as *the* charging decision. It

is usually assumed or implied by the national groups that their standards should apply to the initial charging decision (defined below) which should be controlled by the prosecutor. But these assumptions overlook the substantial diversity in the organization of the charging process and ignore or underestimate the impracticalities of trying to achieve such a standard in many jurisdictions.

This chapter will sort out the issues behind the criticisms of charge bargaining and of "overcharging." It will describe the charging process and show that the criticisms of it are part of a historically evolving debate about three fundamental, interrelated policy questions: whether there should be any plea bargaining at all; what role the prosecutor should play in the criminal justice process; and how the screening of criminal cases in the post-arrest-pretrial stage of the criminal justice process should be done (by whom, at what point in the process, and according to what standards). This debate consists of differing opinions about the optimum (fairest, most efficient and effective) way to respond to the reality that the overwhelming majority of cases referred to the courts (in medium to large jurisdictions) must be disposed of without trial.

The emergence of the prosecutor

The long-term trend in the development of the urban (and suburban) criminal justice system has been for the public prosecutor to emerge as *the* official. He or she has become the official responsible for resolving the discrepancy between ever-increasing caseloads and insufficient court capacity. This trend is the logical solution to the organizational and legal fragmentation of the American criminal justice system. The partitioning of that system into subunits divided by legal, geographic and political restrictions represents (partially by design) a major obstacle to an efficient or coordinated response to the crime problem. The detection and apprehension functions of law enforcement are performed by police and sheriff agencies organized on town, city, or county bases. These agencies turn their cases over to court systems that are usually organized on a county basis but often have their operations subdivided both geographically and substantively. Many jurisdictions divide their court systems into two tiers with several "lower" tier courts scattered throughout the county. The substantive jurisdiction of these "lower" courts is usually limited to setting bail; determining probable cause for felonies; accepting guilty pleas to misdemeanors; trying misdemeanor cases; and binding felony cases over to the superior court for formal accusation and trial if probable cause exists. The superior courts are usually located at one central location and can accept guilty pleas to felonies or try them.

In contrast to the fragmentation among police agencies and within the two-tier court systems, prosecutors' offices are typically organized on a countywide basis. They usually do not have their substantive jurisdiction split between felonies and misdemeanors (U.S. Bureau of the Census, 1978). Also, in contrast to the court system where each judicial officer is an equal among equals with respect to deciding legal matters,[1] assistant prosecutors are subject to the policy preferences of the chief prosecutor. He or she can specify what standards he or she wants followed in which kinds of cases. Thus, because it is organized on a countywide basis, because it spans the work of the numerous separate police agencies most of which will never be consolidated (Skoler, 1978), because it covers the justice process from postarrest through sentencing, and because its policies are subject to the control and review of one chief executive, the prosecutor's office is structurally in the most feasible position of any justice agency to control the criminal justice process. It can bring efficiency, uniformity, and effectiveness to the justice process. The two primary levers for doing this are through the charging and the plea bargaining processes.

However, while the prosecutor's office is theoretically best suited to assume this position of chief coordinating and policymaking agency of the justice process, only a few prosecutors' offices have moved to fully implement this role, and even their moves are of comparatively recent (late 1960's) origin. The slowness of prosecutors

to assume this role can be attributed to a variety of factors.

One fundamental reason is historical. The prosecutor's office is the last of the main agencies of the justice system to develop into a major organizational force. The prosecutor's office has traditionally been a small and often part-time operation (McDonald, 1979; Jacoby, 1980a). In the last century prosecutors were used to write indictments and to try felony cases (or dismiss or plead them). The justice process was largely controlled by the police and the judiciary. Prosecutors were absent from the lower courts, often referred to as "police courts," where the police served as prosecutors. If cases were screened out of the system at all, it was done by the judicial officer at either the initial appearance or the preliminary hearing (or by prosecutors nol-prossing (dismissing) cases after they were indicted). These arrangements still exist in many jurisdictions [2] or have only recently been changed. Until the early seventies in Chicago, for instance, the police controlled the initial charging decision (to be defined) and the preliminary hearing served as the major screening mechanism in the system. In 1967 about 80 percent of the 1600 cases which the police had charged as felonies were dismissed or reduced and disposed as misdemeanors at the preliminary hearing (McIntyre, 1968).

One obstacle to the full realization of prosecutorial control of the justice process has been the unwillingness of the police to yield control of the initial charging process and of the lower courts. In Monroe County (Rochester), New York, 5,800 of the 7,000 felony cases filed by the police in 1978 were disposed of as misdemeanors or dismissed by the grand jury.[3] The chief prosecutor hopes to eventually take control of the initial charging decision, but feels he must gradually prepare the smaller, out-county police departments to accept the move. Otherwise the political resistance would be too great. In Madison County (downstate), Illinois, the chief prosecutor took his chances and unilaterally announced to the local police that either they get his office's approval before filing cases with the court, or he would not prosecute the cases. The Chicago (Cook County) prosecutor's office managed to get the police to yield control of the initial charging decision but had to agree to leave with them the power to reverse the prosecutor's decision in serious cases if the police disagreed (McDonald et al., 1981). The Philadelphia District Attorney was unable to

---

[1] As distinct from administrative matters which are typically decided by a chief judge.

[2] An official known as a "police prosecutor" still officially exists in 74 agencies in 23 states (U.S. Bureau of the Census, 1978).

[3] Source: Field notes from the Police Prosecutor Relations Study, W. F. McDonald, Project Director, Georgetown University Law Center.

persuade the police to let his office do the initial charging, so he secured a Supreme Court rule which permits any prosecutor's office to require that the police obtain its approval before filing cases with the courts.

In other jurisdictions, like Henrico County (suburban to Richmond), Virginia, the prosecutor's office has the authority to control the lower court processes, but the shortage of manpower sometimes results in police officers conducting the proceedings by themselves. In still other jurisdictions prosecutors have not taken full control of the justice process either because they have not yet seen it as their responsibility to assume that pivotal role or they would prefer not to be burdened with additional political risks which it entails.

A critical aspect of the emerging role of the American public prosecutor is his office's relationship to the charging process. This relationship must be examined from two perspectives: the way in which the charging process is organized in a jurisdiction and the standards used in making the charging decision. These two perspectives are addressed below.

The organization of the charging process

The charging decision cannot be identified with any one decision at a single point in the criminal justice process. Rather it is better conceived of as a process, a series of interrelated decisions culminating with the filing of formal charges (Miller, 1969:12). That process includes not only the decision as to which offense(s) to charge but also the degree of crime; the number of charges arising from a single criminal event; the number of counts arising from separate criminal events; and whether to charge the defendant with being a habitual offender, sexual psychopath, bail violator or other condition that makes him eligible for a more stringent sentence.

The charging decision is not wholly within the control of the prosecutor. The actual division of control varies among and within the states according to variations in legal, structural and policy differences. In about half the states (mostly eastern ones) the formal accusatory instrument (charging document) is the indictment of the grand jury (Katz et al., 1972). In the rest it is accomplished by the prosecutor's filing of an information. The prosecutor controls the decisions regarding both of these instruments.[4] The number, degree, and type of charges contained in these instruments are the best indications of the prosecutor's policy toward the use of his or her charging power. Some of the criticism of charge bargaining is directed at this formal accusatory decision. But much is directed elsewhere because it is only one part of the charging process. The *effective* charging decision is often made by the police decision to release a suspect after arrest; or by the judge's decision at the warrant application stage or at the preliminary hearing that probable cause does not exist; or the grand jury's decision to no-bill; or by the prosecutor's decision to reject cases at initial screening or dismiss or reduce charges after initial charging or after formal charging.

For misdemeanors the effective charging decision is the initial charging decision because no subsequent indictment or information will be filed. Also, for felonies that are disposed of as misdemeanors or dismissed *before* the case is referred to the grand jury (or for the drafting of the felony information) the initial charges will have served as the formal charges. In many jurisdictions much of the "felony" caseload is disposed of before reaching the formal accusatory stage. In Delaware County, Pa., for instance, 53 percent of the cases in which the initial charges were felonies or misdemeanors were disposed of by reductions to a misdemeanor or outright dismissal or withdrawal at the preliminary hearing. For these reasons it should be evident why the initial charging decision has also been a focal point of the concern about charge bargaining.

Jurisdictions differ widely in the organization of their respective charging processes and, hence, in where the effective charging decision is made and by whom. In addition to the de facto charging decisions by which a case is effectively terminated from the system, there are four decisions that are referred to as "charging" decisions. They are the ones regarding the booking charges, the initial charges, the formal charges, and something called the prosecutor's "screening" decision. The relationships among these decisions and other aspects of the overall charging process are presented in a generalized scheme in Figure 2.1.

---

[4] Grand juries are notorious for being "rubber-stamps" for the prosecutor for virtually all routine criminal matters.

Figure 2.1 Generalized scheme of the decision points in the charging process and related matters

Decision Point	Booking Charges	Initial Charges	Formal Charges	
Possible Point of Prosecutorial Review	R_1	R_2	R_3	R_4
Decisionmaker	Police	Police Court Prosecutor	Prosecutor	Prosecutor Grand Jury
Other Significant Activities at This Stage of Process	Plea Negotiations	Bail; Plea Negotiations	Preliminary Hearing; Plea Negotiations; Bail	
Time From Seizure of Defendant*	2–4 hrs.	6–72 hrs./Without unreasonable delay	3–45 days	

* General estimates

After a suspect has been seized and brought to the station, the police enter in their own records the charge(s) which they regard as the crime(s) for which the arrest was made. The booking charge(s) (sometimes referred to as "police" charge(s)) are not ordinarily part of the controversy regarding charging practices. They are, however, occasionally used by researchers as a baseline against which they judge the "accuracy" of the prosecutor's charging decision (Wildhorn et al., 1976). These charges are not without consequences. Their main effect is their impact on the bail decision at the stationhouse. Bail decisions are often mechanically determined by a schedule tailored to the police charge. The booking decision is usually made within a few hours after the seizure and is ordinarily without prosecutorial review or input.

The initial charging decision refers to the choices related to the filing of the initial complaint with the court to begin proceedings. That document will list one or more charges on it. Depending on the jurisdiction the decision to file the complaint and the selection of the charges will be made by one of four officials: the police, the judge,[5] a prosecutor's office with jurisdiction limited to misdemeanor cases and preliminary proceedings in felony cases, or a prosecutor's office with general jurisdiction.

The initial charges carry important consequences for everyone involved. The police are anxious to have the case

accepted and charged at the highest level. They want the felony arrest and clearance statistic, which in some places is linked to whether the case is accepted and initially charged as a felony. For the defendant the initial charges will again heavily influence the bail decision (if stationhouse bail was not set). If the crime is a misdemeanor, the initial charges will constitute the formal charges on which the defendant will be tried. There will be no other charging document (information or indictment) filed. If the crime is a felony and a plea bargain is struck before the formal charges are drafted, the initial charges will be the ones that are negotiated.

The initial charging decision controls the workload of the court system and affects the prosecutor's task in various ways depending upon the law and the prosecutor's policy. As critics of "overcharging" point out, having the largest number and highest degree of charges filed provides the prosecutor with leverage in plea negotiations. Charges can be dropped or reduced in exchange for pleas without giving the whole case away. But this is not the only reason why prosecutors may support the filing of maximum initial charges.

In all jurisdictions the initial charges must be filed without unreasonable delay—which can mean up to 72 hours after seizure of the defendant. Some jurisdictions have adopted time limits as stringent as 6 hours (e.g., Detroit). Obviously such short timeframes limit the amount and quality of information available to the person making the initial charging decision. It restricts the amount of post-arrest–preinitial-charge investigation as well as laboratory testing of physical evidence such as drugs or weapons, and the careful assessment of the witness' credibility

---

[5] While judges are not ordinarily thought of as charging agents, in some jurisdictions, e.g., Knox County, Tenn., initial charging is accomplished by the police filling out a description of the criminal event and the judge choosing the offense covered by the facts—although the police frequently fill in the offense for him.

and commitment to cooperate with the prosecution. If the case were to be initially charged low and later determined to be more serious, then the charges would have to be amended. While this is legally permissible (McDonald et al., 1981) it is regarded as undesirable or impractical administratively. In some places it means dismissing the case and starting over again. In other places it means taking the case out of the normal court processing and then reinserting it with new charges. This adds delay and complication to an already complex logistical task. Prosecutors' officers which are intent on disposing of cases expeditiously (e.g., within 60 days of initial filing) are loathe to add any delays to the process. Everyone recognizes that it is always more efficient to reduce or dismiss charges than add new charges to an existing charging document.

In still other jurisdictions (e.g., Maryland) the law does not permit juries to find a defendant guilty of a lesser offense included within the most serious offense charges. Thus each separate lesser offense must be charged in order to ensure that if the top offense is not proven the defendant will not go scot-free.

The formal charging decision occurs anywhere from 3 to 45 days after the defendant is seized. It has special significance for the prosecutor because of the common (but increasingly antiquated) opinion that the pattern of case attrition *after* the formal accusation is filed is almost exclusively the prosecutor's responsibility. Hence that pattern can be used as a measure of prosecutorial performance. In this view cases dropped or bargained *before* the formal accusation may represent poor police work or inadequate initial charging over which the prosecutor (in many places) has no control. Therefore those cases should not be blamed on the prosecutor.

In addition to these separate charging decision points, there is frequent reference to "the prosecutor's screening decision." This phrase gets used indiscriminantly, sometimes referring to the initial charging decisions or the formal charging decision, or to the hasty adjustments of charges at the preliminary hearing. In its most useful sense it refers to that point in the process where the prosecutor's office carefully and deliberately reviews cases, decides whether to proceed, and selects the charges. As indicated in Figure 2.1 this could occur at any one of four points in the process: prior to booking (R_1); just prior to the initial filing (R_2); shortly after (3–10 days) initial filing (R_3); or just prior to the grand jury or the drafting of the formal information considerably later in the process (up to 45 days) (R_4). Also it may not occur at all.

The prosecutor's office may not systematically review cases at any point in the process. In some jurisdictions the preliminary hearing may have come to serve as a screening mechanism. In others there may be little or no screening until the case gets to the grand jury or beyond. Whatever "screening" does occur at the preliminary hearing in such places amounts to nothing more than a hurried conference between prosecutor and police officer. The prosecutor's power to rationally select charges in such situations is severely restricted both by his lack of clear (to the police) authority to make the charging decision and the lack of time and additional sources of information (e.g., witnesses to be interviewed) with which to make optimal decisions.

The prosecutorial screening recommended by national standard setting groups is that which occurs just prior to initial charging (R_2). The National District Attorneys Association (undated:65) states:

> Screening should commence as close to the time of arrest as practical. It should be completed prior to the defendant's initial court appearance. The defendant should be presented for arraignment on the charge designated by the District Attorney immediately upon the filing of the complaint. This criminal complaint shall be filed within 48 hours of defendant's arrest.

Actually, a closer time to arrest (by a few hours) than the initial filing in court would be just prior to the booking decision, which typically occurs within 2 to 4 hours after the defendant is seized. This location of prosecutor's screening decision is rare.[6]

More commonly, prosecutorial screening programs are located either just prior to initial charging (R_2) or within a few days afterwards (R_3). The available research is in disagreement over which of these two arrangements is more frequent and even on the question of how frequently the police file their cases directly in court or take them first to the prosecutor for a review. Based on a 16.7 percent response rate to a questionnaire mailed to 3,415 prosecutors' offices, the National Center for Prosecution Management (1972) reported that in 87 percent of all American jurisdictions cases involving felony charges are reviewed by the prosecutor before they are filed in court. For misdemeanors only 67 percent of the jurisdictions involved a prosecutorial review.[7]

---

[6] It was tried by the Philadelphia District Attorney's Office. Beginning in August 1971, that office operated a 7-day week, 24-hour program of screening wherein 15 prosecutors were placed in the police station to review cases before booking (Merrill et al., 1973:22). Although the program was described as a success at the time (Id.), it was subsequently discontinued when its Federal funding ended.

[7] The nature of the "review" was not defined in the questionnaire. Traffic cases were excluded.

In contrast, based on a 95 percent response rate to a telephone survey of a 10 percent sample of jurisdictions with a population over 100,000, McDonald et al. (1981:206) found that in most (51 percent) jurisdictions the police file their cases directly with the courts without a prosecutorial review. In an additional 13 percent of the jurisdictions the police either have the option of filing cases either with the prosecutor or the court, or felonies are filed one way and misdemeanors another. In only 36 percent of the jurisdictions did the police file all cases with the prosecutor's office first.

Proper charging and conflicting purposes

Much of the difficulty with defining "overcharging" arises from the fact that there is no clear consensus on what constitutes proper charging. Professor Brunk (1978) was correct in observing that "there seems to be no even theoretical standard of proper charging derivable from the penal philosophy underlying the (criminal justice) system as there is in the case of 'normal sentencing.' " [8] We lack a jurisprudence of charging. This undoubtedly is due to the comparatively recent origin and recognition of the functions that the charging decision is being forced to serve. At one time in the last century it was sufficient for the charging decision to be nothing more than a legal judgment as to the appropriate kind, number and level of charges for which there was probable cause to prosecute. Today the legal standard for charging remains the same. As long as he has probable cause the prosecutor may bring whatever charges he chooses without violating constitutional standards. The Supreme Court reiterated this standard in *Bordenkircher* v. *Hayes,* 434 U.S. 357 (1978), as follows:

> In our system, as long as the prosecutor has probable cause to believe that the accused committed an offense defined by statute, the decision whether or not to prosecute, and what charge to file or bring before a grand jury, generally rests entirely in his discretion.

However, while the legal standard has remained the same, the nature and significance of the charging decision has changed dramatically. Two separate developments account for this. The proliferation of mandatory sentencing statutes as well as habitual offender statutes (especially ones with mandatory minimum sentencing provisions) blurred the functions of prosecutor and judge (or jury). Under these laws the sentencing decision which was once wholly the prerogative of the judge (or jury), was transferred in part to the prosecutor. His charging decision could now effectively limit the judge's sentencing discretion. Thus, the charging decision assumed the character of a sentencing decision and the prosecutor was thrust into a sentencing role.[9] This legitimated and reinforced the growing sentencing role which prosecutors had been informally developing through plea bargaining. Gradually the prosecutor's role in the justice system was transformed from merely that of the attorney for the state and enforcer of the law to sentencer as well. Prosecutors came to look at their charging function from the perspective of someone who is responsible for proper sentencing.

This is illustrated in contrasting ways by the chief prosecutors of New Orleans and Alaska. Harry Connick in New Orleans has restricted charge bargaining but has also made extensive use of the habitual offender law with its mandatory minimum sentencing provisions. His office uses this law to prevent judges from giving sentences that he regards as too lenient. In contrast, Avrum Gross, the Attorney General who initiated the no-plea-bargaining policy in Alaska, expressed concern that his no-charge-bargaining policy was resulting in sentences that were inappropriately severe. The evaluation of his policy (Rubenstein and White, 1979) had indicated that his policy's main effect was to give longer sentences to cases that "deserve" to be treated leniently (the first-time offender, the marijuana user, and the assaults between relatives) while serious criminals received about the same sentences as always. Formerly, the "deserving" cases had obtained less severe sentences through charge bargaining. Gross has indicated half jokingly that if the judges did not adjust their sentences downward for these deserving cases and if there were no other way to achieve greater equity in sentencing he would favor a return to charge bargaining.[10] The concern for sentencing exemplified by Connick and Gross indicates the subtle transformation of the prosecutor's view of charging. The question of what constitutes proper charging has become commingled with the question of what constitutes proper sentencing.

The second major development which has radically altered the significance of the charging decision has been the explosion in the volume of cases entering the court systems. By the end of the last century, as the result of the inauguration of modern professional police departments; the increasing size and urbanization of the popu-

---

[8] His statement was rephrased in the edited, published version of his paper, (Brunk, 1979:547) and lost some of its precision.

[9] For two excellent analyses of the relationship between the sentencing structure and the charging decision see Ohlin and Remington (1958) and La Goy et al. (1979).

[10] Remarks at Special National Workshop on Plea Bargaining, French Lick, Indiana, June 15–17, 1978.

lation; an increased number of criminal laws; and an increasing reliance on the courts for the settling of private disputes, the urban courts could no longer afford to offer every defendant a trial. They were looking for ways to rid themselves of their growing backlogs (McDonald, 1979; and McDonald et al., 1981). Prosecutors responded to this development by nol-prossing (dismissing) many cases and plea bargaining others.[11] By the 1920's after the numerous local, state and national crime commissions had documented the extensive amount of attrition from the courts, the search for a jurisprudence of charging was launched.[12] By then it had become evident to most observers that the charging decision would have to serve a new function. The courts could no longer afford to allow every case for which probable cause existed to even enter the court systems, much less have a trial. The practice of nol-prossing weak cases after they had been charged and allowed to consume court resources was not an efficient answer. Unworthy cases had to be kept out of the court system from the start. The logical solution was to have the prosecutor control case intake at initial charging and to refuse to accept cases unless they met a standard of proof that was something higher than probable cause. The charging decision had to become a screening decision; and prosecutors had to stop passively accepting cases and start actively seeking ways of rejecting them. To the prosecutor's growing role as sentencer was added the role of guardian of court resources. In this new role they were being encouraged to act as legislators effectively decriminalizing certain (unspecified) offenses by not prosecuting them and reducing the probability of other crimes being prosecuted by raising the threshold level of case acceptability.

This view of the charging function and the prosecutor's role was not immediately endorsed by all parties. Some of the state and local crime commissions of that era supported it (see e.g., Pound and Frankfurter, 1922, and Illinois Crime Survey, 1929). But the influential Wickersham Commission (U.S. National Commission on Law Observance and Enforcement, 1931:108) declined to endorse it. Not until 40 years later was a consensus reached that the charging function should be used in this way and the prosecutor should perform the badly needed screening function. But even then the new consensus left unclear many details of how this was to be done and on certain matters the consensus broke down. National groups agreed that the standard of case acceptability should be higher than probable cause but they did

not agree on how much higher.[13] The recommended standards fall into two groups, those approximating what we shall call either a prima facie standard or an even higher convictable, winnable, or beyond-a-reasonable doubt standard. Included in the former group are the standards of the ABA (1971:§ 3.9) which recommended that a case should not be accepted unless the evidence is "reasonably supportable"; the NDAA (1977:§ 9.4), which stated that the evidence should be admissible at trial and capable of being "reasonably substantiated"; the ALI (1975:§ 350b), which recommended there be admissible evidence sufficient to support a guilty verdict"; and the CDAA (1974:7), which required that the evidence be strong enough to "warrant conviction."

This prima facie standard differs from mere probable cause in that it requires that the evidence be admissible and sufficient to support a conviction if not controverted by other evidence. It is a standard familiar to trial judges who must decide at the completion of the state's presentation of its case at trial whether the evidence that has been admitted is sufficient on its face to warrant a reasonable man to conclude that the defendant had committed the crime. Meeting this standard is what prosecutors mean when they worry about whether they can "get a case to the jury." The prima facie standard is higher than mere probable cause but not by much. It certainly does not represent a major dike against the flood of cases drowning the court systems.

In contrast, other groups have recommended a much higher standard. They require that the prosecutor not only determine whether he or she can get the case to a jury but whether he or she can get a jury to return a guilty verdict. If not, the case should not be charged. For instance the Florida Supreme Court (February 4, 1974) in its rulemaking capacity issued the following standard:

> Before filing an information, every State's Attorney should not only seek probable cause in his investigation, but also determine the possibility of proving the case beyond a reasonable doubt. If the latter cannot be accomplished no information should be filed and the defendant should be released.

The NAC (1973:§ 1.1)—the commission that recommended that plea bargaining be eliminated—advised:

---

[11] In Maine prosecutors were nol-prossing so many cases that questions were raised as to the propriety of this practice (Emery, 1913).

[12] See, e.g., Illinois Crime Survey, 1929, and Missouri Association for Criminal Justice, 1926.

[13] The groups referred to will be cited as follows: the American Bar Association (ABA), the National District Attorneys Association (NDAA); the American Law Institute (ALI); the California District Attorneys Association (CDAA); and the National Advisory Commission on Criminal Justice Standards and Goals (NAC).

An accused should be screened out of the criminal justice system if there is not a reasonable likelihood that the evidence admissible against him would be sufficient to obtain a conviction and sustain it on appeal. In screening on this basis, the prosecutor should consider the value of a conviction in reducing future offenses as well as the probability of conviction and affirmance of that conviction on appeal.

The NAC's standard is more flexible than that of the Florida Supreme Court. The NAC does not specify any particular level of probability of conviction. Rather it says the level should vary according to circumstances (e.g., be lower for more serious defendants). The differences in the charging standards among standard-setting groups is reflected in differences in the actual standards being used in the field. A recent telephone survey of a random national sample of jurisdictions with a population over 100,000 found a considerable variety in the standards used, as indicated in Table 2.1.

Table 2.1 Frequency of different charging standards used by prosecutor offices	
Charging standard	Percent of offices using standard [N = 36]
Probable cause	39%
Beyond a direct verdict	14%
50/50 chance of conviction	11%
"High probability" of conviction	14%
Beyond a reasonable doubt	19%
No set standard	3%
Source: McDonald et al., 1981:215.	

From their unanimous insistence that the charging standard be something higher than probable cause, it seems to follow that the national standard-setting groups would regard all cases accepted at the probable cause level as instances of "overcharging" or, at least, of improper charging. This means that not only are individual cases in some jurisdictions improperly charged but for many jurisdictions which continue to accept all cases on nothing more than probable cause the entire charging process is outside the pale of propriety. According to the telephone survey just cited, this amounts to 39 percent of all American jurisdictions with populations over 100,000 (McDonald et al., 1981).

Such a blanket condemnation, however, is not what is ordinarily meant by overcharging. Rather the term refers to certain practices within jurisdictions other than merely accepting cases on minimal evidence. Some of these practices which are regarded by some writers as constituting "overcharging" are specifically condemned by one or more of the national groups. But the two most common meanings of overcharging, namely, filing the most serious charge supported by the evidence or filing all the charges supported by the evidence, are not in themselves considered improper or unprofessional by the standard-setting groups (provided the evidence meets the prima facie level of strength). As we shall see later something more must be present, such as the prosecutor being motivated solely to get a guilty plea.

The relevant standards of four of the major national groups are set forth below.

The ABA (1971) states:

(a) It is unprofessional conduct for a prosecutor to institute or cause to be instituted criminal charges when he knows that the charges are not supported by probable cause.

(b) The prosecutor is not obligated to present all charges which the evidence might support. . . .

(c) The prosecutor should not bring or seek charges greater in number or degree than he can reasonably support with evidence at trial.

The ALI (1975) states:

The prosecutor shall not seek to induce a plea of guilty or *nolo contendere* by exerting such pressures as

(a) charging or threatening to charge the defendant with a crime not supported by facts believed by the prosecutor to be provable;

(b) charging or threatening to charge the defendant with a crime not ordinarily charged in the jurisdiction for the conduct allegedly engaged in by him.

The NDAA (1977) states:

The prosecutor has the responsibility to see that the charge selected adequately describes the offense or offenses committed and provides for an adequate sentence for the offense or offenses.

NDAA further states:

(a) The prosecutor shall file only those charges which he believes can reasonably be substantiated by admissible evidence at trial.

(b) The prosecutor shall not attempt to utilize the charging decision *only* as a leverage device in obtaining guilty pleas to lesser charges.

The NAC (1973) states:

No prosecutor should, in connection with plea negotiations, engage in, perform, or condone any of the following:

1. Charging or threatening to charge the defendant with offenses for which the admissible evidence available to the prosecutor is insufficient to support a guilty verdict.

2. Charging or threatening to charge the defendant with a crime not ordinarily charged in the jurisdiction for the conduct allegedly engaged in by him.

3. Threatening the defendant that if he pleads not guilty, his sentence may be more severe than that which ordinarily is imposed in the jurisdiction in similar cases on defendants who plead not guilty.

4. Failing to grant full disclosure before the disposition negotiations of all exculpatory evidence material to guilt or punishment.

As already noted, all four groups agreed that the case acceptance standard should be at the prima facie level or higher. None of them prohibit the filing of multiple charges or the highest charge for which evidence meeting the prima facie level is available. Three of the groups (ALI, NDAA, and NAC) clearly intend to prohibit certain charging practices which are linked to plea bargaining. The ALI and the NAC specifically prohibit the filing of charges that are not ordinarily filed, just to secure guilty pleas. Prohibiting this practice is of negligible significance, however, because it is not a common method of overcharging. None of the defense counsel we interviewed mentioned this in their complaints about local overcharging practices.

NDAA specifically prohibits using the charging decision *only* as leverage for plea bargaining. But this standard is ambiguous especially when taken together with NDAA's other requirement that the charge(s) selected must adequately describe the offense(s) committed and also must provide for an adequate sentence for the offense(s). Nowhere is the complexity and incompatibility of purposes surrounding the charging decision captured better than in trying to reconcile these three standards.

In order to make the charge(s) fit the crime(s) the prosecutor must file as many (if not all) of the charges and the highest degree of the offense for which he has admissible and supportable evidence. Establishing a public record of the extent of the offender's involvement in criminal activities and the extent to which the crime problem in the community has been solved by the arrest of particular individuals is one of the functions which prosecutors (and NDAA) regard as legitimate and essential. This public accounting function of the charging decision is occasionally highlighted in instances of major crimes as, for example, in a case of a major fraud in

Norfolk, Virginia, in which 360 charges against three individuals were filed but pleas were eventually accepted to only 15 misdemeanors. The prosecutor explained his reasoning in a press release reproduced below.

PRESS RELEASE

DATE: November 16, 1977
FROM: Commonwealth's Attorney, (Norfolk, Virginia)
RE: Charlie Falk

Charlie Falk, Kathryn L. Falk, Fred Hailey and Charlie Falk's Auto Wholesale, Inc. were indicted on November 1, 1976, on three hundred sixty charges arising out of a lengthy investigation. . . .

Indictments were brought against the individuals for conspiracies to obtain money by false pretense, alter certificates of title and to commit forgery. In addition individual charges of the same crimes were brought against three persons for separate instances of the crimes. The defendants could only have been convicted of the crimes, or the conspiracies, but not both. The decision to bring the 198 other charges against the Falks and the 77 against Hailey was a matter of trial strategy, should it have been necessary to try the cases. However, the Commonwealth has pursued the discussions in this case by reference to the eight charges of conspiracy pending against the three individuals.

The Commonwealth has looked to many factors in reaching a decision as to how these cases should be disposed of. Exposure of the defendants and the activities they engaged in was very important. We feel that the indictments brought and convictions obtained accomplish this goal.

The most important factor to consider was restitution; that is, what could we do to help the victims of these defendants. It must be pointed out that the victims whose cars were indicted on were arbitrarily chosen by the Police Department and Commonwealth Attorney's Office, and thus we could not realistically look to only those fifty in terms of restitution. Those whose vehicles the convictions are based on were chosen completely at random from the pending indictments. We feel that the solution we have reached is the fairest under the circumstances. Thus, we have achieved the third aim of the prosecution.

Certain evidentiary problems have arisen recently in the prosecution which made it clear that we had to adjust the original goals we had made. Evidence which was available to us at the time of indictment is now of questionable availability. In addition, the credibility or believability of this evidence have been brought into issue. Our experience indicates that the problems with this evidence are of such a serious nature that the ability of the Commonwealth to obtain convictions, particularly against the individual defendants, is questionable. Thus, the Commonwealth has agreed to accept pleas to 15 misdemeanors rather than the 8 felony conspiracy charges in the cases of Charlie Falk, Kathryn Falk and Fred Hailey, because of the evidentiary problems.

The question of incarceration of the defendants was also discussed, and the Commonwealth considered that any lengthy jail or penitentiary sentences would have hampered rather than helped our victims in their actions for restitution. Since our victims must be regarded first in this type of economic crime, we opted for the 10 day sentence for Charlie Falk.

The problems and considerations involved in an economic crime of this magnitude are great, and are quite different from those involved in a street or violent crime. Society in general is hurt by this type of crime, and we feel that the exposure and punishment of the defendants brings justice to society. The more specific victims can only be helped by making the defendants available and able to make restitution. We feel, based on our experience in prosecution, that all aims of the Commonwealth have been achieved.

In filing the multiple charges necessary to describe the criminality of defendants like the Falks, prosecutors are doing what many people would call overcharging. The prosecutors will know that many of those charges may be dismissed either in exchange for a guilty plea or simply because too many charges make a case cumbersome to try and do not affect the sentence after a certain point. NDAA, however, would not call this overcharging unless the *sole* motivation in filing the multiple charges was to plea bargain them. But, how this state of mind is to be determined in individual cases is unclear.

The other aspect of the mixed signals given by NDAA's standards is evident in contrasting the requirements that prosecutors make the charges describe the crime(s) *and* that they also provide for an adequate sentence. This emphasis on the sentencing function of the charging decision can lead in two directions, both resulting in practices that are regarded as overcharging. On the one hand it is an invitation to reduce charges in those cases where convicting a defendant of the crime he actually committed would result in a punishment which the prosecutor regards as too severe. At the same time it supports prosecutors in filing additional charges, especially ones that prevent judges from imposing sentences that the prosecutor regards as lenient. In brief, NDAA may disapprove of overcharging, but its own standards require

prosecutors to engage in charging practices that for many observers constitute overcharging. This inconsistency reflects the competing and partially irreconcilable demands that have been placed on the charging decision.

The NAC's charging standards are less inconsistent than NDAA's. This is because NAC starts from the position that plea bargaining should be eliminated and then proceeds to prohibit certain forms of charge bargaining. Particularly noteworthy is its prohibition against threatening defendants with more severe sentences if they plead not guilty. As written, this standard proscribes all such threats regardless of whether they are connected to the charging decision. For our immediate purposes the prohibition against threatening to file additional or more severe charges is most relevant. In our sample we found evidence of it only in one jurisdiction, Norfolk; and there it was done by the police.

The difference between securing pleas by threatening to add charges in contrast to offering to reduce or dismiss charges that already have been filed is subtle at best. Yet, some critics regard the former practice as especially reprehensible. The effort to have it declared unconstitutional, however, failed. In *Bordenkircher* v. *Hayes,* 434 U.S. 357 (1978), the Supreme Court declined to provide constitutional support to the NAC's prohibition against threatening to add charges as a means of securing pleas. In *Bordenkircher* the prosecutor threatened Paul Hayes during plea negotiations that if Hayes did not accept the plea agreement being offered, an indictment under the habitual offender statute would be sought. The court held that this was not an improperly motivated prosecutorial act. It was not like vindictiveness for a defendant's successfully appealing a prior case or discrimination on the basis of some arbitrary classification such as race or religion. Therefore, the Supreme Court concluded that the appellate court had erred in ruling "that a prosecutor acts vindictively and in violation of due process of law whenever his charging decision is influenced by what he hopes to gain in the course of plea bargaining negotiation." The fundamental difference between the Supreme Court and the NAC is that the Court approves of plea bargaining and the charge bargaining that is part of it. As the Court reasoned in *Bordenkircher,*

> [t]o hold that the prosecutor's desire to induce a guilty plea is an "unjustifiable" standard, which, like race or religion, may play no part in his charging decision, would contradict the very premises that underlie the concept of plea bargaining itself (Id.: 364).

But the objection to *Bordenkircher* was not necessarily synonymous with being opposed to all plea bargaining

18

or even all charge bargaining. Even after *Bordenkircher* tactics were found constitutional, many prosecutors objected to them. John Van de Kamp, District Attorney of Los Angeles, said at that time that his office would not use them. "In my office, we don't charge low and threaten high" (Farr, 1978:81). Similarly among 200 prosecutors nationwide there was a consensus that the *Bordenkircher* tactics should seldom, if ever, be used (Id.). They objected to the tactics on the grounds that the tactics "were offensive to anyone with a sense of fair play" (Id.).

Given the ambiguity and inconsistency among national standard-setting bodies regarding proper charging, it is not surprising to find a similar lack of clarity and agreement in the literature and in the field regarding the meaning of the term, overcharging. We now turn to that literature and our field studies to explore further the nature and meaning of the complaints about charge bargaining and the feasibility of reform measures.

Overcharging: a misnamed policy debate

Definitional problems. Overcharging has been referred to by different terms such as "overfiling" or "loose filing" (Carter, 1974); "bedsheeting" (Katz et al, 1972:106); and "inaccurate" charging (Wildhorn et al., 1976). But even when the same term is used it often has different meanings. One unfortunate and misleading connotation of the term is that something unlawful or clearly unethical is involved. For instance, Alschuler (1968:85) found that prosecutors "define overcharging as a crude form of blackmail—accusing a defendant of a crime of which he is clearly innocent in an effort to induce him to plead guilty to the 'proper' crime." But, he says, this is not what defense attorneys mean by the term. For them (and most people who employ the term) overcharging does not imply that the prosecutor has filed wholly fabricated charges against someone without evidence sufficient to meet the probable cause standard. Rather, as Alschuler (1968:85) puts it, defense attorneys using the term "refer to different, but *equally serious,* problems." [14]

One of those problems is "horizontal overcharging," the filing of numerous accusations against a single defendant. The problem here is not the level of proof. On the contrary,

> [w]hen defense attorneys condemn this practice, they usually do not disagree with the prosecutor's evaluation of the quantum of proof necessary to justify an accusation. Usually, they concede, there is

----
[14] Emphasis added.

ample evidence to support all of the prosecutor's charges. (Id.).

The defense attorneys' complaint about horizontal overcharging is that the number of charges filed is "unreasonable," meaning, evidently, unfair. It gives the prosecutor a tactical advantage in plea negotiations and at trial. It is "dishonest" in that the prosecutor is not really interested in securing convictions to all charges and when he dismisses some charges in exchange for a plea he is giving the defendant a bogus consideration, "the sleeves from his vest" (Ibid.:95).

The second problem is " 'vertical overcharging'—charging a single offense at a higher level than the circumstances of the case seem to warrant" (*Ibid.*:86). Again, the complaint here is not that the prosecutor charges crimes of which the defendant is clearly innocent; rather, it is that

> they set the evidentiary threshold at far too low a level in drafting their initial allegations. Usually, defense attorneys claim, prosecutors file their accusations at the highest level for which there is even the slightest possibility of conviction.

> The substance of the defense attorneys' complaint is that while prosecutors may apply standards of "substantial evidence" or "probable cause" in deciding whether to accuse the defendant at all, they do not apply that standard in determining what crimes to charge. Indeed the bare possibility that evidence may emerge to justify an allegation usually causes prosecutors to "play it safe" . . . (Id.)

Thus a prosecutor may have a policy of charging every homicide as first degree murder even if he or she initially thinks a particular defendant is guilty of only manslaughter because circumstances might emerge that could make the crime murder. This policy prevents the possibility of the defendant pleading guilty to the inappropriate lesser charge.

Alschuler's definition of vertical overcharging captures only one of the two meanings behind that phrase. He implies that prosecutors need to tighten up their case screening standards in regard to the selection of the highest charge(s). His definition approximates what Wildhorn et al. (1976:40) define as inaccurate charging. According to them a prosecutor has charged a defendant inaccurately if there is insufficient evidence to convict him of the most serious charges filed.

The second meaning of vertical overcharging is the most important of all the definitions of overcharging. Yet it has not clearly surfaced in the literature on overcharging. It refers to cases where the prosecutor has ample evidence to support the highest charge but for various reasons local attorneys feel that the highest charge is not appropriate. One common reason for this is that the fact pattern of the crime and the criminal fit into a typified pattern which local attorneys know will usually end up being treated less seriously than what legally could be done. For instance, a defense attorney from Chicago noted that "barroom-brawl" homicides will be charged as murders but usually disposed of as manslaughters. Thus, he felt that the correct charge for all barroom-brawl-type homicides should be manslaughter from the beginning.

By implication his standard of proper charging is to charge at the level at which a particular type of case is ordinarily disposed of in a jurisdiction. This position seems to imply that it be accompanied by a ban on charge bargaining. Katz et al. (1972:131) apparently have this in mind when they insist that charges should be "truly realistic" and that this policy should be joined with a ban on charge bargaining. Similarly, but in reverse order, the Alaska Attorney General's ban on charge (and sentence) bargaining was accompanied by a policy of "realistic" charging which approximates what our Chicago attorney had in mind—as we shall see later.

Not only defense counsel object to vertical overcharging. Joe Busch, the former Los Angeles District Attorney, reportedly referred to it as "legal-blackmail" (Carter, 1974:66), and prosecutors in a California jurisdiction described by Carter (1974) were split over it. Some prosecutors felt they should "file high and deal down." Their thinking was described by one of them as follows:

> Some [prosecutors] feel we should start out realistically, but my feeling is that for a defense attorney to get his guy to plead, you've gotta give him something. The defense attorney is selling a service, and if his client feels he hasn't done anything for him, then it's not being fair to him. You just file high and then deal it down a notch to what it should have been all along, and everybody's happy. We get what we want. The defendant thinks his attorney is great. The attorney gets his money . . . It's not our job just to go on the ironclad cases. (Ibid.:73).

The type of overcharging being referred to by these prosecutors appears to be vertical overcharging, where the evidence may be sufficient to file a felony, but the cases are almost invariably reduced for disposition as misdemeanors. The prosecutors who objected to this practice did so for the same reason Joe Busch did. They regard it as unfair. One of them put his views as follows:

> To me [overcharging] isn't right all the time. I do it sometimes, but why, if you know he's going to

plead to a misdemeanor, do you file the felony on him and cause him to pay more bail and make him sit longer? To me it's not fair, a lot of people say we ought to stick 'em, but that offends my conscience. And another way he can get stuck is that his attorney will charge more. (Ibid.:70)

Generally, either horizontal or vertical overcharging or both is what references in the literature to overcharging mean. For instance Bond (1981:231) writes:

> Generally "overcharging" connotes the filing of a charge more serious than the one the prosecutor believes is justified by the evidence or the one to which he expects a plea.

Utz (1979:105) says

> overcharging [is] charging more or more serious counts than those on which the prosecutor truly wants conviction.

In its analysis of felony case dispositions in New York City's court the Vera Institute of Justice (1977:137) reported the following:

> Overcharging was particularly evident in the attempted murder, handgun possession and grand larceny cases. In some cases, felony charges appeared to be levelled against defendants, guilty at most of resisting arrest or harrassment, to "cover" use of force by arresting officers. But more generally, overcharging involved levying the highest permissible charge to set the stage for negotiation of a plea to an offense that would, in the police view, be appropriate to the circumstances.

However, other writers have different definitions of overcharging. In his analysis of plea bargaining in Canada, Klein (1976) adopted a definition of charge bargaining akin to the prohibition by the ALI and the NAC against filing charges not ordinarily filed. Klein writes:

> What constitutes overcharging is related more to normative than legal considerations . . . [It is related] to the norm that is operating in a jurisdiction in respect to a charge vis-a-vis the behavioral components (as opposed to the legal components) of an act . . . If the norm in a jurisdiction is to charge an individual who forged and cashed a stolen cheque with only one offense, then to charge him with three offenses in relation to this act would be perceived as overcharging. (Id.:118).

Other foreign writers have apparently misunderstood (or decided to redefine) the common usage of the American notion of overcharging. For example, McCabe and Purves (Baldwin and McConville, 1977:112) report that unlike in America there is virtually no "overcharging" in England. Americans will note, however, that this conclusion depends entirely upon their definition of terms. They do not regard what they call "full charging" as "overcharging." But in McCabe and Purves' description of "full charging" Americans will recognize the old wine of vertical and horizontal overcharging in a new bottle. "Full charging" is defined as

> inserting every charge which could reasonably be said to arise from the situation even when it is clear that it is unlikely that every charge could be proved on the evidence available (Baldwin and McConville, 1977:112).

Perhaps McCabe, Purves, and others are under the misimpression that American prosecutors regularly file fabricated charges to secure pleas.

The existence and extent of overcharging in a jurisdiction is often inferred by Americans by the extent to which charges are reduced or dismissed after cases have been filed (see, e.g., Keppel, 1978). As a rough indicator such a procedure is of some value. But as Wildhorn et al. (1976:41) point out, many things affect the outcome of charges in a case, only one of which is the accuracy of the original charges. Thus, not too much weight can be placed on such rough measures.

One way around this problem was devised by Baldwin and McConville (1977). They had the "commital papers" relating to a sample of cases examined by two independent, experienced case assessors. The assessors were asked to predict the likely outcome of the principal count in the indictment on the basis of the evidence available in the papers. In only 25 percent of all cases was a prediction of acquittal made by at least one assessor, and in only 10 percent of the cases did the two assessors agree in their predictions. Thus, Baldwin and McConville concluded that there was no "overcharging" in the English setting. But once again, their conclusion is a function of their circumscribed definition of charging (which is in effect what Wildhorn et al. have called accurate charging). The more common version of the American notion of vertical overcharging is not what Baldwin and McConville's methodology addressed. It is not that the principal charge(s) could not be sustained if they were allowed to go to trial. It is that certain sustainable cases are regularly reduced for disposition and that, therefore, they should have been filed that way in the first place.

Overcharging and proper charging distinguished. The confusion about overcharging does not end with the multiple meanings of the phrase. It thickens as one tries to determine the relationship between overcharging and proper charging. For instance in Alschuler's discussion it seems that, while overcharging is not improper in the

sense of filing completely fabricated charges, there is still something (admittedly vague) improper about overcharging. Alschuler (1968:86) says "the line between 'proper' charging and 'overcharging' is far from clear." But he and others feel there is a line to be drawn.

The difficulty in making distinctions is compounded by discussions like that of Bond (1981:233) who refers to "legitimate overcharging." He writes that "[s]everal circumstances may justify overcharging," including avoiding being whipsawed by defense into still further concessions which the prosecutor believes are unjustified; "playing it safe" when the prosecutor does not know precisely what offense the facts will ultimately prove; and refusing to exercise discretion to achieve an equitable outcome. In support of his last example, Bond cites some rare case law (e.g., State v. Stevens, 381 P.2d 100 (Ariz. 1963)) that sustains his argument that the prosecutor need not take into account equitable considerations in his charging decision. In so doing, however, Bond leaves the mainstream of the debate about overcharging and screening. That debate has long since regarded legal requirements as too minimal to be of much help in restructuring the charging process to meet the contemporary needs of the justice system. It is no longer a matter of what the law requires but what the system needs in order to balance efficiency with fairness and effectiveness. The law may not require prosecutors to exercise an equity function at charging, but observers like Graham and Letwin (1971); Katz et al. (1972); Alschuler (1968); Miller (1969); the crime commissioners of the 1920's (e.g., Cleveland, Missouri and Illinois); and the standard-setting groups of the 1960's and 1970's agree that not only could prosecutors perform such a function but that the future quality of justice in American criminal courts depends upon their doing so and that the charging function must be performed in more than a merely legal, technically correct manner.

Unfortunately Bond does not make clear what illegitimate overcharging would be. He cites some case law in support of the view that the prosecutor may not overcharge to induce a plea (Heidman v. United States, 281 F.2d 805, 808 (8th Cir. 1960)) and Brady v. United States, 397 U.S. 742 (1970)). But the thrust of these rulings has been overturned by the Supreme Court's holding in Bordenkircher v. Hayes, 434 U.S. 357 (1978). His only clear example of illegitimate overcharging is his inclusion of the ALI's prohibition against charging crimes not ordinarily charged. It is noteworthy that he does not condemn horizontal or vertical overcharging, nor does he invoke any of the other charging standards of the major national groups.

If we now examine each of the types of overcharging identified above from the point of view of the charging standards of the four national groups, we can further illustrate the inconsistencies, ambivalence, and inchoate nature of the developing jurisprudence of charging. First, charging a defendant without probable cause for any of the charges filed would be unanimously condemned by all four groups. For that matter, charging a defendant with evidence that would sustain probable cause but would not be admissible at trial is regarded by each of the groups as improper. Charging a defendant with charges for which there is admissible cause evidence but which are not ordinarily charged in a jurisdiction is condemned by two of the groups (ALI and NAC). Horizontal overcharging in either of its two forms [15] presents an ambiguous situation. Assuming there is admissible probable cause evidence and the charges are not out of the ordinary, then horizontal overcharging becomes improper to NDAA if the charges are filed *solely* to obtain leverage in plea bargaining. However, the *failure* to horizontally overcharge *would also be improper* according to NDAA if the additional charges were needed either to adequately describe the criminality of the offender or to provide for an adequate sentence! Since a prosecutor could almost always claim these latter two motives for his or her horizontal overcharging, he or she could never be in violation of the only-for-plea-bargaining standard.

By the same logic, vertical overcharging of the kind where prosecutors have sufficient evidence for the highest charge but routinely accept pleas to reduced charges does not violate NDAA's standards. Even though he or she knows the case will be routinely reduced, the prosecutor can still claim to be establishing an accurate public record of the conduct involved. Thus his or her motive is not *solely* to secure guilty pleas.

Vertical overcharging of the other kind that Alschuler describes, that is, where there is sufficient evidence to charge some crime, but only the slightest evidence to support the highest degree of crime, is explicitly and unanimously condemned by all groups. As the ABA (1971:§ 3.9c) puts it, "[t]he prosecutor should not bring or seek charges greater in number or degree than he can reasonably support with evidence at trial."

---

[15] Namely, filing numerous charges arising from separate criminal incidents, e.g., a dozen separate forging and uttering offenses, or filing numerous charges arising from different crimes committed in the course of one criminal incident, e.g., charges of robbery, burglary, larceny, and carrying a concealed weapon arising from one armed robbery in a home.

The organizational preconditions for proper charging. In reviewing the standards of proper charging of various reform groups and other critics, it is crucial to recognize the often unstated assumptions about how the charging process must be organized, staffed, and operated. Accurate charging assumes not only a technical knowledge of the law but also experience in local practice and adequate information with which to evaluate the case. If prosecutors' offices are going to file only charges that can be proven at trial, then they must have a systematic screening of cases based on thorough investigations with cases reviewed by trial-experienced prosecutors preferably with direct access to the witnesses and police officers in the cases. Such screening programs do not exist in most jurisdictions.

Little wonder that Alschuler should find that the primary reason for overcharging (especially vertical overcharging) is the tendency among prosecutors to "play it safe." They "play it safe" because the prosecutors selecting the charges are usually inexperienced and the information upon which they are basing their decisions is often minimal and untrustworthy. It is often nothing more than the police report and the local arrest record. Police reports are universally decried by prosecutors as inadequate and unreliable. Furthermore, getting the police to do postarrest followup investigations is problematic (McDonald et al., 1981). Prosecutors know that the police often omit or distort information in their reports. Therefore, without interviewing the police and witnesses themselves, prosecutors are never very sure about how strong their cases really are.

When prosecutors' offices do establish rigorous screening programs, substantial numbers of cases are either rejected from the system or filed at reduced charges. In New Orleans when the Connick administration initiated screening, a dramatic increase in case rejections occurred.[16] In the Bronx in 1979 the police made 22,500 felony arrests; the prosecutor's office indicted only 2,500 felonies. In Chicago in 1972, the new felony review unit of the prosecutors' office declined to seek indictments in 41 percent of the murder cases brought by the police as well as 95 percent of the armed robberies, 87 percent of the rapes, and 97 percent of the aggravated batteries (McIntyre and Nimmer, 1973:20). In Philadelphia in 1973 an experimental early prosecutorial screening unit found that 41 percent of the 20,000 arrests could be quickly eliminated from the system (Savitz, 1975:262). In 1967 in Los Angeles, the prosecutor's screening process

---

[16] See *infra* for details.

reduced 64,000 felony arrests to only 24,505 felony prosecutions (Katz et al., 1972:112).

In their criticism of overcharging Katz et al. do not stop with identifying the symptom. They identify the cause. They want "realistic" charging and the elimination of charge bargaining, but they note that this requires a major commitment of resources to the early screening process. Their views are interesting not only for the organizational preconditions for proper charging that are recommended but also because their focus of reform is only the formal charging (not the initial charging) of felony cases and, most importantly, because they predict that realistic charging *will eliminate* charge bargaining but *will not eliminate* the incentive for defendants to plead guilty.

Katz et al. would have the police do the initial charging and then within one day of arrest (for defendants held in custody, 5 days for those released on bail) the prosecutor would review his case and meet with the defense attorney for a charging conference. The result of this would be the revision of unrealistic felony police charges (which would be dismissed, diverted, or reduced to misdemeanors and rerouted) and the filing of realistic formal felony charges. Once filed, the felony charges would not be reduced for guilty pleas. Katz et al. assert that contrary to what critics of their proposal predict, realistic charging coupled with a no-charge-bargaining policy would *not* mean that defendants would stop pleading guilty. Their support for this claim, however, seems to be a combination of faith and the problematic assumption that the new rigorous screening would so dramatically reduce the court's caseload that the prosecutor would be able (and willing) to get a conviction at trial in cases where the defendant did not plead guilty. They (1972:132) write:

> Once the prosecutor shows at the inception of this reform that his office is prepared to try cases within the speedy trial requirement, guilty pleas will flow as they do now because the charges will be realistic. Defendants will be as ready to plead then as they ultimately are now, once the opportunity to wait out the prosecutor no longer exists and the prosecutor makes it clear that he is trying cases and convicting defendants.

Other reformers have also suggested a restructuring of the charging process to achieve realistic charging and eliminate charge bargaining. But they also hold problematic views about the relationship between their reforms and the overall practice of plea bargaining. For instance in an article entitled "Abolishing Plea Bargaining: A Proposal," Professors Parnas and Atkins (1978) recommend that *judges* should prevent overcharging through their power to review charges.[17] The deceptive nature of this proposal is that it identifies plea bargaining with charge bargaining. For Parnas and Atkins the elimination of overcharging is synonymous with the elimination of plea bargaining. Having closed the front door, however, they then proceed to open the back. In contrast to Katz et al. they say that once charge bargaining has been ended it will be necessary to provide defendants with some alternative incentive to get them to plead. This, they argue, should be in the form of differential sentencing with pleaders getting a more lenient sentence than those convicted at trial. In their view (but not ours) this is not plea bargaining.

The critical objection to proposals to charge at the level to which a case is ordinarily pleaded is that it leaves the prosecutor nothing to offer in exchange for a guilty plea. While reformers confidently predict that if charges were truly realistic defendants would willingly plead guilty for nothing in exchange, practitioners are rightly skeptical of such predictions. The belief that the state should not unilaterally dismiss or reduce charges without getting something in exchange, like the related belief that guilty pleas would be less forthcoming without such exchanges, is widespread and axiomatic among practitioners. Even the police are staunch advocates of these views. For instance, Alaskan police objected strongly to the no-plea-bargaining policy because it ran contrary to these views. The Alaska Judicial Council (1977:54) reported,

> Police investigators often objected strongly to dismissal of charges by prosecutors. Investigators working with bad check cases cited several examples of cases in which charges had been dismissed, giving the reasons they believed had caused the dismissals. "If a guy pays up on a check case, charges are dropped." "We had a recent forgery case involving numerous checks. The D.A. and defense attorney got together, the defendant pleaded to two charges and the others were dropped." "In the old system [plea bargaining], they pleaded guilty to three out of five charges, without talking to defense counsel." "If there aren't enough judges to go around at calendar call or the D.A.'s are busy, they only take more serious cases and dismiss the others." "If they eliminated plea bargaining entirely, it would be O.K. But if we've got four counts, some shouldn't be dropped." Police were indignant that

---

[17] Their recommendation was endorsed by some seasoned defense attorneys with whom we discussed it at a meeting of the Executive Council of the National Legal Aid and Defenders' Association.

charges were dropped without any concessions in return from the defendant.

Eliminating overcharging: the Alaskan experience. The complexity of the issues surrounding overcharging and the actual impact on plea bargaining of eliminating it are best illustrated by the Alaskan prosecutor's office's attempt to eliminate plea bargaining. That effort was initiated by Attorney General Gross who as a defense attorney had developed a distaste for overcharging.[18] The difficulties of implementing a policy of realistic charging can be traced through a series of his memoranda. The problems he faced were of two main kinds: defining overcharging and getting his assistants to agree to the policy. Notice should be taken of the shifting implicit definitions of overcharging he uses.

His implementing memorandum of July 3, 1975, implicitly defines overcharging as filing cases "which could not be made at trial" (a definition similar to Alschuler's definition of vertical overcharging as well the standards of the ABA, NDAA, ALI and NAC regarding the requirement that evidence be sustainable at trial). The memorandum is ambiguous because it says plea negotiations involving charge reductions are permissible but then tries to split the hair between reductions which are done *simply* to obtain a guilty plea and those which are not (which you will recall is one of the NDAA's standards). It reads as follows:

> Plea negotiations with respect to multiple counts and the ultimate charge will continue to be permissible under Criminal Rule 11 as long as the charge to which the defendant enters a plea of guilty correctly reflects both the facts and the level of proof. In other words, while there continues to be nothing wrong with reducing a charge, reductions should not occur simply to obtain a plea of guilty. An effective screening of cases filed . . . will have to be instituted in order to avoid filing cases which might be "bargained" under the existing system but which could not be won at trial.[19]

Three weeks later he tries to clarify what he means by "not charging simply to obtain a guilty plea." "I stress to you . . . that you should file the charge you can prove."[20] But he does not say what he means by "provable." He continues:

---

[18] Based on interview with A. Gross, French Lick, Indiana, June 1978.
[19] A. Gross, Memorandum of July 3, 1975.
[20] A. Gross, Memorandum of July 24, 1975.

Some charges should not be filed at all. Merely because you are brought a police file does not mean that you are required to file a criminal charge. In some cases the facts simply will not justify criminal prosecution either because it is not warranted in the interest of justice or because technically we could not prove the charge. If that is the case do not file the charge in the first instance. I am not interested in seeing the office file Assault with a Deadly Weapon charges and then reduce them to simple assaults with suspended impositions of sentence with no fine or jail time purely because we never had a case in the first place.[21]

His explanation of what he means by provable introduces yet another definition of overcharging, namely, the prosecutor should not file cases which are not in the interest of justice. This standard is unlike the standards based on exercising a technical knowledge of the law and of local practice. It does not call for an assessment of the provability of a case. Rather it imposes an equity function on the prosecutor at charging. Also, in his clarification he overstates his description of the "nonprovable" charges which his office had been accepting; namely, ones in which "we never had a case in the first place." Undoubtedly he does not mean to imply that his office had been accepting cases which lacked even probable cause. More likely it refers to the second kind of vertical overcharging we described, namely, filing cases as felonies because technically they are felonies (and may even have admissible and reasonably strong evidence) but which are members of a class of criminal acts which as a matter of de facto policy has become reduced to being treated as misdemeanors in the local jurisdiction.

This unofficial downgrading of felonies to misdemeanors is one of the unidentified major premises in many a discussion of overcharging. It, together with the assumption that charging should be used to achieve an equity function, is usually not evident except in some discussions of prosecutors condemning the "overcharging" done or requested by the police. There it is often clear that the prosecutor is rejecting the police charge not because of the strength of the case but because the prosecutor feels that while the higher charge is technically correct it would be inappropriately severe or because that type of crime has traditionally been handled as a misdemeanor.

By "type of crime" we are not referring to any legal category of crime such as burglary but rather to certain

---

[21] A. Gross, Memorandum of July 24, 1975.

typical patterns of criminal conduct, similar to Sudnow's (1965) notion of "normal crimes." Legal categories like burglary cover a wide variety of facts and circumstances from systematic residential burglary of a committed burglar to the breaking and entering of schools by students seeking to do some mischief. Even theft from automobiles constitutes burglary in some jurisdictions. Any one of these fact patterns could be charged as burglary and may be supportable at trial. The police will usually charge them (or want them charged) as burglaries not only to get the felony arrest statistic (see McDonald et al., 1981) but for other reasons as well. The police do not want to officially assume an equity function; [22] also they often are either unaware of or do not recognize as valid the unofficial policy of downgrading of a specific fact pattern to a misdemeanor.

It is this difficult matter of distinguishing classes of typical fact patterns within categories of crime which Attorney General Gross tries to identify in yet another memorandum a year later. But his point gets lost because (as in the general literature on overcharging) he couches the issue of a de facto policy of downgrading certain classes of criminal acts in the language of assessing the provability of cases.

> . . . I want to emphasize the thrust of [my] initial . . . memorandum . . . I wanted charges which were initially filed to accurately reflect the level of available proof at that time and that I did *not* want overcharging . . . I want you to file the charge or charge that you think you can prove and stick with them until and unless you are convinced they are not proper charges . . . *Charges should be dismissed or decreased only . . . when justified . . . and not as a quid pro quo for entry of a plea of guilty.*
> I realize there are times when the elements of the offense may be highly technical, as a result of which two similar type counts are filed to protect yourself dependent upon the way the evidence develops. In that instance you obviously only intend to seek a conviction on one or the other, and therefore it obviously makes sense to dismiss one if a plea is entered to the other count. This is not the situation I am trying to prevent.
> What I am trying to prevent is deliberate overcharging. That will not be easy to change, but I want a real effort made. I know that even if the facts warrant reduction on a charge, some of you will be hesitant to make it if you do not get some sort of implied or express indication from the defendant that he will plead guilty. After all, if the de-

---

[22] Although the police do frequently take the initiative in directing prosecutors to reject charges (Graham and Letwin, 1971).

fendant does not want to plead, why give him the break of reducing ADW [assault with a deadly weapon] to A&B [assault and battery]? The answer lies in the fact that if it is the kind of case that should be reduced to an A&B, it is the kind that should be filed as an A&B or reduced to one if it was initially filed at a higher level.

The critical missing element in this attempt at clarifying what constitutes overcharging is the explanation of how one knows when one has the kind of ADW which "should" be filed as an A&B. The memorandum of June 30, 1976, misleadingly suggests that this is determined by the level of proof. But that is not enough. In addition one must determine whether the fact pattern involved in the ADW fits the typical patterns of ADW's which were alluded to in Gross' earlier memorandum of July 24, 1975. If it is one of those ADW's which in the past have been reduced to simple assaults with suspended imposition of sentence, then the policy applies. Either it should not be filed at all or filed only as a misdemeanor.

Also noteworthy in the June 30, 1976, memorandum is that even with a screening program and an explicit policy of no charge bargaining, Gross expects that there will be times when prosecutors must "play it safe" and file several charges to protect themselves against the possibility of evidence not developing properly. Thus it is not so much the desire to play it safe that is the cause of overcharging but rather the unwillingness of prosecutors to drop or reduce charges to their correct level without getting guilty pleas in exchange.

Two years later Attorney General Gross reported that his no-plea-bargaining policy was a guarded success. He was sure that his prosecutors were no longer engaging in sentence bargaining but he was less sure of his success in eliminating charge bargaining. He reported:

> Sentence bargaining [by prosecutors] has been virtually eliminated in Alaska. Charge bargaining, though, has been much harder to control. The difficulty here is that when a charge is reduced from that originally filed, it is basically a subjective judgment as to whether the charge was reduced because the evidence developed in the case after indictment warranted a reduction, or whether the charge was reduced by the district attorney for the purpose of inducing the defendant to enter a plea. Short of quizzing every assistant district attorney on every reduction of charge, there is no way to completely guarantee that a bargain has not been struck, albeit quietly.

The effort to eliminate charge bargaining initially focused on convincing district attorneys that the ap-

25

propriate charge should be brought in the first instance, or, if subsequent facts convinced them that a charge should be reduced, that it should be reduced independently of an agreement for a plea. There has been some progress in this area and charge bargaining has clearly been reduced. At the same time, no one should delude himself into thinking that after many, many years of plea bargaining a directive from an Attorney General is going to change everyone's past practice and attitudes overnight. There are certainly still some cases where charge bargaining takes place either directly or surreptitiously, but hopefully the practice is on the wane.

Statistical evidence from the evaluation of the Alaska program suggests that the policy of realistic charging did *not* result in the wholesale rejection or dismissal of large numbers of cases. For the three major cities involved (Anchorage, Fairbanks and Juneau) there was a decline in the number of felony charges filed, from 1,815 in the year before the policy to 1,771 for the first year of the policy. Given the tough language of the policy, this is a surprisingly small decrease and, at that, much of it was apparently due to the decline in the actual number of cases being brought in due to the tapering off of the construction of the Alaskan pipeline and its associated crime problems (Gross, 1978).

However, while the number of felony cases filed did not appear to be affected by the accurate charging policy, there was other evidence that the policy was having an impact. In following the transformation of the charges from arrest to disposition, it appeared as though initial charging had become more accurate. The proportion of initial charges that changed to lesser charges at disposition declined (Gross, 1978). The other side of the coin, however, is that while charge bargaining may have ended, plea bargaining did not. It was merely forced back into a *sub rosa* form of differential sentencing through implicit bargaining (see Chapter 5). This suggests Katz et al. (1972) were wrong in their prediction that realistic charging would keep guilty pleas flowing without any substitute inducement.

Charging practices in six jurisdictions

A leading textbook (Chambliss and Seidman, 1971:395) describes the social organization of the charging process in American jurisdictions as follows:

> The typical situation surrounding criminal prosecution is characterized by Wayne LaFave as 'one in which the police make an arrest without a warrant and then bring a suspect to the prosecutor with a request that he approve the issuance of a warrant.'

The decision to arrest is clearly made by the police. The decision as to whether to charge the suspect and the selection of the charge are the responsibility of the prosecutor. The prosecutor's charging decision is manifested by his approval or refusal of the issuance of a warrant.

It should be evident from our prior discussion that this description implies a much greater uniformity in the organization of the charging process than actually exists. The charging process is one of the most diverse components of the American justice system. While there are some commonalities, its diversity is most prominent. This diversity makes national standards of proper charging problematic.

The following section describes the diversity in the charging and screening processes in six jurisdictions. Special attention is given to the relationship between these processes and the nature of plea bargaining. A statistical comparison of selected aspects of the charging process (presented in Table 2.2) highlights some major dimensions of the differences which exist. In addition, Figure 2.2 shows the differences among the jurisdictions regarding relative proportions of charge and sentence considerations in the guilty plea agreements in our samples of robbery and burglary cases. The narrative descriptions of each jurisdiction which follow will set these statistical differences into their respective contexts.

Delaware County (Pa.). The case screening process in Delaware County is dominated by the police decision regarding initial charges. Nowhere in the early stages of the process is there a systematic review of cases by the prosecutor. It is possible for a felony case to be initially charged, bound over at the preliminary hearing, placed in an early diversion program and eventually nol-prossed without a lawyer reviewing the case for probable cause.[23] The initial charges are selected and the cases are filed by the police in the lower courts. These district courts used to be located in police stations and referred to as "police" courts. The district court judges are the former justices of the peace and are mostly nonlawyers.

The prosecutor's office does try to influence the early charging process but its ability to do so is hampered by the fact that cases originate in 32 separate district (lower) courts spread throughout the county. The prosecutor's office has assigned assistant prosecutors only to the district courts in two cities (Upper Darby and Chester) that contribute about 40 percent of the total volume of cases to the county's court system. Those prosecutors, however, act only as resource people for the police.

---

[23] A prosecutor would review these cases but the review would not be for probable cause.

Table 2.2 Selected aspects of the charging process by jurisdiction (robbery and burglary cases that went to guilty plea or trial)

Characteristic	El Paso [N=247] *	New Orleans [N=521] *	Seattle [N=758] *	Tucson [N=571] *	Delaware County [N=654] *	Norfolk [N=632] *
Number of charges in initial complaint						
1	83.0%	48.4%	76.1%	47.1%	1.8%	54.6%
2–3	10.9%	43.2%	21.0%	45.3%	24.0%	28.6%
4+	6.0%	8.4%	2.9%	7.5%	74.1%	16.8%
Number of charges in formal accusation						
1	89.5%	88.9%	61.2%	29.9%	0.7%	22.8%
2–3	7.0%	9.9%	33.8%	53.4%	19.0%	49.3%
4+	3.2%	1.2%	5.0%	16.7%	80.3%	27.8%
Number of charges convicted of						
1	89.5%	91.4%	84.9%	78.3%	72.5%	53.3%
2–3	7.5%	8.2%	13.4%	19.5%	22.6%	33.5%
4+	2.9%	0.4%	1.7%	2.2%	5.0%	13.1%

* N's vary slightly by each characteristic due to item nonresponse.

Figure 2.2 Types of plea concessions in robbery and burglary cases by jurisdiction

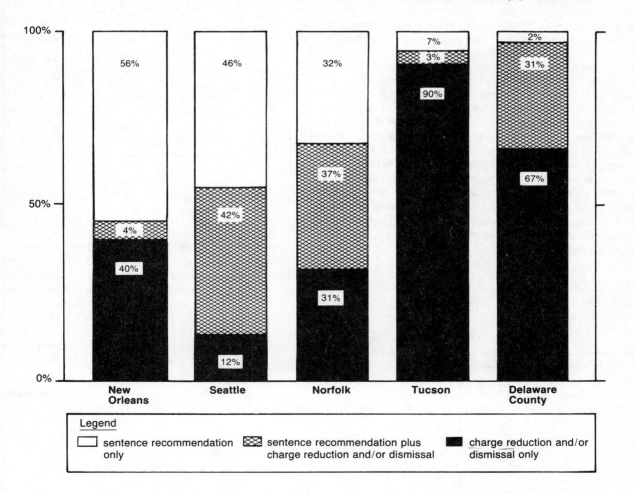

Legend
sentence recommendation only

sentence recommendation plus charge reduction and/or dismissal

charge reduction and/or dismissal only

They will advise them on what to charge if asked. Similarly, there is a "duty man" available by phone 24 hours a day from the DA's office who, if asked, will advise the police serving the other district courts as to what charges to file. The police say they do consult with the prosecutor in serious cases and when they have any doubts; but otherwise the police have no specific charging policies.[24] In two police departments interviewed the procedure is simply to have a supervising sergeant review the case with the arresting officer and help select the charges. One officer with 23 years experience said the police usually "wing it" most of the time. The assistant prosecutors say that when the police do ask for advice about charging specific cases, they usually recommend filing a lower number or degree of charges. Evidently, however, their advice has not had a general restraining influence on the police tendency to file numerous charges. Delaware County has by far the highest number of initial charges per case of any of our six jurisdictions. Four or more charges were filed in 74 percent of the robbery and burglary cases in our sample; see Table 2.2. Within 2 to 10 days after the initial appearance in district court, a preliminary hearing is held at which there will ordinarily be no prosecutor present (except in Upper Darby or Chester) unless the case is of special interest to the prosecutor's office. The office comes to know about such special cases in three ways. It is sent copies of all cases being initiated by the police immediately after their initiation. It may also have been further alerted to an especially serious case either by a call from the police or through the newspapers. For the most part the preliminary hearing will be put on by the police, and the nonlawyer judge will decide whether the case should go any further. Of 7,593 criminal matters (including felonies and misdemeanors)[25] entering the Delaware County court system in 1976, 4,010 (53 percent) were dismissed or withdrawn at the preliminary hearing. It is believed that many of the dismissed cases were arrests initiated by citizens who had filed complaints in the lower courts. Another 10 percent (742 cases) resulted in guilty pleas to summary offenses. The remaining cases (including felonies and level 1 and level 2 misdemeanors) were bound over to the Court of Common Pleas (superior court).

Notwithstanding the substantial number of cases dismissed in the lower courts, it is the opinion of local attorneys that the district judges are virtual "rubber-stamps" for the charges selected by the police. If the prosecutor's office wants different charges filed than those leveled by the police, it either dismisses the case and has it rebrought; or, more likely, it requests special leave of the court to amend the charges. Either way, revising police charges is done only occasionally.

The review in the prosecutor's office is based on the case file forwarded from the lower court, which contains a form filled out by the judge. It states the name of the defendant, the dates of the crime and arrest, the names of the arresting officer, and maybe the witnesses. There is no description of the crime or of the evidence; nor is there information about whether bail was set. This file is reviewed by a nonlawyer in the prosecutor's office to determine whether the defendant appears to qualify for the diversion program (ARD—accelerated rehabilitative disposition). This initial determination is made simply on the basis of whether the charge(s) fit within the District Attorney's list of charges eligible for diversion.[26] If so, the case is given to an experienced prosecutor to review it even further using additional information (primarily arrest records) to determine whether the case does in fact qualify under the DA's charging criteria and other criteria regarding prior record. If it qualifies, the defendant, his or her attorney, the arresting officer, and the victim are notified and a date is set for hearing on the diversion recommendation. If placed on diversion, the defendant may serve up to 2 years on preconviction probation; and if he or she meets the terms of diversion,[27] the case will be dismissed. In 1976 between 847 and 1,000 cases were placed in the diversion program.[28]

If a case does not qualify for diversion, then the nonlawyer prepares the formal charges by simply filing the charges listed by the police and bound over by the district judges. These cases are then submitted to the prosecutor's "screening" attorney who reviews the charges and the police file; sees if the charges are appropriate; sets the priority of the case and assigns it to a trial team. If the prosecutor wants to change the charges he may request special leave of the court to do so. But this rarely happens. In our sample, the number of charges filed by the prosecutor was identical to the number filed by the police 97 percent of the time (see

---

[24] Except that one department will *not* file charges for violating the Sunday blue laws or for gambling (bingo) at church carnivals or fairs. A former chief had been fired after doing so.

[25] Misdemeanors in Pennsylvania are graded into three levels with the first level being punishable by up to five years of incarceration and the second level up to two years.

[26] For list see Appendix A.

[27] E.g., drunk drivers must attend the alcoholism council for testing; drug users must be tested; indecent exposure offenders must get psychiatric testing.

[28] Systematic data on case flow in the Delaware County court is not computerized. Both the court and the prosecutor's office keep their own statistical records, which do not always agree.

Table 2.2 for comparison with other jurisdictions). The prosecutor is more likely to dismiss cases (nol pros) than alter charges. During the case review and preparation process and later (up to the time of trial) cases are nol-prossed. In 1976, 552 of 2,841 (19 percent) of the cases bound over to the Court of Common Pleas were disposed of in that manner. After the review the case is presented at a formal arraignment conducted by a layman who reads the formal charges to the defendant. The arraignment occurs about one to two weeks before trial.

Some plea bargaining occurs at various stages of the process, but the bulk of it occurs on the day of trial in what attorneys describe as a "panicky" atmosphere at the back of the courtroom. A lot of guilty pleas come only after a trial has begun. The plea bargains involve both charge bargains and sentence recommendations. The amount of charge reduction is enormous. Most cases start out with many charges and end up convicted of few. However, defense attorneys were in general agreement that the charge bargains were rarely of any value. It is the sentence commitment that concerned them. Most of them said things like: "A charge reduction is always immediately available but they're not worth anything to the defendant. It's the time he is concerned about."

Another lawyer said: "They reduce charges in almost all the cases but that's not the heart of the matter. If the man is charged with six crimes, you don't care if he's convicted of all of them because the judge only needs one conviction to put him in jail. So I don't worry about the number of charges."

Because most Delaware County defense attorneys see charge bargaining as being largely irrelevant to the sentence, they are generally not upset at the overcharging which, most of them (10 of 13 or 77 percent) believe goes on. As one public defender put it when asked about prosecutorial overcharging, "They do, but I wonder if it matters. They seem to put on more than is necessary for prosecution but they get dropped through a plea bargain, nol pros, or suspended sentence. It doesn't have any effect—with the possible exception of a hidden fine."

The defense attorneys accept and expect the police to overcharge because they figure the police do not know how to charge correctly. The phlegmatic attitude of the Delaware County defense attorneys towards overcharging by police and prosecutors stands in sharp contrast to earlier reports of the widespread condemnation by attorneys of the practice.

Norfolk City (Va.). The charging process in Norfolk is divided among the police, the prosecutor, and the district (lower) court. Initial charges for both felonies (arrested without warrants) and misdemeanors are initiated by the police by obtaining a warrant from a magistrate (formerly, justice of the peace). The police decide whether the case is a felony or a misdemeanor and set it on the appropriate court docket. The police are under virtually no guidelines in selecting charges other than to pick the charges which seem to fit the facts.[29] Typically they pick the highest charge. For example, drug possession cases are always charged as "possession with intent to distribute" no matter how small the amount of the drug. The police use overcharging to accomplish several goals. One officer stated, "Yes, generally I charge higher in order to hold it over their heads. It helps to up the (bail) bond and it also helps in plea bargaining."

As for the number of charges, our sample of cases indicates the police most frequently file only one charge (55 percent) but almost as frequently file multiple charges (45 percent). In a small but substantial proportion of cases (17 percent) they file four or more charges per case. While this is considerably less heavy multiple charging than that of the Delaware County police—who filed 74 percent of their cases with four or more charges—it is two to eight times higher than that of the other four jurisdictions (see Table 2.2). It is no coincidence that this high degree of heavy multiple charging occurs in the two jurisdictions where the prosecutor's screening mechanism does not involve an early review of cases or a direct interaction with the police regarding the charges.

All cases are usually presented within 24 hours in the (lower) District Court (referred to as the "police court") for an "initial appearance." At this point most misdemeanors are acted upon. Many are disposed of by guilty pleas.[30] But many others are tried, convicted, and appealed to the (upper) Circuit Court for retrial.[31] These misdemeanors are presented either by the police or the court clerk. Prosecutors are rarely involved. Felonies will have a preliminary hearing date set for 2 weeks later.

---

[29] One exception is homicide. The police have a policy of charging all homicides with first degree murder.

[30] See Chapter 6 (Judicial Supervision) for a description of the rapid disposition of these misdemeanor cases.

[31] Almost as many misdemeanors as felonies reach the Circuit Court. In 1976, a monthly average of 291 misdemeanors compared to 507 felonies were commenced in the Circuit Court, according to court statistics for five months.

The preliminary hearing constitutes the main prosecutorial screening mechanism. Prosecutors reduce many felonies to misdemeanors in exchange for guilty pleas and some cases are dismissed completely. This charge modification and disposition process at the preliminary hearing is considered the primary form of clearing cases. Unfortunately, no statistics are available on the extent of the felony reduction and dismissal at preliminary hearing. Some observers believe that most of the adjustments of the cases are in the form of charge bargains rather than outright dismissals. One court watcher estimated that less than 10 percent of the felony cases are dismissed outright. Everything that can be reduced or dismissed will be. Prosecutors note that there are important advantages to adjusting cases before they are bound over to the Circuit Court. As one noted, "if you are going to reduce a sale (of drugs) to accommodation, then try to do it in Police Court. You get a lot less exposure there, plus it saves time and money. In Circuit Court there might be a reporter present."

Prosecutors also believe, however, that there are some cases which "must" be allowed to proceed to the Circuit Court even though they will be plea bargained to misdemeanors or dismissed. Such cases are not delineated by any explicit office policy and do not constitute any specific class of offense (except possibly homicide) but rather are identified on an individual basis. They are ones where the charges are too serious to reduce; or there is a lack of information in the file; or there is pressure from the community or the victim to have the case handled seriously; or other circumstances dictate that the case should be given fuller treatment.

Cases that are bound over to the grand jury and forwarded to the prosecutor's office are assigned to individual prosecutors who select the formal charges to be filed. Their choices are approved by a supervisor, but this review is not guided by any explicit charging standards. Generally, prosecutors add more charges (of a lesser-included kind) to the most serious charge filed by the police. One assistant prosecutor explained, "For example, they will come in with a charge of burglary. We will then add grand larceny and possession of burglary tools on the indictment." By the time of the formal charging decision of the prosecutor, the police are supposed to have completed any postarrest investigation needed in the case and forwarded that information to the prosecutor. (This information is typically not available to the prosecutor during the "screening" at the preliminary hearing.) The ineffectiveness of the preliminary hearing screening is evident by the fact that at the Circuit Court

level 23 percent of the felonies are dismissed by the prosecutor.[32]

The case screening process in Norfolk is notable for the unusual and somewhat inconsistent views that local attorneys have of it. The prosecutors and defense attorneys tend to define the screening function as a responsibility shared between the prosecutor and the court but with the court holding the major share of the responsibility. Most defense attorneys reported that both horizontal and vertical overcharging occurs; yet they were also of the opinion that the prosecutor's office did a fairly good job of screening! They blamed the overcharging on both the police and the prosecutor; but they attributed the perceived inadequacies of the case screening process to the District Court judge. They blamed him (not the prosecutor) for failure to eliminate more cases at the preliminary hearing. No one seemed to think that the prosecutor should take the initiative in dismissing more cases. As for the overcharging, the defense attorneys were almost unanimously pleased with it because of its advantages to them. They noted that it gives them something to take back to their clients. One stated, "We have to sell things to our clients. However, if he is a professional, then he will tell you about overcharging." Most noted that getting "overcharges" reduced or dismissed makes them look good in the eyes of their clients and makes the defendants feel that they are getting a good deal. (Obviously, it is this potential for deception and manipulation which has contributed to the concern of some critics of charge bargaining.)

Norfolk prosecutors also blamed the failure in the screening process on the District Court judge. The prosecutor's office had established a screening division at one time but according to prosecutors it did not succeed because the District Court judge was unwilling to cooperate. They did not define screening as an independent prosecutorial function.

In addition to whatever screening is done by the Commonwealth Attorney's Office there is an unknown amount of unofficial screening and charge bargaining done by the police. They use their charging powers to obtain informers, confessions, and guilty pleas. One officer stated, "If there is a felony arrest it must go to Police Court. Unofficially, I will not make an arrest if I think he can be of service [as an informer], thus bypass-

---

[32] Based on Circuit Court caseload statistics for January, February and April, 1977.

ing the official procedure." Another stated, "If I see someone who might be a possible informer in the future, we will charge that individual with a lesser offense and treat it as a misdemeanor." One defendant reported that he pleaded guilty because "the police told me they would help me as much as they could and they would drop the strong-arm robbery charge. They said I would end up with 36 months."

Another explained, "I did it to keep from getting other charges. I was nervous at the time. I gave a statement since there was no use in going to court and pleading not guilty."

A third said, "The police told me that if I put away all my connections, they would guarantee me 12 months."

Yet another defendant reported, "I pled guilty to five counts of statutory burglary. The police told me if I didn't make a statement, they would give me 15 more charges of burglary."

Over half of the police officers interviewed said they engage in plea negotiations with defendants. The basic forms of plea bargaining by the police are either the threatening to add charges or the offering to dismiss charges and then putting in a "good word" with the prosecutor. The deal is usually made directly with the defendant during the questioning period after arrest. The defendant is told he will be charged with many more crimes if he does not make a statement. After making his statement the defendant goes to police court, has an attorney appointed, and is told by him that there is very little that can be done unless the statement can be suppressed—which rarely happens.

The police role in plea bargaining is further enhanced by the fact that the prosecutor's "screening" is done in the "police court" at preliminary hearing. Much of this "screening" is just plea and dismissal bargaining. Defense attorneys know that the key to successful plea bargaining (or outright dismissal) is getting the police officer to agree to the disposition. Unlike that in New Orleans where prosecutorial screening involves a private discussion between the police officer and the prosecutor in the prosecutor's office, Norfolk's screening is done in open court with police officers, defense attorneys, and prosecutors milling about trying to strike agreements on dispositions and exchanges. Defense counsel approach police officers for information about their cases and for their approval of certain "screening" decisions. Case strength is not a major consideration in this combined screening, bargaining and dismissing process.

The police importance in charging (and plea bargaining) extends even into the Circuit Court. The Commonwealth Attorney's Office has a policy of contacting the police officers in a case before plea bargaining and requesting their recommendations. A few other jurisdictions have similar policies, but in Norfolk it appears to be more than a matter of professional courtesy or even of checking for additional information. The police opinion of the correct charges and dispositions seems to carry considerable weight. All police officers interviewed stated that they usually were contacted by the prosecutor's office before the indictment is filed and asked for their recommendations or comments. One officer went on to say, "If they don't contact us about a case that we want reduced, then we will contact them. They usually go along with our recommendations."

The power of the police regarding charging and plea bargaining was emphasized by one private defense attorney who had served as a local prosecutor for two years. In his view, "the real prosecutor in Norfolk is the police officer." He explained:

If the police officer won't agree to deal there is no deal. You really negotiate with the detective (in felony cases). You go down there and tell him, "I promise my man won't be back this year." Then he'll say, "No. We've got to have some time on this man." Or, "We don't feel this guy has to have any time." Or, "This guy is high on our list. He's a real bad actor. We have to put him away." Those police officers sound just like lawyers, the haggling they go through.
Then you go see the assistant prosecutor and tell him "The detective doesn't feel too bad about this case." The prosecutor will then call and check with the detective and confirm what you've reported. And the prosecutor may then say to you, "Well, if the judge will go along with it then I'd accept it." Then you'll see if you can fly it by the judge.

This attorney noted that charge bargaining (or plea bargaining generally) by police differs from that of prosecutors. Factors relevant to case strength are unimportant to the police in setting the terms of the deal.

The policeman is only concerned with what he wants to do with the guy and who you (the attorney) are. You don't argue about is it a good search or good arrest. To police officers every search is a good search. Every arrest is a good arrest. They are afraid to admit any error in the arrest because they fear it will be based against them in trial. If you point out an error they are likely to say, "Well, we'll see about that."

Tucson (Pima County, Ariz.). In Tucson screening of cases by the police before referral to the prosecutor's office is minimal. All cases are sent to be reviewed by the County Attorney's Office. Depending on whether the case is referred by detective squads or uniform police officers, an investigative prosecutor or police liaison officer will review the case. Detective squads take the case directly to the investigative prosecutors while all other officers refer their cases to the police liaison officer in the County Attorney's Office. The function of the liaison officer is to coordinate the investigations of the police officer with the County Attorney's Office. If a case is rejected by the liaison officer, it is returned to the sergeant at the police department. If the case is again referred to the County Attorney, it bypasses the police liaison officer and goes directly to the investigative prosecutors. Estimates suggest that only 2–3 percent of cases are screened outright by the police liaison officer.

Police officers stated that the only policies for screening cases are those in the prosecutor's office (2:2).[33] However, the role of the police officer can be important in the disposition of cases. Officers are routinely consulted by the prosecutor before an indictment is issued if the prosecutor wants clarification of arrest information (2:2). In addition, they are approached by defense counsel prior to final disposition in approximately 80 percent of all cases (1:2). Defense counsel sometimes encourage them to agree to a plea bargain or, at least, not to object to a plea bargain (1:2); but counsel rarely ask them to "tone down" reports or "withhold information" (2:2).

Police officers play a very limited role in their contacts with the defendant. They stated that they never engaged in plea bargaining with defendants (other than informants). They do not try to persuade defendants that they will "do better" by pleading guilty. The officers said that in order to bargain a defendant into being an informant, permission must be obtained from the prosecutor before making the deal. (Several interviewed defendants noted that police officers or narcotics agents had informed them of the possibility of dismissed charges in exchange for information. The typical plea agreement with informants was a dismissal or reduction of charges in exchange for evidence in three other cases.)

The County Attorney's Office screens cases through its Issuing Team of four experienced attorneys who are in charge of investigating cases. In 1977 the team issued approximately 55 percent to 65 percent of the cases referred (compared to 51 percent of the cases in 1976). Prosecutors said their standard in accepting cases was "evidence strong enough to get the case to trial." The County Attorney hoped that he had established the policy of indicting people on provable charges and on enough counts to "impress" the jury. By this he meant that if the defendant had a pattern of 20 robberies then the indictment should show that the defendant is a multiple offender. However not all 20 robberies should be included because that could confuse the grand jury and hinder successful prosecution. He did not feel that his office overcharged.

The views of defense attorneys regarding the charging practices in the prosecutor's office disagree with the County Attorney's. A majority of defense attorneys stated that the prosecutor's office *usually* screens out cases that have serious legal or evidentiary weaknesses (7:10) and accepts cases that are strong enough to get to trial (10:10). However, most defense attorneys also felt that the prosecutor's office accepts some cases that would not withstand a motion for a directed verdict of acquittal. These cases are accepted because of the prosecutor's belief in the factual guilt of the defendant, or the nature of the crime, or the background of the defendant (8:10). Counsel noted that prosecutors attempt to get a guilty plea to a lesser included offense in such cases.

Notwithstanding their belief that the prosecutor usually only accepts cases with evidence greater than probable cause and despite the fact that 35 to 45 percent of the felonies are rejected by the prosecutor's screening unit, 9 out of 10 defense attorneys claimed that the prosecutor's office overcharges! Examples of overcharging included adding "kidnapping for—" charges to rape or robbery charges, or charging someone with "burglary" when the evidence suggests "possession of burglary tools." Overcharging was believed to occur because it increases the prosecutor's leverage in plea negotiations or otherwise increase the number of guilty pleas (8:10). Also it was believed that police officers sometimes pressure the prosecutor's office to indict on particular charges if the officer is involved in developing the case (2:10). Almost half (4:10) of the defense counsel suggested that vertical overcharging was common. Others stated that horizontal overcharging (3:10) or a combination of both (2:10) occurred. Regardless of the type of overcharging, most defense counsel stated that it was *routine in all cases* (7:10)!

The perceptions of defense counsel regarding widespread overcharging are undoubtedly linked to the fact that charge bargaining is the major form of plea bargain-

---

[33] The first number in the parenthesis refers to the number of persons agreeing with the preceding statement. The second number refers to the total number of persons questioned about the specific topic.

ing in Tucson (see Figure 2.2). In the Superior (felony) Court sentence agreements are rare.[34] Charge reduction and dismissal as well as agreements not to file habitual offender charges account for almost all of the plea bargains according to judges and defense attorneys. Our sample of cases confirmed this perception. Ninety-three percent of the plea agreements involve charge bargains (either exclusively or with sentence considerations). The latter occurred in only 16 percent of our cases. Charge reduction was reflected in the substantial decrease in the number of charges per case between formal accusation and ultimate conviction. Seventy percent of our Tucson sample had 2 or more charges listed in the indictment, but only 22 percent of the cases resulted in convictions on two or more charges. Most convictions (78 percent) were on only one charge (see Table 2.2).

Tucson defense attorneys indicated that overcharging influences the advice they give their clients. If a case is vertically overcharged and the evidence is strong, they feel that a guilty plea to a lesser offense is usually the best available option for avoiding a harsh sentence. On the other hand, if the evidence is weak they are more likely to seek a dismissal or advise their client to plead not guilty. In contrast, horizontal overcharging does not usually affect the advice of counsel because there is no consecutive sentencing in Tucson.

The prosecutor's office operates a Serious Offender Bureau (SOB) which is related to charge bargaining and screening in important ways. The goal of the SOB is to "devote special attention to career criminals and serious offenders, to minimize delay, and to prevent manipulation of the weaknesses of the system. . . . [S]elective and vigorous prosecution of serious and habitual criminal offenders, along with a clearly defined and limited plea bargaining policy, will utilize existing judicial resources to their fullest extent, and insure swift justice to the criminal who deserves it. . . ."[35] The initial selection of potential SOB cases is made by the prosecutor's Issuing Team (screening unit) using an "objective rating system applied to all incoming criminal cases" (Op. cit.:2). This evaluation system is based on the seriousness of the offense and the seriousness of defendant's prior record. As to the matter of case strength, the Office Manual explains, "In order to avoid unnecessary waste of SOB and judicial resources, the strength of the case will also be considered, but will not be the controlling factor" (Id.).

The final decision as to whether a case will be given SOB treatment is made by the Bureau Director.

SOB cases can be plea bargained but the terms must meet the minimum SOB guidelines, which are designed to achieve the twin goals of accurately reflecting the original offense and placing "the defendant within a sentence range sufficient to deal with the degree of criminality involved" (Op. cit.:2). The guidelines focus primarily on what charges may not be dismissed or reduced. The policy is as follows:

PIMA (ARIZONA) COUNTY ATTORNEY'S OFFICE

MINIMUM GUIDELINES FOR SOB PLEA NEGOTIATIONS (1977):

GENERAL:

(a) There will be no plea agreements designating probation or limiting prison time to less than the maximum provided by law.

(b) Provable priors [offenses] will not be dismissed unless the defendant's exposure to Arizona State Prison is at least ten years without the prior on a single count.

(c) Aggravation hearings will be held where appropriate and will not be waived by plea agreements.

(d) The sentencing judge will not be designated by agreement.

(e) Plea negotiations will be terminated at least ten days prior to trial in all cases.

VIOLENT OFFENSES; ARMED OFFENSES; RESIDENTIAL BURGLARIES:

(a) Defendant may plead to the count against *each* victim carrying the highest *minimum* prison sentence, or,

(b) Defendant may plead to the two counts in the indictment or information carrying the highest *minimum* prison sentence.

OTHER OFFENSES:

Defendant may plead to the county carrying the highest *minimum* prison sentence, provided that maximum exposure is at least ten years, or to any combination of counts necessary to raise maximum exposure to at least ten years, where possible.

NOTE:

These are *minimum* guidelines. Stricter terms may be set by the assigned deputy in appropriate cases with the approval of the Bureau Director. In no event will more lenient terms be agreed to without

---

[34] In contrast, in the (justice) misdemeanor court, sentence agreements occur in about 70% to 90% of the guilty pleas, according to estimates of the judges.

[35] (Pima (Arizona) County Attorney's Office, Operations Manual for Serious Offender Bureau, 1977, p. 1.)

the approval of the Bureau Director *and* the County Attorney.

Seattle (King County, Wash.). The Seattle (King County) court system has two tiers, a District (lower) Court of limited jurisdiction and a Superior (upper) Court of general jurisdiction. Until the mid-1970's all felonies and misdemeanors were filed in the District Court. Prosecutors used the preliminary hearing of the District Court to screen felony cases. If a case looked strong, it was bound over or refiled in the Superior Court. Otherwise it was reduced to a misdemeanor and disposed of in the District Court. This changed when a new 60-day speedy trial rule made a "dry run" at the preliminary hearing an unaffordable luxury. Since then only "expedited" (minor) felonies are filed in the District Court and are expected to be disposed of there as misdemeanors.[36]

This will typically happen at the preliminary hearing, where the prosecutor will move to reduce the charge to a misdemeanor, usually in exchange for a guilty plea. These expedited felonies as well as the misdemeanors are initially charged on the basis of a complaint filed by the police. (One defense attorney claimed he sometimes is able to convince police officers to file felonies as misdemeanors.) All other felonies are filed directly in the Superior Court.

The police bring these felonies to the appropriate "filing" deputy prosecutors. If the case involves a sex of-

---

[36] "Expedited" cases are specifically defined by the King County District Attorney's Plea Bargaining standards (pre-June 22, 1977) as follows:

"Expedited Crimes" are:

(a) larceny of any type where the total value of all property taken pursuant to a common scheme is less than $250, except

(1) from the person, or

(2) as part of a business enterprise, or

(3) where the property possessed was stolen in a residential burglary and circumstances exist which give probable cause to believe that the defendant committed the burglary, or

(4) where the property possessed was stolen in more than one criminal incident.

(b) forgery when the total face value of all instruments forged is less than $250, unless two or more different identities are involved.

(c) credit card forgery where the total value of all items charged is less than $25, unless two more different identities are involved.

(d) credit card theft where the possession involves the cards or identification of one person only.

(e) joyriding where the vehicle was abandoned within 24 hours of the theft, no stripping occurred or where there is no evidence of intent to permanently deprive.

(f) possession of marijuana in quantities less than 250 grams.

(g) possession of dangerous drugs in quantities less than:

(1) amphetamine—50 tablets

(2) barbiturates—10 capsules

(3) others—quantities sufficiently small to indicate personal use as opposed to sale

(4) Class I controlled substances are always treated as felonies.

---

fense, the police bring it to a member of the prosecutor's Morals Unit. These are experienced attorneys picked for their ability to handle sensitive cases. All other cases are brought to the prosecutor's Filing Unit, composed of deputies with at least a year's experience who serve on the Unit for 3 months and then go back to trial practice.

According to the chief criminal deputy, the official filing standard is "whether the case will get to a jury." He added that deputies like to win cases and consequently the actual standard is probably even higher, something close to being winnability at trial. Defense attorneys generally agreed that the prosecutor's evidentiary standard at screening is high. Six described it as "getting to a jury" or stronger. Two described it as "pretty strong." Only one said it was *not* "getting the case to a jury. Rather," he said, "it was 'we think they are guilty.' "

Evidently the detectives in the Seattle Police Department have learned and incorporated the prosecutor's high filing standards.[37] About 90 percent of the cases they bring over are accepted. The Seattle detectives prescreen their cases and do not bring them over if they do not meet the filing standards (except for homicides and politically sensitive cases, all of which are brought over). According to the legal counsel for the Seattle Police Department, there are no official policies about the kinds of cases to screen out (except for the prosecutor's guidelines about filing "expedited" cases and misdemeanors in the District Court). Typically, the detective does not bring the case over until it has been thoroughly investigated. The detectives will be told by the deputy prosecutor if the case is to be filed or declined or needs further investigation before they leave the filing conference.[38] The charging decisions for both minor ("expedited") and serious ("high impact") felonies [39] are governed by explicit policy. Minor felonies are all to be filed in the District Court by the police.

All "high impact" crimes are to be filed in the Superior Court. The guidelines controlling the charging and plea bargaining of high impact cases attempt to achieve the triple goals of evenhandedness, appropriate sentence, and an appropriate record of the actual offenses committed. Plea bargaining is not prohibited but is regulated to

---

[37] Officers from other departments in King County with small caseloads have had less experience with the filing unit and tend to bring weaker cases over.

[38] They can appeal declinations all the way to the chief prosecutor.

[39] Murder; manslaughter; assault in the first degree; rape; robbery; kidnapping in the first degree; residential burglary; and arson in the first degree or involving a residence. King County (Washington) District Attorney's Office Policies, Section 1051(1), pre-June 22, 1977.

---

achieve these goals. Proper charging and charge bargaining (as defined by the King County District Attorney, Christopher Bayley) are a critical part of the guidelines. The filing policy is as follows:

SECTION 1052: FILING

HIGH IMPACT CRIMES

(1) All high impact crimes will be filed directly in superior court unless there are specific evidentiary reasons for a preliminary hearing.

(2) If weapons were used or were present and capable of being used in the commission of the crime the appropriate special allegation will be charged in all cases. This applies whether or not an individual defendant actually possessed the weapon.

(3) If a defendant has two or more prior felony convictions which have resulted in prison sentences, and if the present charge includes a high impact crime, an allegation of habitual criminal status will be made in the original information. See Section 1320 for specific procedures on charging and handling habitual criminal allegations in other cases.

EXPEDITED CASES

(1) All expedited cases will be filed in district court as felonies. The only exception will be those cases where the defendant's prior record is such as to require the imposition of a sentence involving loss of liberty for more than six months. These cases will be filed direct in superior court.[40]

The disposition guidelines specify what sentence recommendations shall be made and what charges may not be bargained away. The deliberate filing of multiple charges of the horizontal type (i.e., separate criminal incidents as well as different criminal acts committed as part of one incident, e.g., vandalism in addition to damage done when burglarizing) is an important feature in this plea bargaining policy. Multiple charges are to be filed but not for the purpose of being traded away. Their purpose is to assure either an appropriate sentence or an appropriate record of conviction (even if it does not increase the sentence). For instance, one will notice that Standard 4 (below) insists that charges arising from separate criminal incidents for certain offenses may not be dismissed. But then Standard 5 (below) directs deputies to recommend that conviction for these separate counts be served *concurrently*. The standards are as follows: [41]

---

[40] King County (Washington) District Attorney's Office Policy Manual, pre-June 22, 1977.
[41] Only those standards relevant to charges are presented here.

SECTION 1053: DISPOSITION

HIGH IMPACT CRIMES

(1) Sentence recommendations pursuant to these standards will be made in all rape, robbery and residential burglary cases. All sentence recommendations in these cases will involve some loss of liberty. The amount of loss of liberty to be recommended will be determined by reference to the attached recommendation standards for the crime involved. The only factors which are relevant to the amount of loss of liberty are the nature of the present crime, any aggravating factors which may be present, and the defendant's prior criminal record.

(2) Aggravating factors will be applied in the following manner.

(a) Multiple Incidents—One additional step will be added for each additional incident up to a maximum of two additional steps.

(i) Uncharged criminal incidents will not be considered unless probable cause exists to believe the defendant committed the uncharged crime.

(b) Physical Injury Resulting—One additional step will be added for each victim who is physically injured.

(c) Weapon Used—One additional step will be added if a weapon was used in the commission of the crime. Only one additional step may be added in the category.

(d) Prior High Impact Crime Conviction—One additional step will be added if the defendant has previously been convicted of a high impact crime. Only one additional step may be added in this category.

(e) Vandalism Present—One additional step will be added to residential burglary recommendations where the residence was vandalized in addition to damage resulting from the entry and the theft. Only one additional step may be added in this category.

(3) In rape, robbery or residential burglary cases firearm or deadly weapon allegations where the weapon was used or was capable of being used in furtherance of the crime and habitual criminal allegations are not the subject of bargaining and will not be dropped for any reason other than our inability to prove the specific allegations.

(4) In rape, robbery or residential burglary cases counts representing separate high impact criminal incidents shall not be dismissed.

(a) "separate incidents" mean independent crimes *i.e.,* two robberies of different victims at different locations are separate criminal incidents; the robbery of two victims at the same time and location is one criminal incident.

(b) multiple counts arising from a single criminal incident, including crimes committed while withdrawing, may be dismissed as part of a plea bargain, *i.e.,* grand larceny of property taken in a burglary, an assault committed in the course of a robbery, or the robbery of several different victims at the time and place.

(5) Concurrent maximum terms of 20 years in the case of rape, robbery and burglary in the first degree and 15 years in the case of burglary in the second degree will be recommended.[42]

The policy allows for exceptions in all cases but they must be approved in writing by certain senior prosecutors. The dropping of allegations requiring mandatory sentences is allowed only for one of the following reasons:

(a) where proof problems make conviction on the original charge unlikely or,

(b) where the defendant is able to provide information or testimony that will reasonably lead to the conviction of others who are responsible for more serious criminal conduct or who represents a greater danger to the public interested or,

(c) where specific factors present require the reduction or elimination of punishment on the grounds of mercy.[43]

Turning now to expedited felonies, the charging and disposition policy for them involves that second kind of vertical overcharging discussed earlier. It is not that these cases lack ample evidentiary strength. Rather, it is that they are routinely filed as felonies and reduced to misdemeanors in exchange for pleas. The policy is institutionalized as follows:

SECTION 1053: DISPOSITION

EXPEDITED CASES

(1) The defense attorney will be informed that upon an agreement to plead guilty in District Court the defendant may enter a plea to the crime listed below. Preliminary hearings will not be held in expedited cases. If a plea of guilty has not been entered by the date of the preliminary hearing the case will be dismissed and filed directly in Superior Court.

---

[42] Ibid., Section 1053.
[43] Ibid., Section 1054.

Crime charged	Crime reduced to
Larceny	Petit larceny
Forgery—checks	Petit larceny
Credit card forgery & theft	Petit larceny
Joyriding	Petit larceny
Possession of marijuana	Possession of marijuana
Possession of dangerous drugs [44]	Possession of legend drugs

When we asked local practitioners about the amount and kind of overcharging that occurred, the responses were mixed and conflicting. Prosecutors did not see their District Court policy as a form of institutionalized overcharging. As for Superior Court cases, they said their filing standards are very high. Defense attorneys generally agreed about the high standards in the Superior Court. Nevertheless, 4 of 10 defense attorneys also said that the prosecutor's office overcharges! (Three said overcharging was both horizontal and vertical. One said it was mostly horizontal.) Two other attorneys said that the Criminal Division (of the DA's Office) does not overcharge but the Fraud Division does (horizontally). Another attorney believed that the prosecutor does not overcharge except in habitual offender cases. When asked to clarify what he meant, he gave an unusual definition of overcharging. He said that prosecutors "overcharge" on the habitual offender allegation in that they use it *as if* there were insufficient legal basis for the charge.[45] Two attorneys described practices which might be regarded as *sub rosa* overcharging. They said that in some cases the prosecutor does not file all the charges that the available evidence would support. These unfiled charges are later used to encourage guilty pleas. Prosecutors threaten to file them or to "sling mud" at sentencing if the case goes to trial.

Our sample of robbery and burglary cases shows a comparatively small amount of horizontal charge bargaining. Most cases (76 percent) were initially charged with only one charge. In a few cases (15 percent) extra charges were added to the formal accusation and in some cases (23 percent) charges were dropped at conviction (see

---

[44] Id.
[45] This response was most surprising because prosecutors regularly complain about the habitual offender proceedings being so much trouble. They say that such charges are usually not filed unless careful documentation is available.

Table 2.2). This conforms with the general view that the dominant form of plea bargaining in the Superior Court is sentence recommendations (see also Figure 2.2). In our sample 46 percent of the guilty pleas involved sentence recommendations alone. Very few (8 percent) involved charge modifications alone. Inasmuch as our sample involved two crimes covered by the office policy of filing multiple charges for separate incidents and not bargaining them away, one would not expect much dismissing of charges. Thus, the decrease in the proportion of cases with two or more charges from 39 percent at formal accusation to 15 percent at conviction seems high given the policy.[46]

New Orleans (La.). In Louisiana the initial charges in a case are decided by the police but the decision to file formal charges belongs solely to the district attorney.[47] In all but capital cases and those punishable by life imprisonment, the district attorney may proceed by bill of information rather than grand jury indictment.[48] Unlike some other states,[49] a magistrate's finding of probable cause is not a necessary prerequisite to the filing of a formal charge. If after a preliminary hearing a magistrate finds no probable cause, the only necessary result is that the arrestee is freed from custody. Prosecution is *not* barred.[50] The prosecutor's charging decision awaits receipt of the police report, delivered anywhere from 1 to 10 days after arrest.[51]

On the day after the arrest or initial hearing, the Screening Division sends notices to the victim and the witnesses[52] to come to the District Attorney's Office. Before accepting or rejecting any charges, the screening attorney interviews the victim and as many "necessary"[53] witnesses as possible. The number of witnesses interviewed varies with the attorney and the demands of the case.

In the vast majority of cases the arresting officer is interviewed. He or she is sometimes pivotal to the charging decision. If he or she does not bring over the case in person, the screening assistant may interpret this to mean that the officer does not really care about the case (unless, of course, the officer is working midnight shift). If present, the officer may be able to prevent the refusal of a case by providing information to the screening attorney's questions which are not adequately answered by the police report. As one screening prosecutor noted, sometimes a case does not look so bad after talking to the officer. On the other hand, the fact that an officer wants to charge an arrestee (or sometimes wants his case refused) is not decisive. At times various officers get quite frustrated by the office's refusal to prosecute "bad actors" whom they have arrested. Yet again, they are sometimes upset for the opposite reason. If strong evidence is present, the screening attorney may accept the case over an occasional officer's objection. One officer complained he had been unsuccessful in getting the Screening Division to refuse certain drug cases which he thought should not have been prosecuted because of certain factors in the arrestee's favor.

Some officers generally have their cases accepted; others rarely do.[54] In many cases, the police officer's credibility determines how much weight the screening prosecutor gives to his input. The prosecutors ask themselves whether the officer generally "makes good cases"; accurate investigations; legal "busts"; and whether he or she tells you "how it really went down."

---

[46] However, this disparity might not represent a breakdown in policy. The charges dismissed could be charges other than the ones covered by the policy. Also, many of the burglaries in our sample are nonresidential and therefore not restricted regarding charge dismissal.

[47] Louisiana Code of Criminal Procedure, Article 61.

[48] Ibid., Art. 382.

[49] See, e.g., *Coleman v. Alabama*, 399, U.S. 1 (1970).

[50] Louisiana Code of Criminal Procedure, Article 386. Informally, the New Orleans magistrates have adopted an unwritten policy regarding release of arrestees against whom timely charges have not been filed. The prosecutor must accept or reject charges against an arrestee within the shorter of two possible time periods: 1) within 10 days after the initial appearance (which is a bond hearing held within a few hours of booking); or 2) within 3 days after the preliminary hearing (set by the magistrate only on request of the defendant anywhere from 1 to 7 days after the initial appearance depending upon the schedule of the arresting officer).

[51] If charges have not been accepted during this period of time, the magistrate may grant an extension if the arrestee is on bond. With jail cases, the magistrate may grant a release on recognizance if the crime is not serious. For a more serious crime, the magistrate is likely to grant an extension even though the defendant is in jail. If the magistrate refused an extension in a serious case, the assistant district attorney present would probably file some charge against the arrestee simply to prevent his release and to allow the screening division the time needed to review the case.

---

[52] If the police report has not arrived, the screening division gets the names of at least some witnesses from the arrest register which is available to the prosecutor at the initial appearance from the police.

[53] Certain persons listed as witnesses, usually certain police officers, are not "necessary" because they cannot testify to anything in court. In the case of police officers, they may be listed as witnesses although they only transported the arrestee to police headquarters and could not be used to testify to anything at trial unless the arrestee gave a statement while in their custody.

[54] For an analysis of the difference among police officers in getting cases accepted, see Forst, Lucianovic and Cox, 1977.

The length of the delay is related to the complexity of the case and to whether or not the police department is currently paying its officers overtime. According to one screening prosecutor, when overtime pay is not available, a backup in the flow of police reports occurs.

The screening prosecutor may also hear from the defense attorney but the defense attorney must initiate the contact.[55] The value of defense counsel's involvement at the New Orleans screening is problematic. Most of the information which he or she might bring to the attention of the screeners would probably be found out by them eventually.[56] One possible value noted by a defense attorney is the locating of alibi witnesses. He claims that people in lower class, high crime neighborhoods will talk to defense attorneys but will not cooperate as readily with police and prosecutors.

Although the police have no formal screening authority, they may in fact informally screen cases in several ways. Some officers, e.g., narcotics officers, may tend to screen out cases thought unworthy of prosecution, e.g., possession of marijuana, simply by not arresting persons who have committed the offense. At times, officers may agree not to arrest in return for information. This constitutes a type of plea bargaining. If the officer were to arrest the person and then attempt to get his charges reduced or dismissed, he would have to go through channels by getting a letter from the police superintendent's office to the district attorney requesting such consideration. For some misdemeanors, the police have the option of charging the defendant with the appropriate municipal offense rather than the corresponding state charge. By sending the case to Municipal Court, the police can avoid the District Attorney's Office and deal, instead, with the City Attorney's Office. This is done at times either for convenience or because a police officer thinks the District Attorney's Office will refuse a charge.

Under prior district attorneys, the screening of cases was minimal. A very small proportion of the prosecutor's manpower was devoted to "the desk" where incoming cases were accepted or rejected. Approximately 75 to 85 percent of the incoming cases were accepted. The result was a glut of cases in the court system. Many cases sat dormant for years in file drawers. There was no systematic docket control.

After assuming office in April 1974, the new District Attorney, Harry Connick, gave priority to controlling the flow of cases. An inventory recorded over 7,500 open cases, many old and some dating as far back as 1936. Within 6 months approximately 5,000 cases were nol prossed as unprosecutable. Next, the prosecutor's office established an extensive screening system.[57] Connick built his other policies (most notably his limited plea bargaining policy) around this strategy of intense screening.

The Screening Division has the responsibility to fully investigate cases before acceptance or rejection. The screening prosecutor must interview the victim and essential witnesses (police and lay) before deciding on charges. Theoretically, the screening attorneys accept only charges that can be proved beyond a reasonable doubt at trial without any reduction for plea purposes.

As part of an overall policy of accountability the Screening Division maintains a system of review. The screening assistant must record his reasons for the refusal of every case not accepted. In turn, a supervisor reviews all refusals. As for acceptances, when at a later stage a trial assistant desires to nol pros a case, he or she must get approval from the screening attorney who accepted the case as well as from the Chief of Trials and the First Assistant. This holds the screening attorney responsible for judgment calls and uses his or her knowledge of the case as a check against the trial assistant's judgment of the same case.

The emphasis placed upon screening requires that the screening be done by more experienced trial attorneys. Only they can be expected to know whether a case can be proven to a jury. Traditionally, however, assistant district attorneys have preferred the "action" of the courtroom to the responsibilities of the "desk." Accordingly, Connick employs incentives in terms of pay and status to entice experienced trial assistants to the position of screening attorney. As a result, the less experienced

---

[55] If the defendant is not yet represented by counsel, of course, no one will appear on his behalf. In the case of indigents, counsel is appointed at the initial bond hearing and again at the preliminary hearing. This attorney, however, is not the one who will later represent the individual if charges are accepted against him. Particular counsel is not generally appointed until arraignment on the formal charges. Between arrest and this arraignment an indigent is not actually being represented except at his appearances in Magistrate Court.
The question naturally arises as to whether the indigent receives "unequal treatment" as a result of the lack of representation at the screening stage. The answer to this is unclear. No doubt in some cases private attorneys gain concessions for their clients that are not generally available once a case is accepted. In such cases, the paying defendant is being represented. In other cases, defense attorneys agree on behalf of their clients to enter pleas at arraignment to what appears to be a charge lower than what might otherwise have been accepted. In fact, however, according to certain assistant district attorneys, some of those cases are ones that otherwise would have been *rejected!*

[56] This is in sharp contrast to the situation in other jurisdictions where prosecutorial screening is less aggressive. In Greenville, S.C., for instance, a defense attorney who is a courthouse regular reported that one of his most important services to his clients is in supplying the prosecutor's office with information which they need to screen out or properly assess the case. He might produce a hotel receipt showing the defendant was out of town on the date in question. In New Orleans the screening prosecutors would be expected to find such receipts through their own investigations.

[57] Funded by the Law Enforcement Assistance Administration of the U.S. Department of Justice.

attorneys generally staff the individual trial courts. Not all of the experience, however, has been drained from the courtroom. A separate division, the Career Criminal Bureau (CCB),[58] composed of more experienced trial attorneys, screen as well as try the more serious cases.

CCB forms another basic building block in Connick's overall policy. CCB combines the functions of the trial and screening attorneys. Experienced attorneys target arrestees who have five or more felony arrests and/or convictions. When a "career criminal" is arrested, a CCB attorney takes charge of the investigation, often at the point of arrest, decides whether the case will be accepted or rejected, and follows the case from the first appearance through trial of the case. The CCB unit also maintains its own system of supervisory review.

Under Connick's policies, a large number of cases is screened out of the system. The impact of these policies can be seen in Table 2.3 below which includes a partial comparison with the screening practices of the previous administration.

Table 2.3   Case rejection at initial screening, New Orleans, 1972–76

	1972	1973	1974 *	1975	1976
Acceptances:					
Cases	6756	7937	6312 (59%)	6375 (60%)	5063 (56%)
Defendants **	NA	9127	7642 (58%)	7605 (58%)	6057 (54%)
Counts ***	NA	NA	NA	NA	7454 (38%)
Refusals:					
Cases	NA	NA	4363 (41%)	4884 (40%)	3919 (44%)
Defendants	NA	NA	5483 (42%)	5454 (42%)	5142 (46%)
Counts *	NA	NA	NA	NA	11,885 (62%)

* The Connick administration assumed office on April 1, 1974.

** Not available.

*** Joinder of offenses was not generally permissible in Louisiana until September 1975. See La. C.C.R.P. Article 493.

---

[58] Also Federally funded.

As indicated in Table 2.3 there was approximately a 20 percent decrease in the number of cases accepted in both 1974 and 1975 as compared with the last calendar year of the previous administration, 1973. Also the number of cases accepted in both 1974 and 1975 is slightly lower than even the 1972 figures.

Connicks' policy specifies that only strong, triable cases are to be accepted for prosecution. The rationale for the policy is to avoid glutting the system with cases that cannot be tried and hence must be either plea bargained or nol prossed. Connick believes the screening policy makes it possible to enforce a tough, "no" (limited) plea bargaining policy because the prosecutor is always in the position to go to trial. Consequently, once a case is accepted for prosecution, office policy dictates that the defendant either plead guilty as charged or go to trial. Connick has not tried to eliminate plea bargaining. He believes it is a legitimate tool in limited circumstances. His purpose has been to eliminate the atmosphere of "dealing" between prosecutor and wrongdoer. He wants plea bargaining to be the exception rather than the rule and he wants to see serious criminals given appropriately severe sentences.

Given Connick's screening and plea bargaining policy one would not expect to find any overcharging. This was generally borne out both in the opinion of defense attorneys and in our sample of cases. However, several attorneys thought a little bit of horizontal overcharging occurs. However, as Table 2.3 shows, the District Attorney's Office accepts a much smaller percentage of the counts (police charges referred to the office) (38 percent) than it does cases (56 percent) or defendants (54 percent). This reflects the difference between the police tendency to list two or more crimes in their initial charging papers and the prosecutor's tendency to go with one charge.[59] This difference can also be seen in Table 2.2 wherein 52 percent of the cases contained two or more charges on the initial complaint but only 11 percent of the cases contained two or more charges on the formal accusation.

Table 2.2 also appears to indicate that Connick's no-plea-bargaining policy is successful. There is almost no change in the proportion of cases with only one charge at the formal accusation (90 percent) compared to conviction (91 percent). In other words, it appears that defendants are pleading as charged. This is true but deceptive. It does not reflect the whole picture. It does not include the reduction in the habitual offender allegations

---

[59] The prosecutor's charging practice in this regard is influenced by the rules of joinder of offenses in one indictment. A defendant upon motion can routinely get a severance of offenses (*State v. McZeal*, 352 So. 2d 607 (1978). Thus each count must stand on its own. Obviously, this minimizes horizontal overcharging.

nor does it reflect sentence recommendations. Our data (which include those matters) indicate that charge reductions or dismissals alone occurred in 27 percent of the cases and sentence recommendations alone occurred in 56 percent (see Figure 2.2). (Still more of each occurred in combination with each other.) One common form of charge bargaining not reflected in the formal accusation or conviction statistics is the agreement not to file the "multiple bill" (habitual offender provisions) or to reduce the number of prior convictions alleged in the multiple bill.[60] This has a direct consequence on the sentence because the multiple bill places a mandatory minimum on the sentence which is increased with every additional prior conviction alleged. Through the use of the multiple bill the prosecutor's office is able to get defendants to plead as charged while simultaneously controlling the sentencing of judges who are considered too lenient.

The main complaint about charging in New Orleans was not about overcharging but about *undercharging*. The police and defense attorneys believed the prosecutor's office undercharged cases. By this they meant two things. The office rejected cases that should have been accepted; and it filed lower charges than were appropriate, for example, simple robbery when a basis existed for armed robbery with an implied weapon (finger in the pocket).

Police complaints about the charging practices of prosecutors are common in most jurisdictions (McDonald et al., 1981). But in New Orleans where the case rejection rate went from about 20 percent under the old administration to about 45 percent under Connick, they reached a peak. The Police Department publicly declared that they refused to believe they were "wrong" in almost half of their arrests (Times-Picayune, 1974). A summit meeting between the two agencies was held at which the District Attorney's Office presented a report showing the reasons for the rejections of the cases. For many cases the reason was that the victim/witness did not want to pursue the matter. For these cases the prosecutor's office had written "sign off" statements from the victims/witnesses. The Police Department has evidently been appeased. It has now begun a case review process of its own in which it records the disposition it expects in a case. When these expectations were compared to what actually occurred, they were largely (90 percent) in agreement with the prosecutor's office's actual decisions.

---

[60] For further analysis of the use of the habitual offender law in Louisiana, see Subsection G on that general topic herein.

Assessing the validity of the complaint by defense attorneys that the Connick administration undercharges is difficult. It again raises the uncertain nature of what constitutes proper charging. Rather than some objective standard the definition of proper charging ultimately involves an ethical choice. One must first indicate what overall penological strategy one is attempting to accomplish. Then "proper" charging can be defined in relationship to that objective. The charging standards of the national groups do not address this first order issue. They deal with second order issues which set certain ethical limits on the means by which the overall strategy is pursued.

One oversimplified but fundamental choice in designing an overall strategy is between giving a little punishment to a lot of cases or a lot of punishment to a few, selected cases. Connick believes in the latter strategy. His critics seem to be upset for either one or both of two reasons. They believe the former strategy is in the better interest of community safety; or they cynically believe that the main reason for pursuing the latter strategy is its political benefits. It allows the prosecutor to accept only cases he can win and thereby gives his office a good "track record."

El Paso County (Tex.). El Paso County has two separate prosecutors' offices. The District Attorney handles felonies in the District Court and the County Attorney handles misdemeanors in the County Court. In El Paso City, a third office, the City Attorney, handles violations of municipal ordinances. Initial charging is done by the police, who are under no guidelines regarding the degree or number of charges to file. Generally police officers seem to select charges based on a literal reading of the penal code for the maximum crime(s) that fit(s) the offense(s), as suggested by the following interview with a patrolman.

> Q: How do you charge? Do you include all things you can?
> A: We had a case where these people stole a car and robbed two guys. We charged them with "stolen auto" and "aggravated robbery."
>
> Q: Do you know what the D.A. finally charged these people with?
> A: I am sure they went for the aggravated robbery. But the stolen vehicle was kind of shaky.
>
> *Note:* The D.A. did not charge aggravated robbery; nor was the stolen auto charged. Only robbery was charged.

Occasionally, a specific policy comes into being as a way of trying to deter a particular problem. According to a robbery detective, the patrol officers "used to charge those guys who go into convenience stores and take six-packs of beer with 'theft.' Now they're charging them with 'robbery' because it's happening too much."

The initial charges that the arresting officer wants filed are reviewed at the booking desk in the police department by his supervisor. The nature of this review depends entirely upon the individual supervisor on duty. As one patrolman explained,

"Some will go over it carefully and tell you if you have a good case. Some guys will go over it for spelling only. They're not concerned with the content at all. Some supervisors, you take it in there, lay it on the desk, and they don't even look at it. My supervisor will want to know everything about the case and what we want to file."

Supervisors who do review cases check to see if the elements of the crime are there and whether the report is understandable. Some warn patrolmen against blatant overcharging, as one patrolman reported:

"Some will tell me to go another charge. Like some times in class C cases, I bring a guy in; I file drunk, disorderly conduct, interfering, all this; all the way down the line—[somebody gave me a real hard time]. And, the [supervisor] will say, 'Why don't you go "drunk and disorderly" because the prosecutor will think you're "picking" on a guy.' "

Cases will be reviewed again within the Police Department by detectives who decide whether a case should be sent to the District Attorney or the County Attorney's Office. One detective explained,

"We have good working relations [with the D.A.]. They leave a lot of initial screening up to our discretion * * *. There are different offenses that range down from C misdemeanor on up to first degree felony. It's a matter of whether or not it would be impractical to all parties concerned to present a case to the D.A. when it should have been presented to County Attorney's. So we use discretion where to send a case. * * * Of course if anything does come up in investigations that a case should be changed to a felony, then it will be sent up to the D.A. But initial screening is right here in our office."

These officers have developed a detailed knowledge of the legal requirements of specific offenses and the kinds of proof problems which occur. They differ from many police officers in this degree of detailed knowledge of the law. But they are similar to police officers everywhere in that they lack an experienced prosecutor's feel for the subtleties of case strength. They can recognize when they don't have a case but for the most part their screening is based on a mechanical application of penal code definitions to the facts of particular cases. Interviews with the police officer in charge of the CAP (crime against persons) unit and the Head of the Sex Crimes unit reveal how adroit the police can become at screening. These officers do not appear intent on overcharging. Rather, their sophistication suggests that with training and adequate supervision experienced police officers could serve as effective initial screeners.

Q: So you make the [screening] decision based upon the arrest report whether a given case should be sent on or to whom it should be sent?
A. (CAP Officer): At the point that it comes into our office for screening, from the original field officer's report, at that point we determine what type of investigation should be initiated * * *. Some cases involving assault we won't know how to specifically handle it until we see or talk to the persons involved to determine the type of injuries or the means of the offense committed.

Q: What types of things do you look for on deciding if a case should be screened out?
A. (CAP Officer): We look for elements that constitute that particular penal offense. There may be one element that's decisive whether it should be sent to the D.A. or County Attorney.

A. (Sex Officer): We have about the same problem screening cases [as does CAP]. Yet age is the most important part of any sex offense.

Q: In what way?
A. (Sex Officer): The difference in age between 16 and 17, say in an exposure case, is the difference between a Class C misdemeanor and a third-degree felony.

We have a lot of cases where a boyfriend is accused of raping a girl and after a few days she has second thoughts on it and decides, "Well I don't want to get him into all that trouble, get him sentenced to jail."

Q: What if you have an 18-year-old kid who is with his date and pulls off her underwear then she jumps out of the car screaming? What do you do with that?
A. (Sex Officer): Well, it's attempted rape. But, how are you going to prove it? What were his intentions? Well, you can't prove he intended to rape her. Maybe he wanted to look at her. Attempted rape is an impossibility to make.

Q: In this case what would you do? Forward it on to the D.A.?
A: We'd probably have an assault by contact case. When it boils down to it, that's all we got. That's assuming she'll press charges. We don't have any

sex violation. I might add that, again, in the screening process you're trying to read elements to fit laws of our state.

Q: You look for the elements that constitute an offense?

A. (Sex Officer). Right.

Q: If there aren't elements, you'd drop the case at this point?

A. (Sex Officer): No. We can change the charge. Say we don't have grounds to prove a rape, then we have sexual abuse or some other charges we can put it under. Might be lesser charge or sometimes a harder charge.

Q: Are there any formal or informal policies regarding screening? For example, are there crimes that are not routinely processed?

A. (CAP Officer): No. Generally we go strictly by guidelines in the Penal Code. It's very clear.

These officers do *not* screen out cases in which an arrest has been made. All such cases, even ones which they know will have to be terminated, are transmitted to the D.A. (or other prosecuting official) who takes responsibility for the actual termination. All felony cases are delivered to the D.A.'s Screening Bureau, which is located in the same police building. It is staffed by two attorneys who have had some trial experience and two investigators from the Police Department. Their view of cases relies largely upon the information provided by the detectives, who will usually have spoken to the prosecutors already about the investigative needs of the cases as the detectives were screening them. The prosecutors may still ask for further investigation (e.g., clarification of a witness' statement) before deciding what formal charges to bring. The prosecutors themselves do not usually meet with victims and witnesses. They rely on the police to make those important judgments about the credibility and reliability of these people. One robbery detective explained, "Most of the time he'll [the prosecutor] ask us if he's a 'good' victim, credible, reliable. Does he gotta good record? Not a good record? Does he *have* a record?"

Prior to the establishment of the Screening Bureau in the early 1970's the preliminary hearing ("examining trial") was used as the main screening mechanism. Now preliminary hearings are held in about 5 percent of all felonies. Instead the District Attorney takes his cases directly to the grand jury. The standard of case strength used by the Screening Bureau is whether a case can be won at trial. Approximately 60 percent of the cases forwarded to the Bureau are rejected. According to the Chief of the Bureau, the detectives do a good job of catching the

blatant weaknesses in a case, such as a lack of statements from witnesses or a failure to substantiate the elements of a crime. But they are unable to anticipate how a case will look at trial and how local juries will perceive witnesses. The cases his Bureau rejects are not ones where there is no evidence linking a defendant to a crime. They are ones where the evidence is not enough to make a conviction very probable.

Local defense attorneys generally agree that there is no overcharging by the District Attorney's Office. Rather (as seems to be typical in places where prosecutors operate vigorous screening standards) defense counsel accused the District Attorney's Office of accepting only "pure gold" (very strong) cases in order to protect its conviction record. Our sample of burglary and robbery cases indicates that the police rarely file more than one charge per case (17 percent); the District Attorney's Office rarely changes the number of charges; and charges are rarely dropped at conviction. Of course, it must be recalled that the District Attorney's Office does no plea bargaining of any kind.

One additional fact about the screening of felonies by police and prosecutors in El Paso is of particular note. When the District Attorney decided to end all plea bargaining by prosecutors, the judges were left with the job of supplying defendants with the incentive to plead. Rather than assume that responsibility they established a point system by which defendants could assess whether they would get probation or incarceration if they pleaded guilty. One of the key determinants of the score a defendant received in the point system was the seriousness of the charge in the instant offense. In addition the seriousness of charges in his prior record also influenced the points. Under this system the charging decision assumed a new significance. Given the popular notion that restricting discretion at one part of the justice process only shifts it to another part, one might have predicted that either the police or the prosecutor might have used their newly enhanced charging power to decide the sentencing fate of defendants. But such a prediction would have been wrong. The police were generally unaware of the point system or how it worked; and the screening prosecutors' overriding concern was the triability of cases.

The handling of misdemeanors in El Paso differs from felonies. There is no followup investigation. Disposition decisions are usually made on the basis of the police report alone. The charges are those filed by the police. There is no screening as such. Rather cases are briefly reviewed for disposition which frequently is either a quick dismissal or a "slow" dismissal (after diversion) or a guilty plea. One key determinant of whether the outcome is a dismisal or a guilty plea seems to be whether or not the defendant can afford counsel. Dismissals are usually obtained by defense attorneys by contacting the County Attorney's Office between the time the case is initially filed by the police and the Friday "arraignment" session. Counsel may argue that the case is weak or the penalty would be too severe. The County Attorney's Office appears to be less interested in case strength than in the impact of the conviction on the defendant. For example, if the defendant drives a truck for a living and is charged with driving while intoxicated, the case will almost always be dismissed.

Misdemeanor defendants who do not have attorneys will discuss their cases directly with the Assistant County Attorneys who generally advise them to plead guilty to avoid being "creamed" if they go to trial and in order to get probation or diversion right away. These cases do not ordinarily get dismissed outright. They either get diverted and then dismissed or they plead guilty and get probation. One assistant County Attorney reported that dealing directly with defendants is more difficult than dealing with attorneys and that this affects the ultimate disposition.

> I try to treat each case as it comes along. On reflection, though, there may be some categories, types of responses that I usually have to certain cases. One thing, it's more difficult to deal with defendants who are unrepresented because they don't understand what's going on . . . Those defendants with lawyers come out better because I feel safer in discussions with attorneys.

Later when asked how he would handle a case where the evidence falls apart after the case is in the system, this prosecutor replied:

> My response to it varies depending on whether there is a defense attorney involved in the case. If there is a defense attorney, I'll dismiss it . . . If there is no attorney I'll try to get the defendant to plead guilty.

Charging habitual/repeat offenders

One aspect of the charging process which requires separate mention is the use of the "repeat" or "habitual" offender laws. Most states have special sentencing provisions which either permit or require more severe sentences for repeat offenders (Tappan, 1960:742). These laws are notable for two main reasons: their lack of use and their involvement of the prosecutor in the sentencing process. Typically the sentence-enhancing effect of a habitual offender law can only be applied if the prosecutor has charged the defendant with being a habitual offender. This usually involves filing documents which es-

tablish that the defendant is a person who has been previously convicted of one or more felonies. The effect of these charges vary by jurisdiction. Some increase the maximum sentence allowable; others impose a mandatory minimum. Experience has shown that where these laws are used at all they usually have been employed as bargaining chips to be traded away in exchange for pleas rather than to secure severe sentences (Tappan, 1960:473). But by and large, the laws are not used. Even in jurisdictions where the law requires that prosecutors file habitual offender proceedings against eligible offenders district attorneys refuse to file the charges (Miller, 1970:380).

All six of our jurisdictions have habitual offender laws. All but Pennsylvania provide for enhanced penalties upon a second conviction of a felony. In Pennsylvania a third penitentiary sentence of more than one year triggers the habitual offender statute, as does the commission of a second crime of violence within 5 years of the instant offense. In Arizona the commission of a second felony doubles the maximum which can be imposed. In Virginia it authorizes any term up to life imprisonment. In Washington conviction for a second felony triggers a minimum 10-year sentence. In Texas it makes the maximum sentence for the second crime the mandatory sentence. In Louisiana prior felony convictions impose mandatory minimum sentences which increase with every additional felony conviction. If one prior conviction is established, the mandatory minimum sentence is not less than one-third and not more than twice the maximum for the instant conviction.[61] For two prior convictions, the mandatory minimum is not less than half the maximum. For three, it is not less than 20 years or the maximum, whichever is longer, and not more than life.

The infrequent use of the habitual offender laws was reconfirmed by our research. In five of the six jurisdictions, substantial proportions (from 22 percent to 50 percent) of the defendants in our sample had records of prior felony convictions within five years;[62] yet, few had their sentences enhanced (see Tables 2.4 and 2.5). Of the 968 defendants in all six jurisdictions combined who appeared to be eligible for enhancement only, 14.1 percent had the habitual offender laws applied to them. Only in New Orleans was the habitual offender law invoked against a substantial (56.1 percent) proportion of the eligible defendants. As noted earlier, this is due to

---

[61] Louisiana Revised Statute Annotated, 15:529.1. The statute was held constitutional, *State v. Vale*, 252 La. 1056, 215 So. 2d 811 (1968).

[62] The within-5-year qualification is not required by law but we added it because in our experience older prior records tend to be disregarded by decisionmakers. This restriction means our findings underestimate by a slight amount the size of the population eligible for habitual offender proceedings.

District Attorney Connick's policy of using the mandatory minimum provisions of the habitual offender law as an important plea bargaining and sentencing weapon. By agreeing to reduce the number of prior felonies alleged in exchange for a plea, Connick's office can obtain a plea "without reducing the charges." The structure of the Louisiana habitual offender sentencing provisions gives the prosecutor's office powerful levers to induce pleas.

Table 2.4 Frequency of prior felony convictions within 5 years of instant offense among defendants who pleaded guilty or were tried for robbery or burglary by jurisdiction

	El Paso	New Orleans	Seattle	Tucson	Delaware County	Norfolk
Number of prior felony convictions within 5 years of instant offense	(N=197)	(N=321)	(N=735)	(N=474)	(N=605)	(N=515)
None	77.7%	56.6%	66.5%	50.2%	57.8%	54.8%
1–2	18.3%	37.4%	29.8%	31.7%	30.1%	30.5%
3+	4.0%	5.0%	3.7%	18.1%	12.1%	14.7%

Table 2.5 Frequency of habitual offender enhancements of sentences of defendants who pleaded guilty or were tried for robbery or burglary and had one or more prior felony conviction(s) within 5 years by jurisdiction *

	El Paso	New Orleans	Seattle	Tucson	Delaware County	Norfolk
Was defendant sentenced as habitual offender?	(N=44)	(N=180)	(N=246)	(N=236)	(N=73)	(N=233)
Yes	22.7%	56.1%	3.2%	5.1%	8.2%	0.0%

* For Delaware County only defendants with three or more prior felony convictions are included.

Formalization and plea bargaining

Analysis. Along with the trend of the prosecutor assuming greater importance in the administration of criminal justice there has been a trend toward increasing formalization of the prosecutor's office. The larger offices have established centralized managerial control through the issuance of written policies and the hierarchial structuring of the chain of command and of case review. The difference among offices in this regard is a matter of degree. In smaller offices formalization has not occurred to any substantial degree. Policies, procedures, chain-of-command, and review of decisionmaking are not well developed or systematically observed and applied. The ideology of management in such offices is that every prosecutor is a professional person who can make his or her own decisions without specific policy guidance except for the "important" decisions which are to be made by the chief prosecutor. But staff attorneys are often left with little guidance as to which decisions are important enough to be referred to the chief. The guidance provided by one chief prosecutor makes this point. He tells his assistants, "You're right until you're wrong."

The effort to exert managerial and policy control over assistant prosecutors has been met with resistance and resentment. It conflicts with assistant prosecutors' images of themselves as professionals. The hallmark of professionalism is the authority to exercise one's individual judgment and discretion. Policies that restrict discretion are lampooned as turning expensive legal talent into paper-pushing clerks.

A second objection is even more fundamental. It is the pervasive belief that every case is unique and therefore discretion is a necessity and specific policy guidance an impossibility. The kernel of truth in this assertion often gets nourished into a general objection to written guidelines and policies on the grounds that policies cannot decide individual cases.

These objections together with the historically small size of prosecutors' offices probably account for the slow development of explicit prosecutorial policies of control and review. But that is changing [63] and some observers would believe this is for the better (e.g., Brietel, 1960; Davis, 1969; and Jacoby, 1975, 1980a, 1980b, and 1980c). The broad discretion of the American prosecutor has long been worrisome both because of its potential for abuse as well as its consequences for the evenhandedness of case dispositions. Reformers have believed that these dangers can be minimized by policy controls.

As shown earlier, prosecutors' offices that have developed the greatest degree of formalization have included policies governing both the charging and the plea bargaining decisions. This formalization should be related to numerous aspects of case processing, especially those having to do with the consistency of case handling. One would also expect that greater formalization would be positively correlated with the swiftness and efficiency of dispositions as well as the thoroughness of case record-keeping. Also, inasmuch as formalization has meant higher charging standards (at least in New Orleans and Seattle) one would expect less charge bargaining and generally stronger cases (among those that are accepted).

We examined some of the correlates of the degree of formalization of the prosecutor's office using the sample of robbery and burglary cases. In this analysis five of our six jurisdictions [64] were rank ordered along a scale of degree of formalization from highest to lowest as follows: New Orleans, Seattle, Tucson, Delaware County, and Norfolk. This ranking is not based on any quantified formula but rather on our judgments. The extent to which one or more of the following conditions were present was used in deciding the rank order of the offices: the use of a managerial information system (either computerized or manual); the existence, specificity and comprehensiveness of office guidelines for case disposition decisions; the presence of specialized decisionmaking units; the use of required sign-off and review procedures; and the degree of use of written documentation of

decisions and their rationales. The five jurisdictions differed in many other ways besides the degree of formalization, most notably by the size of the office and of the caseload. Given our sample of only five jurisdictions, these other factors could not be held constant. Thus, this analysis can only be regarded as exploratory. The relationships that were found must be verified with a large sample.

The degree of formalization of prosecutors' offices was found to be significantly related to selected aspects of case processing (see Table 2.6). In the jurisdictions with the more formalized prosecutors' offices the number of police charges were lower. (Possibly the police had adjusted their charging practices to those of the prosecutor.) The amount of charge bargaining was lower. (There were fewer charges on the indictment/information; there was a lower probability that the charges on the indictment/information would be reduced; if formal charges were dismissed, fewer were involved in the dismissal; the plea bargain was more likely to include a sentence recommendation; and the total number of charges at conviction were fewer.) The cases which go to guilty plea or trial were stronger. (They were more likely to have physical evidence and more likely to have an eyewitness.) [65] Guilty pleas were more fair and open to review in the sense that there is a greater probability that a record of the plea agreement will be in the files. Cases were disposed of more quickly (with the difference being due primarily to a shorter time from arrest to indictment).

Discussion. While this statistical analysis is only suggestive of possible correlates of formalization, its findings consistently agree with the impressions we developed through our observations and interviews. The character of plea bargaining differs from one jurisdiction to the next based on the role the prosecutor chooses to play in the system. One crucial aspect of that role is the nature of the screening process.

Plea bargaining in jurisdictions where (a) cases have been rigorously screened by (b) trial-experienced prosecutors (c) using a high threshold level of legal proof and (d) having direct interactions with the police who investigated the cases (e) as well as with victims and witnesses is qualitatively different from plea bargaining in other jurisdictions. Several of the institutional weaknesses of plea bargaining as a method of dispensing criminal justice are significantly offset by such a system

---

[63] For a report on one attempt to screen cases using a quantitative scale based on office policy, see Jacoby, 1975.

[64] El Paso was excluded because of its no plea bargaining policy.

[65] Note that this does *not* mean that the police in those more formalized jurisdictions are bringing in stronger cases. Rather it reflects the efficacy of the prosecutor's screening practices. That is, his office only allows strong cases to go to guilty plea or trial at the felony level.

Table 2.6   Relationship between degree of formalization of the prosecutor's office and selected aspects of case dispositions*

If there is a high degree of formalization of the prosecutor's office, then:	N	df	x^2	gamma	P<.01
1. there is a lower number of police charges filed;	3136	16	1734	0.31	*
2. there is a lower number of charges in the indictment/information;	3120	16	2052	0.58	*
3. it is less likely that the number of charges in the indictment/information will be reduced;	2953	4	357	0.15	*
4. in cases where some charges are dismissed after indictment, then fewer charges are involved in this modification;	3084	20	1922	0.53	*
5. the total number of charges on which the defendant is convicted will be fewer;	2997	12	312	0.45	*
6. the plea bargain is more likely to include a sentence recommendation (either alone or in combination with a charge dismissal or reduction);	1681	4	711	0.38	*
7. it is more likely that there is physical evidence in the case;	2994	4	217	0.28	*
8. it is more likely that there is an eyewitness identification of the defendant in the case;	2804	4	216	0.21	*
9. it is more likely that there will be a record of the plea agreement;	2014	4	211	0.41	*
10. the time from arrest to disposition is shorter (the difference being due primarily to a shorter time from arrest to indictment).	3009	48	1155	0.31	*

* Based on robbery and burglary cases that went to guilty plea or trial in New Orleans, Seattle, Tucson, Norfolk and Delaware County. El Paso was not included because of the no plea bargaining policy.

of rigorous case screening. In unscreened systems the evidentiary strength of cases varies enormously and ordinarily is not subject to an impartial testing. Whatever challenge of the evidence that does occur happens in the context of plea negotiation. There each side is trying to convince the other of its strength. In contrast, in rigorously screened systems the strength of the evidence in a case is independently scrutinized by prosecutors with the intent of eliminating weak cases.

The extent to which rigorous case screening approximates the same degree of impartial and thorough scrutiny of a case that would occur at trial is arguable. Skeptics would say that prosecutors are inevitably biased in favor of prosecution despite their ethical obligation to seek justice, not convictions. However, the experience in New Orleans and Seattle suggests that, assuming this is generally true, it can be modified by appropriate incentives. Prosecutors in the screening unit in New Orleans are rewarded for ensuring that weak cases do *not* go forward. Prosecutorial skill is defined in terms of thorough case investigation and accurate assessment of case strength rather than in compiling a long list of convictions. Weak cases which slip through the screening unit are traced back to the screening prosecutor and regarded as an error on his part.

This kind of check on the judgments of prosecutors may not be equivalent of the challenge that is possible in an adversary process. But, on the other hand, observers familiar with biased juries and ill-prepared defense counsel suspect that the trial process itself is often not the most

impartial and thorough means of testing evidence. Many a tried case may have had its evidentiary strength tested more thoroughly by a rigorous screening unit than what was done at trial. Of course, even if rigorous screening is something less than a thorough challenge of the evidence, there is always the possibility that residual weaknesses will be discovered later by defense counsel.

The significance of rigorous screening is that it increases the degree of confidence we can have that the guilty plea process is convicting *provably* guilty defendants. It partially restores to the justice system those values associated with ideas about legality and the requirement of proof beyond a reasonable doubt. Those concerns are eroded by wide open plea bargaining in unfiltered systems. Moreover, the fact that only strong cases are allowed to proceed also minimizes the influence of case strength on plea bargaining outcomes. This enhances evenhandedness and restricts the influence of this penologically irrelevant factor. In addition, the integrity of the charging function is maintained. Accurate, supportable charges can be filed and maintained so that pleas will be to charges that will both correctly reflect the crimes committed and allow for appropriate punishment.

The main concern about screening programs with high threshold levels of case acceptability is that they reject cases that could have been convicted through plea bargaining. For those who believe that a little bit of punishment for a lot of offenders (regardless of the seriousness of their crimes or their prior records) deters more crime than the selective prosecution of a smaller number of serious offenders, rigorous screening is not regarded as a progressive reform.

Conclusion

That part of the controversy over plea bargaining which focuses on charge bargaining has been mired in the semantic quicksand of discussions about "overcharging." Underlying that controversy are three fundamental interrelated policy issues: whether there should be any plea bargaining at all; what role the prosecutor should play in the criminal justice process; and how the screening of cases in the postarrest-pretrial stage of the criminal justice process should be done (by whom, at what point in the process, and according to what standards). Historically, plea bargaining has been used as the main device by which cases were screened and disposed of. However, since the 1920's there has been a growing consensus that the screening of cases should be a separate function performed by the prosecutor at an early point in the process using an evidentiary standard of case acceptance that is higher than the constitutionally required standard of probable cause. Cases that do not meet this higher standard should be rejected outright (or returned for further investigation). They should not be allowed to enter the system and disposed of by guilty pleas. The fact that these cases have been allowed to enter the court system and then disposed of by guilty pleas is behind a lot of what is meant by the complaint about "overcharging."

That ambiguous term has been misunderstood by some people to mean the filing of charges for which there is not even enough legal proof to meet the probable cause standard. Others define it as filing charges not ordinarily filed. More commonly it is defined as filing many charges arising from separate incidents (horizontal overcharging) and filing the highest charge relevant to the offense (vertical overcharging). In both of these kinds of overcharging it is granted that the prosecutor has at least enough evidence to charge the defendant with some offense. In our view all of these definitions are misleading. The question is not one of legal proof. For instance, nine defense attorneys from four jurisdictions who said they thought the prosecutor's usual charging standard was at least a submissible case or stronger also said that "overcharging" is routine! Eight more who believed the prosecutor's charging standards were that high said that overcharging occurs occasionally. For these attorneys overcharging was nothing more than filing all (or many) of the charges that could lawfully be filed. Their complaint about overcharging is not about law but about policy. The underlying question is about how many charges should be filed when there are many charges which could be supported by admissible evidence. The implied answer of some critics of "overcharging" is that after a certain point the piling on of extra charges even though they are supportable is wrong.

A second issue is whether charges should ever be dropped or reduced in exchange for guilty pleas. In other words, should charge bargaining have any role in the disposition process or is the charging function to be something which should be kept separate and distinct from the plea negotiating process? This question does *not* necessarily presume that plea bargaining should be eliminated. Prosecutors might still be allowed to negotiate over sentences or judges might either plea negotiate or establish differentials for pleading.

At stake here are the practices in two kinds of jurisdictions. In some jurisdictions virtually all the plea bargaining is done through charge bargaining. Charges for all crimes at all levels are routinely dropped one or more grades in exchange for pleas regardless of the quality of the evidence. Eliminating this system would not necessarily eliminate plea bargaining in those jurisdictions but would require dramatic adjustments. This issue sometimes gets lost behind discussions of vertical overcharging because one of the practices it addresses is similar to vertical overcharging (although it has never been correctly identified). This unidentified practice consists of the routine reduction of charges in exchange for guilty pleas *regardless* of the quality of evidence. In some jurisdictions this occurs in virtually all negotiated cases. In many jurisdictions it occurs in certain types of cases which have been unofficially downgraded from the legal category in which they properly fit to something less (e.g., burglary of motor vehicles may not be treated as a burglary when the evidence is overwhelming). This downgrading serves not only to reduce caseloads but also to fine tune the broad categories of the penal code to the different degrees of seriousness of criminal activities that technically fall within the same legal category.

The complaint about this kind of "overcharging" is not about levels of proof but about the use of the charging mechanism to secure pleas. Charging cases at one level knowing that these cases will be routinely reduced in exchange for pleas is regarded by critics as "legal blackmail" and a corruption of both the charging process and the criminal justice system's record of information about the true seriousness of crimes committed. Reformers argue that "truly accurate" charges are the ones to which the case would be reduced after plea negotiations and that these charges should be the ones filed originally. Some believe that if truly accurate charges were filed originally there would be no need to offer defendants anything to induce them to plead guilty. Others believe that something else would have to be substituted to

47

induce guilty pleas. (They recommend sentence differentials—more lenient sentences for pleaders than those convicted at trial—which they do *not* regard as "plea bargaining.")

National groups have attempted to define proper charging. However their standards have confounded rather than resolved the issue. They recognize in the charging function two potentially conflicting goals. Generally, according to these standards prosecutors do not have to file all charges and should not file any charges unless they have evidence greater than probable cause. Also prosecutors should not file charges solely for the purpose of securing guilty pleas. Yet at the same time, they are supposed to file an adequate degree and number of charges to establish a proper record of the crime and of the seriousness of the defendant, and they are to charge in a way which allows for a proper sentence. These latter two standards can effectively put the prosecutor in the position of having to file the highest degree or greatest number of charge(s) to establish an adequate record but then to reduce the charge(s) in order to assure an appropriate sentence. The dual responsibility of establishing an adequate record and assuring an appropriate sentence is an invitation to charge bargain (although theoretically charges could be dropped unilaterally without being exchanged for pleas). In addition, the national groups specify or imply that prosecutorial screening should occur between arrest and initial charging. However, this standard needs reconsideration. It does not seem feasible in jurisdictions with numerous outlying lower courts which the prosecutors' offices cannot afford to staff, and it may be less effective than a review conducted at a later point in the process when a fuller investigation can be completed. The jurisdictions in our sample with the most rigorous prosecutorial screening conducted that screening 3 to 10 days after arrest. In those jurisdictions that have responded to the call for truly rigorous prosecutorial screening the nature of plea bargaining in *felony* cases differs in important ways from those which have not. Charge bargaining is reduced although not eliminated. "Accurate" charging has not eliminated the need to offer defendants an incentive to plead guilty. Cases are stronger and disposed of more rapidly. The influence of case strength on the terms of any plea negotiations is reduced because of the uniformly high case strength. Thus, this penologically irrelevant factor is minimized in the negotiation process. Moreover, the fact that cases are reviewed by experienced prosecutors who are rewarded for keeping cases out of the court system provides a major protection against one of the crucial weaknesses of plea bargaining as an institution. It restores in part that crucial principle of Anglo-American jurisprudence that before penal sanctions are imposed there must be proof beyond a reasonable doubt. In jurisdictions with truly rigorous screening we can have a greater degree of confidence that defendants convicted by plea bargaining are *probably* guilty defendants.

With regard to misdemeanors (and sometimes minor felonies) the situation is different. In jurisdictions we studied, those cases continue to be largely unscreened; controlled by the police; maximum charged; and routinely reduced for pleas. The reforms of the charging and plea bargaining processes that are being applied to felony cases are not being extended to petty offenses. The same prosecutor's office that has tried to eliminate maximum charging in felony cases has institutionalized a policy of maximum charging for the purpose of reducing charges for pleas in minor cases. The double standard of justice depending upon seriousness of offense is commonplace. Equal justice for the accused does not require perfect equality of treatment between the pettiest and the most serious case. But it does require a mitigation of the existing double standard.

Our data suggest that charge bargaining and the "overcharging" of felony cases can be controlled by policies short of prohibiting all plea bargaining by prosecutors. In implementing these policies the quality of justice is enhanced and certain important dangers of the plea bargaining system are minimized. Similar policies could operate at both the felony and the misdemeanor levels.

Chapter Three
Prosecutorial Bluffing and the Case Against Plea Bargaining

Introduction

One of the sources of concern about the institution of plea bargaining is the belief that gamesmanship plays a substantial role in the disposition of cases. That is, cases are often disposed of not on their merits but on the ability of the attorney for either side to outwit the other. Of course, the fate of cases that go to trial is sometimes determined by trial tactics. But the gamesmanship in plea bargaining is of a different kind. The concern is not about the inevitable differences between attorneys in legal skill but the unethical and otherwise inappropriate practices believed to be integral to the plea-negotiation process. A variety of questionable tactics have been reported. Defense attorneys are reported to extract lenient plea bargains by threatening to "court-bust"—take all of their cases to trial (Mills, 1971). Prosecutors are reported to bluff defendants into pleading guilty even when the state has no case (Alschuler, 1968). We attempted to determine the frequency of and attitudes toward each of these two practices in our interviews with defense attorneys and prosecutors. Our findings regarding the court-busting proclivities of defense attorneys are reported in Chapter 4. Our findings regarding bluffing by prosecutors are described below.

The only report on the latter practice is by a leading plea bargaining abolitionist, Professor Albert Alschuler (1968). He lists it [1] among the "horrors" (1968:64) of plea bargaining he presents in order to "justify" (1968:64) his "admittedly unorthodox position that plea bargaining should be abolished" (1968:52). He found that "very few

prosecutors apparently disapprove of bluffing" (1968:67) and that some prosecutors "freely avow their own practices of bluffing, concealment, and telling only half the truth" (1968:68). Bluffing, he says, is part of a routine phenomenon of "deceptive sales practices" (1968:67) that are not effectively checked either by judicial inquiries at plea acceptance or by defense counsel. The latter "are not equal competition in the game of deception" (1968:68); "it is not always easy to 'call' a prosecutor's bluff" (1968:66) especially "when he resorts to deliberate misrepresentation in an effort to sustain it" (1968:66).

Two aspects of bluffing as described by Alschuler do indeed sound horrendous. One is his report that bluffing is used to secure convictions in cases which he characterizes as "no case at all," "hopeless" cases that are "effectively unconvictable" (1968:65). A typical example of this "ultimate in a weak case" is the situation "in which a critical witness has died, refused to testify, or disappeared into the faceless city" (1968:65). "In this situation," he says, "plea negotiation *commonly* becomes a game of bluffing" (Id.).[2] Given the frequency with which this situation occurs,[3] the inference is strong that a lot of bluffing is going on.

---

[1] Alschuler disclaims our characterization of his report on bluffing.

[2] Emphasis added.

[3] We have no direct measures of the frequency of this event, but estimates are possible. Brosi's (1979:14) comparison of PROMIS data from 12 jurisdictions found that from 13 percent to 46 percent of felony cases are dropped after filing. One of the two main reasons for this was "witness problems" which covers a variety of subcategories. The subcategory "unable to locate/unavailable" accounted for 50 percent of the "witness problems" in Indianapolis and 19 percent in the District of Columbia. If one adds to this the cases of witnesses who refused to testify, the majority of cases dropped due to witness problems are ac-

The other disturbing part of Alschuler's report is his findings regarding the willingness of prosecutors to engage in deliberate misrepresentations to sustain their bluffs—sometimes going to considerable lengths. He quotes a Philadelphia prosecutor who admitted that he had "sometimes misrepresented the facts in an effort to induce the compromise of constitutional defenses" (1968:67). He says that "[p]rosecutors sometimes go to the point of empaneling a jury before dismissing a hopeless case, hoping all the while to exact a guilty plea" (1968:66). A Pittsburgh prosecutor told him of an occasion when he induced a guilty plea by "telling the defense attorney that a missing witness was waiting in his office for a chance to testify. After the guilty plea was offered the prosecutor put the arresting officer on the witness stand, and the officer presented hearsay evidence concerning the missing witness' version of the facts" (1968:67).[4] A San Francisco defense attorney reported that he had sometimes received telephone calls from prostitutes after he had been retained to represent their pimps. He says the prostitutes told him that the D.A. "bribed" them to make a statement (1968:65). And finally, a Houston defense attorney recalled an occasion where a prosecutor threatened to go to trial if he (the attorney) forced him (the prosecutor) to produce a missing witness. The prosecutor claimed the witness had been located and served a subpoena. The subpoena return was on file but because the attorney had been unable to locate the witness himself he "suspected that the process server had been made a party to the bluff and had filed a fraudulent return" (1968:67). When he refused the prosecutor's offer the case was dismissed.

Alschuler's portrayal of bluffing undoubtedly would give pause to even the staunchest supporter of plea bargaining. The image of prosecutors out to get something from every defendant; exhibiting a remarkable disregard for false conviction; magnifying pressures to plead guilty in cases where the evidence is most dubious; and lying, bribing and filing fraudulent returns in order to convict defendants in cases that are effectively unconvictable, is indeed a frightening prospect. In our view this portrait cried out for verification. We set out to determine the pervasiveness of bluffing and its susceptibility to remedial control. Our findings lead to a less abhorrent view of

prosecutorial ethics and of the role of bluffing in the plea bargaining process.

Findings

In one respect our findings agree with Alschuler's. The majority of our prosecutors approve of bluffing and most would bluff to obtain a guilty plea. But what they mean by bluffing differs in important respects from what Alschuler implies. Prosecutors regard only some bluffing as clearly improper and other bluffing as not only proper but desirable. In addition, there is a gray area where prosecutors disagree among themselves as to where to draw the line.

Bluffing of a certain kind and in certain circumstances is common, but most bluffing does not appear to be as unseemly as Alschuler suggests. Bluffing accompanied by deliberate misrepresentation and elaborate fraud did not appear to occur in our study sites with any frequency. The premise for Alschuler's criticism of what he seems to regard as the most deplorable type of bluffing—bluffing when the prosecutor has "no case at all"—is problematic. Our prosecutors did not agree that his "noncase" was "fatally defective." In order to make these points clear, it is necessary to provide some distinctions and to review the various circumstances under which bluffing might occur.

Central to bluffing is the notion of a weak case. The essence of bluffing is to pretend that one's case is stronger than it actually is. Cases can be or become weak for various reasons and bluffing could be resorted to under any of these circumstances. The bluffing that Alschuler condemns does not encompass all situations. Rather, it is limited primarily to the case which is so weak as to be "no case at all." We shall distinguish that case from other situations.

One kind of weak case is that in which completely groundless charges are brought against an unquestionably innocent defendant. A prosecutor who bluffed in such a case would clearly be acting not only unethically but illegally. We found no indication of this type of bluffing. There is little doubt that bluffing under these conditions would be unanimously condemned by prosecutors.

A second kind of weak case is one in which there is some evidence but it is weak. The key to the propriety of the prosecutor's decision to proceed with this type of case is whether he made a good-faith judgment that the case met the legally required standard of probable cause. If the prosecutor believed that it did not meet that standard but accepted it anyhow, he would have indulged in

---

counted for (in Detroit, Los Angeles, the District of Columbia, New Orleans, and Indianapolis). Of course, if Alschuler is right, then for the most part these cases represent only *unsuccessfully* bluffed cases. The successes are listed among the guilty pleas.

[4] This ruse succeeded, Alschuler implies, because "[t]he defense attorney raised no objection; he and everyone else involved in the proceedings were interested only in concluding the 'formalities' as rapidly as possible" (1968:67).

a bluff that was virtually as illegal and unethical as our first example. This type of bluffing was also not found.

Some cases are or appear to be quite strong at initial charging but subsequently become weak. Two types of weaknesses occur. One is related to the inherent quality of the evidence. For instance, a reliable alibi witness may be discovered; the prosecutor's star witness may not be able to pick the defendant out of a lineup; or a subsequent interview may reveal that a witness is confused and inconsistent. These kinds of weaknesses must be distinguished from those generated by logistical and administrative problems that may affect whether the case can be proved. For instance, the physical evidence may be lost or the witness may not have been notified to appear at a court hearing. This distinction between inherent and administrative weakness in a case is important. It is the basis for one of the informal courthouse norms regarding the limits of proper bluffing. Most prosecutors have no compunctions about hiding weaknesses caused by administrative problems, but they do have reservations about suppressing information regarding the inherent quality of the evidence.

The range of potential deceptiveness in bluffing varies widely from the mild puffery of an offhand remark, such as "We've got the goods on your client," to much more elaborate frauds. Some of this territory is governed by law and by codes of professional ethics. However, it is not until one reaches the territory that lies either outside of or on the boundary of that area which is clearly governed by official norms that bluffing practices become problematic.

There exist legal restrictions on bluffing. Prosecutors may not legally file charges where the evidence does not meet the probable-cause standard. Also, they are no longer permitted to hide certain aspects of their cases. Upon request of defense counsel, prosecutors must make available the results of ballistics tests, chemical analyses, lineups, statements made by the defendant to the police, and other aspects of the case (*Brady* v. *United States*, 373 U.S. 83 [1963]). In addition, prosecutors have a duty to turn over any exculpatory evidence, even without a prior request having been made for it (*United States* v. *Aqur*, 427 U.S. 97 [1976]). Thus if a bluff involved suppressing discoverable or exculpatory evidence, it would be illegal.

Alschuler does not suggest that prosecutors are suppressing discoverable evidence. As for exculpatory evidence, his findings are less clear in part because of the ambiguity of the notion of exculpatory evidence and in part because his study was done before the Supreme Court imposed this rule on prosecutors. We found no evidence that prosecutors were suppressing discoverable evidence

(although we regularly heard that prosecutors will make the discovery procedure more cumbersome for certain defense attorneys whom they disliked or distrusted). In regard to exculpatory evidence, the situation is more difficult to assess because exculpatory evidence is not clearly defined. Some evidence is clearly exculpatory (for example, reliable evidence showing that the defendant was at some other place at the time of the crime). But as one moves away from this polar situation, the notion of what is exculpatory becomes clouded.

Most prosecutors take a narrow view of exculpatory evidence. They feel they must produce evidence indicating factual innocence, and they also feel obliged to deal with certain aspects of legal guilt—for instance, ensuring that the statute of limitations has not expired. But most do not feel any obligation to notify the defense about logistical or administrative problems that may reduce the probability of obtaining a conviction. Here is where they part company with Alschuler.

The situation he describes as "no case at all" is not one involving a factually innocent defendant. It is a case where evidence exists that might support a conviction if the case went to trial. But then something happens, such as the accidental loss of the physical evidence; or a break in the chain of custody of the evidence; or witnesses refuse to testify or cannot be located or die. In Alschuler's view, these developments reduce the probability of conviction to zero. But prosecutors who have bluffed in such situations disagreed that these cases were "fatally defective." In their view, just because a witness cannot be found does not mean he is absolutely unlocatable. Citing the occasional case where they had flown a witness from Africa or other remote place, they pointed out that if the state really wants to go to the expense of locating someone, they can. As for the reluctant witness, they noted that such witnesses can be and are occasionally made to testify (e.g., Kiernan, 1981:B1). They could also think of possible ways around other supposedly fatal defects. Of course, there was no guarantee that their tactics would work or that the state would be willing to go to great expense to find missing witnesses or force reluctant witnesses to testify. But the fact that these options are available transforms what sounds like a black and white issue into a cloud of gray.

Prosecutors pointed out an important reality underlying plea bargaining and justifying their views on bluffing. There are no cases with a zero or a 100 percent probability of conviction. There is *nothing* certain about case outcome! It is possible that an innocent individual can be successfully prosecuted even with quite flimsy evidence. Similarly there is no such thing as a truly dead-bang case. Experienced lawyers all know of instances illustrating these points. They have seen juries acquit defendants who did not have a chance of winning and convict people whose innocence seemed clear. They have located unlocatable witnesses, and they have seen evidence admitted in one court that might not have been admitted in another. It is precisely this uncertainty that causes some attorneys to be cynical about the justice process and to compare it to a game of Russian roulette. Even though these cases are the exception, not the rule, the principle they establish has important consequences. The fact that nothing is certain becomes an important incentive for plea bargaining and an equally important justification for bluffing.

We presented prosecutors with the distinction that Packer (1968) makes between factual and legal innocence together with the argument that bluffing is a means by which the state secures convictions in cases that would have been lost at trial. We argued further that bluffing is, in effect, a way of convicting legally innocent defendants, and hence defeats the basic principle of legality.

This argument was regularly dismissed on two grounds. The first was the uncertainty of case outcome. Since any case might result in conviction, legal innocence is not undermined by plea bargaining or by bluffing. That notion itself is predicated on the idea that outcomes in criminal justice are only probabilities. Our examples of the dead witness or the lost drugs were not regarded as all that weak.[5] Many prosecutors had had or had known of weaker cases that had gone to trial and been convicted. They did not feel that plea bargaining in such circumstances subverted the principle of legality. They did not regard bluffing in such cases as wrong provided that the bluff did not include withholding exculpatory evidence and (for many of them) provided that it did not require them to cross an imaginary line between legitimate puffery, posturing, and gamesmanship, on the one hand; and outright lying, on the other. Many of them draw that line at the same specific point. They would not stand up in court and say they were ready for trial if a critical witness or piece of evidence were lost.[6] But

they might do things short of that to make the defense think that they were ready for trial. Many of them said they would willingly admit to defense counsel that they were not ready for trial if counsel had asked that question directly. But prosecutors say counsel never do.

A major incentive for not crossing that line between legitimate puffery and outright deceit is self-interest. An attorney's personal credibility and reputation are at stake. Credibility is essential for lawyers, particularly in the criminal courts. There seems to be no middle ground. One is trustworthy or not. Once lost, credibility is hard to regain. Without it, the practice of law can be considerably more difficult. Much of what lawyers do, especially in plea bargaining, depends upon trust between parties to represent the truth and to honor commitments. Ironically, although truthfulness is demanded, some deception is both expected and tolerated. The boldfaced liar, however, finds that other lawyers will respond with whatever informal sanctions are available. Notoriously deceitful defense counsel will have to pry all discovery out of prosecutors through the time-consuming process of filing motions. Informal sanctions can be severe. Judges occasionally bar defense attorneys or assistant prosecutors from practicing in their courts because of past deceitful acts.

Thus prosecutors are restrained in bluffing by their awareness of the occupational norms regarding the limits of honesty and the importance of credibility. They are guided by general rules known to courthouse regulars that define the limits of the occupational norms concerning acceptable bluffing. Some of those limits are congruent with those set by the law of discovery and the law on the production of exculpatory evidence. But some areas are not covered by law. Prosecutors indicated, for instance, that they were frequently aware of constitutional weaknesses in cases due to questionable arrests or searches, but they did not feel ethically or legally compelled to tell defense counsel about them. That, they said, would be doing the defense counsel's job.

Even more often prosecutors were aware of administrative problems that weaken their cases and were often the prime reasons for plea bargaining. Many prosecutors did not seem to feel that they have or should have any obligation to inform defense counsel of these weaknesses. In their view, the notion of legal innocence means that defendants are entitled to all of the due-process guarantees that the constitution provides and that a factually guilty person may be found legally innocent if one of those guarantees is infringed. But it does not and should not mean, in their view, that a factually guilty person should be allowed to slip through the criminal justice system because of administrative or logistical errors. The use of

---

[5] They claimed that there are several ways of salvaging such cases. For instance, in the case of the dead or missing witness, they said they were permitted by law to use the transcript of that witness' testimony at the preliminary hearing and at trial if necessary. See *Barber v. Page.*, 390 U.S. 719 (1968).

[6] In one jurisdiction, the chief prosecutor had even issued guidelines specifically dealing with the matter of announcing ready for trial. They read: "Trial: (A) Announcement of Ready; (1) Never announce ready until all witnesses are present or on standby. (2) Make sure contraband has been analyzed and the chain of custody is intact. . . ."

plea bargaining and what they might call legitimate bluffing seemed in their view to be entirely proper, even indicated, in such circumstances.

In our in-depth study of six jurisdictions, we pursued the matter of bluffing systematically. We attempted to estimate the frequency of bluffing in situations where the prosecution had no case at all. Defense counsel were asked how often, if at all, they had had cases in which an indictment (or information) had been filed, the prosecutor had made a plea offer that was refused, and the case had been subsequently dropped by the prosecutor. Of course, this set of facts by itself does not mean that the prosecutor had been bluffing. Therefore we also asked defense counsel who reported having had such an experience whether they were able to determine why the case had been dropped. This question provided some grounds for judging whether there had been a bluff.

Responses to these questions are shown in Table 3.1. Particularly striking is the general infrequency with which defense counsel reported having cases dropped after an offer had been made. Also remarkable is the fact that this practice does not appear to vary by the degree of formalization of the prosecutor's office.[7] One might have expected that in jurisdictions with a low degree of formalization, there would have been more of a need to bluff due to a higher incidence of administrative or logistical errors and a lower sense of accountability among assistant prosecutors. However, these data suggest that this is not the case.

Table 3.1 Defense attorney responses to question relating to case dismissals by city

Have you had cases where after an information has been filed or an indictment returned, the prosecutor has approached you with a plea offer which, upon your client's refusal to accept, resulted in a dismissal of the case by the prosecutor? How often? Were you able to ascertain why the case was dismissed? Why? Was it dismissed?

El Paso

"No, I've never had cases where that happened to me. I always approach the county attorney with an offer."

Both on a misdemeanor and felony level, counsel has never seen this happen.

"No, I always approach them. They never approach me."

"No, that's never happened. Do you mean, are they trying to get something for nothing? No, I don't think they are. If the case is bad, I would never accept an offer unless the defendant wants to, but I would advise against it."

"That's never happened to me."

Counsel indicated that he always approaches the prosecutor and so he has never been approached by them with a plea offer. He was referring both to the county attorney's office and the district attorney's office.

"No."

New Orleans

It is very rare for the district attorney's office to offer a reduced charge. But in eight of ten cases where a charge reduction was offered and this attorney refused to deal, the charges were eventually nol-prossed. This was generally because a victim or witness was unavailable or unwilling to testify.

Yes, it happens, but not frequently. Counsel could not think of a particular case.

Yes, this may happen when they accidentally overcharge or are conned by a witness. Counsel does not believe this is bluffing because the prosecutor has acted in good faith. This occurs in perhaps 15 percent of all cases. It usually results in witnesses' changing testimony or discovery that the witnesses were lying.

Counsel could think of only one incident. It involved a defendant charged with accessory to fraud. The district attorney wanted the defendant to go into a diversionary program. The defendant rejected the offer, and the prosecution dismissed the case.

Yes, this has happened 5 to 10 times in 4 years. It occurs because the prosecution has no case. This usually occurs if the information the prosecutor has is not valid; for example, someone made a mistake in screening.

Yes, 2 times in 4 years. In one of the cases, counsel recalls he knew that from the trial of the codefendant, the evidence against his client was weak.

No. In fact, counsel had had the opposite occur. He had had a case in which he offered to plead guilty to simple robbery on a charge of armed robbery. Instead the district attorney's office dropped the case altogether.

Yes; it's part of the game of bluffing. However, it involves perhaps less than 20 percent of all cases. The usual reason is lack of evidence.

Two or three times in 6 years. Normally counsel knows when in advance that the district attorney does not have anything.

Seattle

Yes, this happens infrequently. Typically it happens when the prosecutor has difficulty getting a critical witness. If it gets to the stage when getting the witness is impossible, they have to tell counsel. Sometimes you find out when your client holds out in an impossible case (the state's case is very strong) and suddenly the case is dismissed.

---

[7] See Chapter 2 for our ranking of each of the jurisdictions doing this variable.

53

Have you had cases where after an information has been filed or an indictment returned, the prosecutor has approached you with a plea offer which, upon your client's refusal to accept, result-ed in a dismissal of the case by the prosecutor? How often? Were you able to ascertain why the case was dismissed? Why? Was it dismissed?

This happens on occasion. Counsel doesn't know how often, but it's probably more than he has found out about.

No.

No. Counsel would be shocked if it had occurred.

Yes. Not very often, and usually they won't try to get very much. For example, they'll try to get a little information in exchange for a dismissal.

This has not happened to counsel. "I don't think prosecutors bluff much. It would hurt their credibility. I don't bluff either. The closest thing I have had was a rape case where we ended up winning in trial. The prosecutor didn't want to try the case, but because there was a complaining witness, he would not drop it. Several plea offers were made prior to trial.

Counsel has had offers of pleas where the case was ultimately dismissed but he does not think the prosecutor was bluffing. "For example, a DWI case usually has one witness, the cop. If the cop doesn't show up, the prosecutor doesn't try to bluff." Rather the prosecutor will tell this attorney what has happened. The attorney in turn will plead his client to physical control to avoid the risk a judge will grant a continuance.

The prosecutor doesn't usually approach the defense. "If the case is bad, I don't go to negotiate. I go to trial." They almost never voluntarily dismiss a case. They dispose of it in some other way. This occurs because they almost never change their minds about the strength of the case. About the only time they dismiss is when a witness disappears. This just happened in a murder case.

Tucson

Yes. Counsel has had this happen but it only happens in about 1 percent of the cases. The prosecutor will usually make a very good offer and this will suggest that something is wrong. If one prosecutor in particular makes any offer at all, you know something is wrong with the case.

Counsel has had this happen in two cases.

Counsel has had a few cases where this has happened, and he believes they were ones in which the witnesses were not cooperative.

Yes, counsel has had these cases. In one case the prosecutor offered to have the defendants participate in a diversion program. The defendant refused, and the case was dismissed.

Counsel has had lots of these kinds of cases. He estimates that approximately 5 percent of the cases he handles fit this category. They are equally divided between cases that were weak initially and those where a crucial piece of evidence was subsequently lost.

No. Counsel has never had this happen. Prosecutors don't want to lose face, so they simply schedule for trial. They may then dismiss without prejudice so it looks as if the case was strong.

Counsel has had one case of this kind.

Yes, counsel has had cases of this kind, but he believes this is a very rare occurrence.

Counsel could not remember any such cases.

Counsel has had a couple of these cases.

Delaware County

Counsel has had one or two of these cases in 2 years; they had absolutely no evidence.

Counsel has had no such case. If a district attorney had a case like that, he would probably try to continue it. He would rather do that than admit he didn't have his witness.

Yes, but counsel couldn't recall a specific case. "Certain district attorneys, whether because of personalities or attitudes, will say 'I don't have my witness.' The district attorney's job is not to convict but to prosecute with what they have. But then there are others who will do anything. They are after you with jail time, long sentences. It's embarrassing. But you can laugh at them or walk away if you know your own case and if you know the district attorney."

Yes, counsel has had such cases. "In most cases like that, the district attorney knows he would be embarrassed; maybe it's a case of police brutality. They don't want to get mixed up with that. So they'll come in with a deal. Often you won't know who's telling the truth about the beating, but the client will say, 'No deal, I didn't do it.' Then the district attorney will go huddle and come back and ask if he'll pay court costs. I had one guy refuse to pay the 60 bucks, so they dismissed it. They'll stonewall it out as long as they can. But then sometimes I'll get a better deal than I deserve."

Yes, it has happened a couple of times. In one case, "they couldn't have proven the case if it went to trial because their witness had left the area, but I didn't find out in time—not until after the guilty plea. I was [annoyed] with myself on that one, but in my opinion you can't get mad at the district attorney. You're blaming him for something you should have done. He's just playing loose."

Norfolk

Yes, it happens, but it's rare. Counsel had one robbery case 3 years ago in which the prosecutor said, "This isn't any big deal. We'll let him plead to a reduced charge." "We wouldn't take it. So they moved to nol-pros. It turned out that they didn't have any witness."

It is very rare. "If they have a missing witness, they will tell me and try to get a continuance. If not, they may reduce it to a less severe offense."

"It rarely happens to me. It gets back to my relationship with the people in the prosecutor's office."

Table 3.1 Defense attorney responses to question relating to case dismissals by city—Continued

Have you had cases where after an information has been filed or an indictment returned, the prosecutor has approached you with a plea offer which, upon your client's refusal to accept, result-	ed in a dismissal of the case by the prosecutor? How often? Were you able to ascertain why the case was dismissed? Why? Was it dismissed?

"Yes, it does happen but not very often. You might have a case where the state's witness or victim has disappeared. You might find out depending on how friendly you are with the prosecutor."	"Yes, but not very frequently. Usually I can find out, and in most cases it's a witness problem." "No, I have not had any cases." "It's only happened a few times that I can remember." "Yes, but nothing comes to mind right now."	"Yes, I think so. However, it doesn't happen a lot. They will come with an offer and I or my client will reject it. They will then dismiss the case. We usually already know why." Yes, but none were very serious charges.

References are to plea-bargaining practices of the misdemeanor prosecutor's office.

Note: Some responses are not verbatim but summaries or paraphrases of responses unless indicated by quotation marks.

Of course, our findings are subject to plausible alternative explanations. Perhaps counsel were trying to save face with us. They might not have wanted to admit that they had been successfully bluffed. Hence our findings might underestimate the true extent of the problem. We discount this possibility, however, on the ground that the responses of defense counsel were largely paralleled by those of prosecutors in the same jurisdiction (at least to certain questions).

Prosecutors were asked to recall their last 10 cases in which there had been plea bargains. For those cases, they were asked to estimate the probability of conviction in those cases had they gone to trial. An attempt was made to have the respondents answer in terms of specific probabilities or ranges of probabilities that could be coded as follows: cases in which the probability of conviction is 91 percent or higher, or "dead-bang" or "airtight;" probability of conviction from 70 to 90 percent, or "strong" cases; probability of conviction between 41 to 69 percent, or "could have gone either way;" probability of conviction from 21 to 40 percent, or "strong enough to beat a directed verdict but defendant probably would have been acquitted;" probability of conviction from 10 to 20 percent, or "probably would have resulted in a directed verdict of acquittal;" and probability of conviction less than 10 percent, or "definitely would have resulted in a directed verdict of acquittal or might have even been unable to establish a prima facie case."

It is arguable as to when a weak case is so weak that it is no case at all. But because weak cases can be won, we feel that the most appropriate category to use for approximating the no-case-at-all is those cases with less than 10 percent possibility of conviction. Such cases were rarely experienced by prosecutors (Table 3.2). Only 4 of 40 prosecutors indicated that they had secured plea bargains in cases with less than a 10 percent probability of conviction. Their combined experience in this regard amounted to 7 cases. Given that eleven prosecutors in one area were asked this question and that the question referred to their last 10 cases, a total of 110 cases were in effect covered by the question. Thus in 7 out of 110 cases (6 percent) covered by this question, the cases were so weak as to approximate being no case at all. But this percentage gets even smaller if one considers that forty prosecutors were asked about their last ten cases and only four of them said they had had the no-case-at-all situation.

Calculating the probability of conviction is risky under the best of circumstances, much less when one is trying to recollect one's last ten cases. Thus we realize that these calculations cannot be regarded as anything but rough indicators. All we claim on their behalf is that they are an advance over the method that was previously used to estimate the scope of this problem. Our estimates convey the general sense that plea bargaining in "nonexistent" (as opposed to merely "weak") cases is not pervasive. This, in turn, suggests that bluffing to hide "nonexistent" cases must also be infrequent.

Table 3.2 Prosecutors' responses to questions referring to probability of conviction at trial, by jurisdiction

Referring to your 10 most recent felony cases in which there were plea bargains agreed to, please estimate what the probability of conviction at trial would have been for each

New Orleans

30-percent chance of winning.

50-percent chance of winning.

33-percent chance of winning. In some of those cases, the defendant refused the deal that was offered; the case went to trial and he was convicted.

"It is very hard to get any sort of percentage figure reflecting the probability of winning a case."

In those cases prosecutors plea-bargained because of a possibility of losing a case; the probability of any conviction at all (as charged or even a reduced charge) was between 20 and 30 percent.

In very few cases did prosecutor have no chance of conviction. In most cases, it was 50 percent of some conviction (either as charged or to a lesser included offense).

"There is a certain small percentage of cases that . . . prove to be unwinnable." If, nevertheless, there is no doubt about the defendant's guilt, prosecutors would like to get a plea. But given the anti-plea bargaining policy in the office, defense counsel are likely to suspect that there is a problem with the case when the office is willing to plea bargain. Moreover, if there is any doubt in the prosecutor's mind about the defendant's guilt, she or he would nol-pros rather than take a plea.

There are only a few cases that are not winnable. If a case is really not winnable, those cases are usually nol-prossed.

If there is no chance at all of winning the case, she would probably nol-pros the case rather than take the plea.

Seattle

Six of them had between 91 and 99 percent probability of conviction; 3 between 71 and 90 percent; and 1 between 41 and 70 percent.

None of this prosecutor's cases are between 91 and 99 percent probabili-

ty of conviction. This prosecutor said there was never a certainty that a case was open and shut. Eight of this prosecutor's last 10 plea bargains were cases that had between 91 and 99 percent probability of conviction; 1 between 41 and 70 percent; 1 between 21 and 40 percent.

This prosecutor's remarks were all directed toward plea bargaining in the misdemeanor courts. All 10 of this prosecutor's last plea bargains had a probability of conviction of between 91 and 99 percent. "District court cases are usually pretty simple and pretty straightforward. Police could probably win most of them without a prosecutor. There are some cases where the police make a bad charge or a wrong charge, but not too many."

It is hard to answer this question but most cases were "strong."

Tucson

75 to 80 percent probability of conviction in all 10 of the last felony plea bargains.

70 to 90 percent chance of conviction in 8 of the last 10 plea bargains. Four of these had a 90 percent chance; two had an 80 percent chance, and two had a 75 percent chance. In addition, he had two cases with about a 50 percent chance of conviction.

Seven of ten of the last felony plea bargains had between 70 and 90 percent chance of conviction.

Three of the last felony plea bargains had between 91 and 99 percent chance of conviction; five between 70 and 90 percent; one about 50 percent; and one between 21 and 40 percent.

Seven of ten had between a 70 and 90 percent chance of conviction.

Precise estimates could not be given. He did say that in general even if a case is weak, prosecutors always have a chance of winning at trial. They will not take a case to trial if

they know they have almost no chance of conviction unless there is a very serious crime and a serious offender. In such cases, they will either dismiss the case or try it.

All ten had between 95 and 100 percent chance of conviction.

Seven had between 91 and 99 percent chance of conviction. Two had about 50 percent chance of conviction; and one had between 10 and 20 percent probability of conviction.

Delaware County

"I can't remember any case where I wasn't convinced that it wouldn't be a conviction."

He could not remember his last 10 cases but felt they probably all would have been convicted if they had gone to trial.

"All of my recent plea-bargains would have been convicted at trial. They were a prosecutor's dream—every witness ready, or we had statement by the defendants, or else heavy circumstantial evidence."

The prosecutor could only remember the last three cases. The first the probability of conviction was "high." "We had him cold." The second case the probability of convictions was "pretty sure." "The victim wasn't so great. He was a bum." The third case was "iffy." "I would have had difficulty proving the burglary. . . . I didn't trust the witness (victim). He was a friend of the defendant. The defendant had stayed with him a couple of nights."

The prosecutor could not remember the 10 last cases but referred to a few cases that he could remember. In a recent case of bad checks, he offered the defendant the option to enter a pretrial diversion program. The defendant declined. The case went to trial and resulted in a hung jury. The defendant might still be convicted in the case because the prosecution has the option of retrying the case.

All of them would have been convicted. "The evidence was there." Several "were defense motivated." They wanted to get it over with. "But I could have convicted anyway whether they believed it or not."

The prosecutor could not remember the 10 last cases but did discuss a few. He said "in general, the chances are 50-50 or better for us. The odds are good for conviction." The first specific case he discussed involved a corporation that dumped a deadly chemical in an area that endangered people living in the neighborhood. He felt there was a 50-50 chance of conviction of the corporation. The second case was a charge of arson. The prosecutor did not believe the sole witness for the commonwealth and felt there would be only a 25 percent probability of conviction. Consequently, he was willing to offer the defendant the option of entering pretrial diversion.

The prosecutor could remember only three cases. One was a rape case with a 40 to 60 percent chance of conviction. "The girl was a bad victim. She was not a very pleasant person, and three males would testify against her character." The second was a murder case that was upcoming and in which he estimated a 90 percent of conviction on at least some charge (not first-degree but at least third-degree murder).

Norfolk

All would have been convicted of something.

All would have been convicted of something.

In eight cases, there would have been about 90 to 100 percent chance of conviction; one about 50 percent; and in one they had the wrong charge.

In most cases, they would have been found guilty. There was one recent case in which a witness was missing that would have been about a zero-percent chance of conviction.

Nine would have been convicted; in one, there was some question.

"I figured that if I had one in three chances of winning a case, then I will go with it. Of the cases that I plea-bargained, I would probably lose 7 of 10 if they went to trial.

Six cases had about 100 percent probability of conviction; two about 80 percent; and two about 50 percent.

Three about 100 percent; two about 95 percent; four about 90 percent; one about 20 percent; one about zero.

One about 100 percent; three about zero; and six about 50 percent.

"That is difficult to answer. I can think of one case where there would not have been a conviction. A percentage would be very inaccurate."

This prosecutor reviewed his docket and gave the following estimates: eight cases about 99 percent chance of conviction; two about 71 to 90 percent; and two about 10 percent.

Note: The question was initially open-ended, allowing respondents to use their own descriptions of the probability of conviction in the relevant cases. However, after the initial response, the prosecutors were presented with the following set of categories and asked to classify their responses into them. The probability of conviction was between 91 and 99 percent (dead-bang); between 71 and 90 percent (strong); 41 and 69 percent (could have gone either way); 21 and 40 percent (strong enough to beat a directed verdict but defendant probably would have been acquitted); 10 and 20 percent (probably would have resulted in a directed verdict); and 0 to 9 percent (definitely would have been a directed verdict).

To explore this issue further, we asked prosecutors how often they had had cases fall apart because a critical piece of evidence or an essential witness had been lost. (This question captures Alschuler's description of the noncase.) We also asked prosecutors how they handled such cases: Did they try to get a plea? Did their handling depend upon the type of crime or type of criminal? Did they think it proper to call ready for trial in such cases in order to bluff the defense into pleading guilty? What should the limits of ethical behavior by prosecutors be in such situations? The answers to these questions are presented in Table 3.3.

Table 3.3 Prosecutors' responses to questions relating to plea bargaining in cases that fall apart

Questions	Total	Questions	Total
Have you ever had a case fall apart, that is, the piece of critical evidence is lost (such as the illegal drugs are lost in the police evidence room or the critical witness dies) and you know that if the case goes to trial, the judge would almost undoubtedly rule that the government had not established a prima facie case?		If yes, does (would) the way you handle it depend upon whether the crime is very serious and/or the defendant a bad actor?	
		Yes (I am more likely to seek a plea if the crime or the criminal is serious)	16
Yes	29	No (It makes no difference)	10
No	4	Do you think it is proper for a prosecutor to call ready for trial (when calendar is called) in order to convince the defense to plead in such cases? (Sometimes answered as if the question had been: "Have you or would you do this?")	
If yes, how often?			
Only one in my career or rarely or "not very often"	7		
About once every six months	1	Yes	10
About once a month or more often or other	3	No	20
More than rarely but otherwise unspecified (for example, "enough," "occasionally," "a lot")	9	What should be the limits of ethical behavior by prosecutors in this type of situation? (The question was open-ended. More than one answer may have been given by the respondent)	
How have you usually handled it, or how would you handle it?			
Try to get a guilty plea	22	Always tell defense counsel	1
Dismiss it	10	Do not lie in open court (or call ready when you are not)	14
It depends on (who the defense counsel is; the crime or criminal; whether evidence is permanently lost; whether I want to take a chance at trial anyway; if I thought defendant was guilty)	20	Disclosure of this type of information should not be ethically required	5
		It depends on the crime and the criminal	2
		Tell defense counsel if a witness or evidence is permanently lost	1'
		Tell defense counsel if a witness has lied	2
		If there is not evidence present or available for state, prosecutor should nolle prosequi	1

Note: Some respondents did not answer all parts of the questions or gave uncodable answers. Therefore, the number of responses in a jurisdiction varies.

Twenty-nine of the thirty-three prosecutors (89 percent) indicated that they had been in a situation where either a critical witness or critical evidence was lost and the prosecutors felt they no longer had a prima facie case. However, as Table 3.3, question 2 shows, this type of situation is not pervasive. Seven prosecutors had had it happen only once or rarely in their career. An additional three prosecutors said it happens about once a month or more often. Nine prosecutors said it happens more often than rarely, but they did not specify how often.

We were surprised and perplexed by these responses. In the first phase of our study, it had appeared that cases fall apart with much greater regularity than was being suggested by these responses. Upon further reflection, however, we realized that there is no necessary conflict between our early impression and the data presented

here. The data in Table 3.3 are not about weak cases in general, but about a special class of weak cases: the extremely weak or nonexistent case. It may be true that there are a lot of weak cases in the system, but they are not all impossibly weak or nonexistent cases. The many weak cases we heard about were apparently only moderately weak. This conclusion puts a new light on the importance of case strength as a factor in plea bargaining. It contradicts the impression that the state could never have won a lot of plea-bargaining cases if they had gone to trial.

The next question asked (question 3 in Table 3.3) is about how prosecutors have usually handled these cases that have completely fallen apart. (In a few cases the responding prosecutors had never had such a case; consequently the question was rephrased to ask how that person would handle one if he did get it.) Fifty-two prosecutors answered this question. Ten said that they would definitely dismiss it; 22 said they would try to get a guilty plea; and 20 gave mixed or qualified responses. They said they would either dismiss the case or try to get a plea depending upon one or more of the following conditions: the defendant's prior record; who the defense counsel was; whether the evidence was permanently lost or just misplaced; whether the prosecutor wanted to take a chance at trial, and whether the prosecutor was certain that the defendant was guilty. It is clear from the pattern of responses to this question that prosecutors are far from unanimous in their views as to the proper way of handling a case that falls apart. This is as true within individual jurisdictions as it is among them.

The fact that 81 percent of the respondents indicated they would try to get a plea (at least in certain cases) indicates that the majority of prosecutors are willing to do a certain amount of bluffing even in very weak cases. But this is not to say that they would deliberately lie or file fraudulent service returns in order to sustain their bluffs. How far a lawyer will go in bluffing is governed by courthouse work norms and ethics. The rule frequently used is whether the prosecutor would call ready for trial. We asked prosecutors if they would call ready for trial in this situation where their case falls apart. As question 5 in Table 3.3 shows, 20 of the 30 prosecutors said either that they had not or would not answer ready for trial in these cases. Thus, the majority say they have not or would not engage in what might be regarded as a small bluff—calling ready for trial—much less engage in the kind of elaborate fraud suggested in Alschuler's anecdote about the process server's phony report. Even calling ready for trial falls short of being an elaborate fraud. Most prosecutors, however, said they would not do this. Their major rationale seems to be indicated in the responses to question 6 in Table 3.3. Most prosecutors who gave some opinion as to what the limits of ethical behavior should be when dealing with the noncase said the line should be drawn at lying in open court. In addition, the next most frequent response to this question was that prosecutors should not be ethically required to inform defense counsel when the prosecutor's case has fallen apart. Thus, what most prosecutors regard as ethical and proper gamesmanship, when the state's case has fallen apart to the point of no longer being even a prima facie case, lies somewhere between keeping it a secret and engaging in the bluff of announcing ready for trial.

Conclusion

That part of the case against plea bargaining that is built on objections to the practice of bluffing needs to be reconsidered. Bluffing does not appear to be as unseemly as it has been described. It typically does not involve violations of legal or ethical norms, elaborate frauds to sustain deceptions, or cases in which there is no chance that the defendant would be convicted at trial.

Prosecutors appear to abide by the law relating to discovery and the production of exculpatory evidence (as required in 1976 by the Supreme Court), but they interpret the latter in a narrow sense. They do not feel they have or should have any obligation to tell defense counsel about weaknesses in their cases that arise from logistical or administrative problems, such as the accidental loss of drugs or the failure to notify a witness of a hearing. At the same time, a number of prosecutors said they would willingly give an honest answer if defense counsel asked them specifically if they had lost the evidence or if the witness was present in the courthouse.

Prosecutors are restrained in their bluffing not only by law and professional ethics but also by the unofficial norms of the workplace. The last is a powerful restraint because it is related to the self-interest of individual prosecutors. Lawyers must protect their reputations for honesty in negotiations if they are to maintain smooth relations with other lawyers. As several prosecutors pointed out, bluffing that involved outright lies would hurt their careers more than it would help. If it were true that prosecutors were regularly obtaining convictions by bluffing in situations where they had what Alschuler calls "no case at all," then this would indeed be a strong argument in the case against plea bargaining. But our data suggest that this is not the case. Very weak cases, ones which approximate being no case at all, occur infrequently. Forty percent of the prosecutors indicated that they had experienced only one such case in their entire careers. What is more, while the majority of prosecutors (82 percent) said they would try to obtain a conviction in an important case that fell apart, most also indicated that they would stop far short of even the officially prescribed limits of propriety in bluffing. Many of them (20 of 30) indicated they would not even go so far as to announce ready for trial at calendar call in order to sustain the appearance that their case had not developed a serious weakness. None of them mentioned a willingness to bribe witnesses, file fraudulent service returns, or empanel a jury. One who said he would answer "ready for trial" at calendar call even though he did not have his witness available did not regard this as a lie or even a half-truth. He felt he would in effect be saying that he was ready to have his case dismissed by the judge once the witness' absence was discovered.

Undoubtedly, some prosecutors do exceed the bounds of fairness and honesty in bluffing defendants into guilty pleas. But this is not an inherent weakness in the institution of plea bargaining. It can and has happened in cases that went to trial (see, e.g., *Miller* v. *Pate,* 386 U.S. 1 (1967), where an Illinois prosecutor convicted a man for the sexual attack and murder of a young girl on the basis of a pair of shorts covered with red material which the prosecutor contended was the victim's blood although he knew it was paint).

Whether prosecutorial lying is more likely to occur in plea bargaining than in trial cases depends on where one draws the line between bluffing and lying—something which practitioners do not find easy to do. If all bluffing is lying, then plea bargaining probably loses. But such a view would be completely at variance with that of the majority of prosecutors. They regard bluffing (short of deliberate misrepresentation) as one of the tactics of negotiation which defense counsel are expected to understand and counteract. If counsel fails to do so it is not substantially different than if he had failed to counter a prosecutorial tactic at trial. If lying is defined as deliberate misrepresentation of the clearly unequivocal kind, such as filing fraudulent returns and bribing witnesses, then the evidence of prosecutorial lying is thin at best. We did not uncover any instances of outright lying or deliberate fraud.

As a whole, the practice of bluffing is not as capricious and unscrupulous as it may sound. The best protection against a bluff is a defense attorney who knows that before agreeing to a plea offer he must check the strength of the prosecutor's case. He must ask a series of simple and direct questions about whether the prosecutor is really ready to go to trial. If the case for abolishing plea bargaining is to be made, it will have to rest on more persuasive grounds than the unseemliness of bluffing.

Chapter Four
Evaluating the Case: Determinants of the Plea Bargaining Decisions

Introduction

Studies have identified many factors that are believed to influence plea bargaining decisions. However, because of the limitations of method or sample, these studies have raised many questions but left them unresolved. Are certain factors relevant to all plea bargains? How much of an impact do specific factors have? Do their respective impacts vary under different conditions? Do prosecutors evaluate cases differently from defense counsel? How consistent is plea bargaining? This last question has several meanings, one of which refers to whether different attorneys (depending upon whether they are acting as prosecutors or defense counsel) would evaluate the same case the same way.

The research presented in this chapter is based on interview data as well as a decision simulation technique. It addresses those questions listed above regarding how the plea bargaining decision is determined. It focuses upon the evaluation of cases for plea bargaining, that is, the process of sorting and weighing information in order to decide whether to plea bargain and on what terms. A comparison is made to determine whether prosecutors do this differently from defense counsel. The importance of two factors, namely, the strength of the case and the seriousness of the criminal, are given special attention. They are analyzed in two ways: first, to determine consistency (i.e., do different attorneys evaluate these factors the same way); and secondly, to determine how much of a difference variations in these factors make in the evaluation of the case.

Methods

Research on plea bargaining decision-making has been based primarily on interviews and observations (Alschuler, 1968; Mather, 1974; Rosett and Cressey, 1976; Newman, 1956; Newman, 1966). A few studies have been based on statistical analyses of available records (Bernstein et al., 1977; Heuman, 1975; Rhodes, 1978). One had prosecutors and defense counsel give standardized ratings of 11 dimensions of actual cases they were mutually involved in (Horney, 1980). Two studies have used simulation techniques of substantially different kinds. Jacoby (1980b and 1980c) developed a set of 279 hypothetical cases of varying type and seriousness, and presented them to 855 prosecutors in 15 jurisdictions. In contrast, LaGoy et al. (1976) adapted the information processing analysis technique ("information board") developed by Wilkins (1965). Substituting plea bargaining for the sentencing decisions, LaGoy presented two hypothetical cases to 20 prosecutors from one state. Unlike Jacoby's method, this technique allows one to follow the information sorting patterns of the decisionmaker. Our research presented in this chapter is based on interviews as well as a modified version of LaGoy's technique which includes a quasi-experimental design. [1]

---

[1] Although we used the same technique as LaGoy, there are major differences in the content of the simulation, the variables used, the nature of the samples involved, and the inclusion of a quasi-experimental component.

Sampling. Some of the interviews with prosecutors, defense counsel and judges are from both phases of our study. The structured interview data, however, are from five of the six sites which were studied in depth and in which plea bargaining was not prohibited. The decision simulation was administered to a total of 138 prosecutors and 105 defense attorneys, of which 46 percent were from the five cities studied indepth. The others are obtained at national professional meetings and at jurisdictions convenient to the District of Columbia.

The simulation. The plea bargaining decision simulation was administered as follows. Respondents were asked to imagine that they were in a hypothetical jurisdiction with certain specific characteristics which were described to them (see McDonald, 1979). It was explained that the use of a hypothetical jurisdiction was necessary because the study was being done nationally, and, therefore, jurisdictional differences had to be held constant. No respondent objected to this requirement or reported that it made the simulation less real. Virtually all the respondents who commented on the simulation reported that it was very realistic. This report was validated by our own observations that virtually all respondents took the simulation seriously.

Respondents were further asked to imagine that a less experienced attorney came to them for advice about whether to plea bargain in a particular case and what the "bottom line" terms of the bargain should be. However, the only things about the case that the senior attorney was told were the charge and the penalty for that charge in our hypothetical jurisdiction. The senior attorney (i.e., the respondent in the simulation) then had to seek as much additional information as he or she felt he or she needed in order to advise his or her less experienced colleague. The respondent was told that the answers to virtually all the questions which he or she might want to know about the case were contained on an "information board" (folder) with which he or she was presented. The folder for the burglary case contained 39 items of information on separate cards enclosed in plastic holders. The cards were fanned out so that only a half inch of the bottom of each card could be seen. On that half inch was written a short descriptive title of the information contained on the upper (hidden) portion of that card.

The respondent was instructed to familiarize him or herself with the labels on the cards and to think of things which he or she would want to know about the case in order to advise his or her junior colleague. He or she was then instructed to pick items of information he or she wanted to know and to stop as soon as he or she was ready to make a decision about what to do with the case. He or she was told that he or she could take as

much time and consult as many items of information as he or she wanted but that he or she should try to act as close to what he or she would do in real life as possible.

The items of information chosen were recorded by the researcher in the order in which they were chosen. When the respondent was ready, he or she was asked to make several decisions. He or she could recommend that the case be dropped altogether from prosecution (only relevant when the game was played with prosecutors) or that it go to trial or that it be plea bargained. If the recommendation was to plea bargain, then the respondent was asked what the "bottom-line" (not the "opening offer") terms of the bargain should be. For prosecutors this meant the most lenient offer they would make before either insisting the case go to trial or dropping it. For defense attorneys this meant the most severe terms they would accept before insisting the case go to trial. [2] Respondents choosing to plea bargain were asked to specify the bargain in terms of type and length of the sentence to be recommended to the court, and the estimated probability of conviction at trial assuming they were attorneys in the case and the case were tried in their local jurisdiction. Each respondent was given two cases to decide: one robbery and one burglary. Prosecutors and defense attorneys were given the exact same sets of facts except that the words "prosecutor" or "defense counsel" were submitted at relevant places.

A unique feature of our simulation is that two variables were manipulated, namely, case strength and seriousness to the offender. Case strength was varied by using two versions of the card entitled, "Evidence—Substance of Available." The seriousness of the defendant was varied by having two versions of the card entitled "Defendant's Prior Record and Police Reputation." (For a description of all items of information used in the simulation, see McDonald, 1979.)

Findings from interviews

Numerous factors have been identified as being influential in plea bargaining. The review that follows discusses those factors reported by other researchers and substantiated by our own interview findings. A second analysis of the same factors based on our plea bargaining simula-

---

[2] Technically speaking, defense attorneys do not accept or reject plea bargains. Their clients do. However, in actual practice, we found that defendants rely heavily on the advice of attorneys and although some attorneys go to great lengths to avoid making a decision for the defendant, most are willing to express their opinion about what the best deal is. Therefore, in reporting our findings here, we shall speak as if the decision were made by the defense counsel.

tion will be presented in a subsequent section of this paper.

Caseload. One of the most common justifications for plea bargaining is the volume of cases. Just how caseload pressures come to influence plea bargaining decisions, however, remains unclear. Some researchers (Alschuler, 1968; and Rhodes, 1978) believe these pressures act at a distance and simply require that some portion of the caseload be plea bargained, but do not determine which cases shall be plea bargained or what the terms shall be. But Mills (1971) describes caseload pressures as having a direct and distressing impact on plea bargaining. He reports how a New York public defender uses the backlog problem as a club to dictate the specific terms of the plea bargains he wants. If the terms are not met, he threatens to take all of his cases to trial. This practice is referred to as "court busting," but it appears to be more of a courthouse myth than a reality. We found virtually no cases in the jurisdictions we visited where "court busting" was an established practice. We heard of only two cases where a defense attorney threatened to take his caseload to trial if he did not get the deal he wanted in a particular case. In both cases the prosecutors were unperturbed by the threat and the situation backfired. The defense attorneys went to trial with their caseloads but were quickly worn out by the heavy doses of trial work. The overwhelming majority of defense attorneys (50 out of 51) told us that they had never tried to court bust and had never heard of it happening. Most of them thought the idea of making such a threat was "ridiculous," "moronic," "very unwise," or "stupid."

Based on our interview data we would agree with the view that caseload pressures act as general determinants of the need to plea bargain but do not determine which specific cases will be bargained or what the terms of the bargains will be. However, caseload does determine in general the kind of cases that are more likely to be plea bargained. The greater the pressure the less attention is given to the less serious crimes. Cases that once might have had some possibility of going to trial if suitable negotiations could not be worked out will be less likely to go to trial and the terms of the bargains may become more generous.

Seriousness of the criminal and the crime. Two aspects of plea bargaining decisionmaking are of special interest. One focuses on the question of what factors influence whether a case will be plea bargained or go to trial (or be dismissed). The other focuses on what factors influence the terms of the plea agreement. Many studies (Alschuler, 1968; Bernstein, et al., 1977; Britt and Larntz, 1980; California Legislature, 1980; Chambliss and Seidman, 1971; Jacoby, 1980b and 1980c; Lagoy et al., 1976; Neubauer, 1974; and Newman, 1966) have found that the

seriousness of the criminal (usually defined in terms of prior record) and seriousness of the crime are influential factors in plea bargaining. But there are some disagreements and strange patterns of relationships between these factors and the plea bargaining decisions. Moreover, there has been little insight into how these two global factors are interpreted and applied in practice.

The question of how the seriousness of the crime affects whether a case will be plea bargained or set for trial has not received much systematic attention. It is generally assumed that misdemeanors are less likely than felonies to be tried and that among felonies the more serious the crime the more likely it is to go to trial. For each assumption there is considerable supporting evidence (Oklahoma Administrative Office of the Judiciary, 1976:140; Jacoby, 1980b:37; Brosi, 1979). But there is also some evidence that among felonies the more serious crimes (e.g., personal vs. property offenses) are not more likely to be tried (Vera Institute of Justice, 1977). [3] One study that attempted to assess which factors determine whether a case goes to trial or pleads guilty concluded in frustration. It reported that " 'the guys who couldn't make a deal' remains perhaps the single most accurate description of the group of defendants who go to trial" (Connecticut Justice Commission, 1980:92).

As for the impact of the seriousness of the crime on the terms of the plea there is considerable agreement that the more serious the crime the less favorable the terms of the plea agreement will be from the defendant's perspective (Jacoby, 1980b; Mather, 1979; Neubauer, 1974). But, Horney (1980) found no correlation between the value of the plea bargain and the seriousness of the crime; and Bernstein et al., (1977) found a strange pattern of relationship between type of felony and the probability of receiving a substantial charge reduction. Among defendants whose final disposition occurred at their first court presentation, those charged with assault were more likely to receive a more favorable reduction than those charged with burglary, robbery, or larceny; and defendants charged with burglary were least likely to receive a more favorable reduction. Among cases whose final disposition occurred after the first court presentation, there was no significant relationship between type of offense and the amount of charge reduction.

Turning to the matter of the seriousness of the criminal, one also finds disagreement and strange results both with regard to the plea-or-trial decision and to the effect on the terms of the bargain. Several studies (Newman, 1956;

---

[3] See also, Bernstein et al., *1977.*

and Chambliss and Seidman, 1971) suggest that recidivists are less likely than first offenders to go to trial possibly because they know the advantages of plea bargaining. Others (Greenwood et al., 1973; Mather, 1974; Baldwin and McConville, 1977; Jacoby, 1980b; Thomssen and Falowski, 1979) have found that defendants with more serious prior records are more likely to go to trial. A study of victimless crimes found that having a prior record was associated with going to trial in only one of four types of victimless crime and at that the independent effect of prior record was small (McDonald, 1977).

As for the effect of prior record on the terms of the plea bargain, studies generally suggest that the more serious the record the less generous the state will be in its plea offer (Jacoby, 1980b; Neubauer, 1974). However, Horney (1980) found no relationship between these two variables while other studies report that there is a relationship but it is not a simple linear one. Britt and Larntz (1980) report that for property offenses, no matter how serious the instant property crime is, there is a bias against incarcerating the defendant as long as his previous record consists of no more than two arrests and no adult felony convictions. They suggest this represents a buffering process preventing prior record from adding to the severity of the sentence until the individual's contact with the criminal justice system has become frequent and/or felonious. The findings of Bernstein et al. (1977) are generally supportive of Britt and Larntz's conclusion up to a point but then add a confusing twist. They found that defendants with prior arrests but not convictions get larger charge reductions than defendants with prior arrests and convictions. But those same defendants with prior arrests and no convictions also got more generous reductions than defendants with no prior records at all! Bernstein et al. speculate that this supports the belief that recidivists use their prior experience with the criminal justice system to obtain better deals than first offenders.

Interviews with prosecutors and defense counsel indicate that seriousness of the offense, seriousness of the crime and evidentiary strength of the case are the three main factors they use in evaluating cases. However, the independent influence of these three factors on the decision as to whether to plead guilty or go to trial was less clear. Generally it seemed that the less serious cases were more likely to be bargained; yet attorneys said that murder cases were regularly bargained as well. Similarly, the attorneys said that defendants with prior criminal records often plead guilty but sometimes they stubbornly want to go to trial and "roll the dice." For three-time losers facing long sentences no matter what happened, going to trial made sense. They had nothing to lose if they could raise a sufficient doubt in some juror's mind.

As for how the seriousness of the offense and the seriousness of the offender affect the terms of plea bargains, our impression based on our interviews was that in both cases the relationship was a simple linear one. Respondents said that less generous deals were being offered to more serious criminals and in the more serious crimes. However there are substantial differences within and between jurisdictions in how seriousness is defined. Some judges permit only prior records of convictions to be used in sentencing discussions, and this policy is carried over by prosecutors in their assessment of cases for plea bargaining. Other judges and prosecutors readily consider arrest records that do not indicate dispositions. Some will even consider police suspicions of a defendant's involvement in criminal activities as the basis for determining the criminal's seriousness.

As for the question how much a unit increase in the severity of the seriousness of the criminal or of the crime affects the severity of the terms of the plea bargain we are unable to provide any precise answers. But the serendipitous findings of our decision simulation shed some light on this matter. During and after the administration of the simulation, we learned how specific items of information are translated by attorneys into increases or decreases in the lengths of time sought in plea bargaining. Occasionally a respondent would flip up one of the information cards in the simulation and groan, "There goes another year." Prosecutors and defense counsel engage in a very fine calculation of moral turpitude. Compared with the layperson, their analysis of moral turpitude is like the difference between measurements in terms of pounds and ounces and those in terms of the finer units of milli- and micrograms. There are subtle shades of nuance that experienced attorneys appreciate but are lost on the layman.

For instance, in the pretesting of our hypothetical robbery with a knife case, prosecutors wanted to know such things as: Was the slashing completely unprovoked by the victim? Had the victim said anything at all or resisted in any way? Was the slashing necessary to accomplish the crime? Was it done out of nervousness or panic or out of simple meanness? When the robber presented the knife, how did he present it? Was there actual contact of the knife with the victim? While the layman may fail to appreciate the distinction between a knife that was used to threaten and a knife that actually struck a victim, attorneys are familiar with hundreds of such cases, and come to appreciate such distinctions and translate them into differences in time to be served.

Prosecutors wanted to know not just whether there had been a slashing but how deep it was, whether there would be permanent injury or ugly scars in visible places such as on the face. This kind of information was used by prosecutors to assess not only how serious the crime had been but also how "mean" or "bad" the defendant was. There was no question that robbery with a slashing was a serious matter and had to be punished, but there was a question about the precise degree of punishment that this particular robbery deserved. While the layman may think that it is enough to know that a person is a "robber who slashes," the experienced prosecutor has learned to make much finer distinctions. Some robbers who slash display a greater disregard for the well-being of their victims than others. In as much as there is not unlimited capacity in the correctional system and since distinctions among offenders must be made, these differences are used as the basis for making them.[4]

Strength of the case. Both the decision to plead guilty rather than go to trial and the terms of the plea agreement are reported by virtually all researchers to be influenced by case strength (Alschuler, 1968; California Legislature, 1980; Horney, 1980; Jacoby, 1980b; Landis, 1974; Mather, 1977; Neubauer, 1974; and Newman 1966).[5]

Alschuler (1968) suggests there is a simple negative relationship between these variables. As cases get weaker plea bargaining is more likely to occur and the terms of the bargain become more favorable to the defendant with the most favorable bargains offered when the prosecutor has "no case at all." Jacoby (1980b) also found that as cases get weaker they are more likely to be plea bargained. But Mather (1974:286) quotes a prosecutor as saying that the weaker a case is the more likely it is to be tried. She analyzed the influence of case strength as it interacts with the influence of case seriousness. Her concept of case seriousness combines the notion of serious crime and serious offender. It refers to the severity of

the sentence that is likely to be imposed in a case. Case seriousness is dichotomized into "serious" and light" cases; and case strength is dichotomized into "deadbang" (strong) cases and "reasonable doubt" (weak) cases. Deadbang, light cases were usually plea bargained; but it was not possible to predict whether reasonable-doubt-light cases would be bargained or go to trial. For serious cases the decision to go to trial in either deadbang or reasonable doubt cases depended upon how good the prosecutor's plea offer was.

Rhodes (1978) also found that contrary to expectations case strength was not strongly and uniformly related to whether plea bargains would occur. He found that neither the subjective estimate of the prosecutors at screening[6] of the probability of conviction nor the existence of facts relating to the objective strength of a case nor the estimated probability of acquittal at trial (based on conviction regressions) were good predictors of whether charges would be reduced in a case.

As for the terms of the plea bargain, Horney (1980) found that the value of the plea agreement was inversely related to the probability of conviction as expected. But, the relationship did not account for a substantial portion of the variance. She concluded there was less individualization of plea bargaining decisions than was previously believed.

In almost all the 31 jurisdictions visited in the first phase of our study and all six of the jurisdictions studied in depth (see Table 4.1) our respondents said the practice was to plea bargain weak cases and take strong ones to trial. But in Kalamazoo, Michigan, the policy was just the opposite. There they "plead the gold and take the dogs to trial."[7]

---

[4] The belief that such distinctions can and should be made is often the basis for objections to sentencing reform proposals that would eliminate or drastically reduce the freedom of criminal justice officials who make these fine adjustments. On the other hand, the belief that these adjustments are not being made evenhandedly has been given as the main argument in favor of such sentencing reforms.

[5] Defense counsel have even told us that the level of effort they put into a case not only at plea bargaining but also at trial depends on their estimate of the probability of conviction.

[6] These prosecutors are not the ones actually handling the plea negotiations of the cases and are usually inexperienced recruits.

[7] The value of such a policy is one which deserves serious consideration. The type of plea bargaining system one would have under it would meet certain crucial concerns about plea bargaining. In theory, at least, it would have several beneficial consequences. It would preserve the trial system for the doubtful cases in which judgment calls about who is to be believed and what actually happened are made by the jury in an adversary setting rather than by attorneys in backrooms. (However, many attorneys would prefer not to have these decisions made by the jury because they do not trust the jury system as much as they trust their own ability to decide what really happened.) It may reduce the risk of convicting innocent persons (assuming this is more likely to happen in plea bargaining than at trial—an assumption not shared by many practicing criminal justice lawyers). It would reduce the size of the consideration the state would need to offer defendants to get pleas. And, it would reduce the impact of case strength on the sentencing decision—thereby minimizing the influence of a factor that no theory of corrections has ever regarded as a relevant consideration in sentencing.

Table 4.1 Prosecutors' reports of the influence of case strength on their plea offers, by jurisdictions
Summer, 1977

[In Percentages]

In cases where the crime is serious, the defendant is a serious criminal, and the case is (strong: weak), what do you usually do regarding plea bargaining?	Case strength (S=Strong: W=Weak)													
	El Paso**		New Orleans		Seattle		Tucson		Delaware County		Norfolk		Total	
	S	W	S	W	S	W	S	W	S	W	S	W	S	W
Require plea as charged; give *no* consideration	50	33	100	0	100	0	50	0	89	33	38	8	68	13
Give *bogus* consideration which has appearance of a *bargain* but no substantive benefit (e.g., drop charges which were either overcharged or would not have affected the sentence anyway)	0	0	0	0	0	0	40	40	11	0	23	8	15	2
Give *minimal* consideration which does not affect length of sentence but may affect other aspects of sentence (e.g., sentence be served in certain prison)	0	17	0	0	0	0	0	56	0	8	0	0	0	13
Give *real* consideration which (probably) will reduce the length of sentence	50	50	0	80	0	100	0	33	0	58	9	23	6	51
Other/combination of above/it depends on case	0	0	0	20	0	0	10	11	0	0	39	61	11	21
(N)	(6)	(4)	(10)	(10)	(5)	(3)	(10)	(9)	(9)	(12)	(13)	(13)	(53)	(53)

*This question was asked only of prosecutors in the County Attorney's office which is separate from the District Attorney's office and was not participating in the no plea bargaining policy.

With regard to the influence of case strength on the terms of the deal we found that the vast majority of prosecutors (21 of 24) report that they make their most generous offers in their weakest cases. But we also learned that contrary to the impression from the literature the "exploding, plastic character" of deals offered by prosecutors is not unlimited. Prosecutors will continue to sweeten the plea offer up to a point. But, if the defendant continues to hold out, then prosecutors will either try the case or dismiss it.[8] They say they would not offer ridiculously reduced charges or lenient sentence recommendations just to assure a conviction. It would be foolish to do so because the defense would "smell a rat"; the judge would not approve the deal; and nothing would be gained even if they succeeded.

Accuracy. Given the crucial importance of the ability to evaluate cases, there is surprisingly little research as to whether attorneys can accurately predict whether a case will be convicted if it goes to trial.[9] The one study of its kind is encouraging. Inexperienced prosecutors working with only that amount of information that is available in cases within 24 hours after arrest were able to predict the actual probability of conviction at trial within a few percentage points for four different offenses (Rhodes, 1978).[10]

---

[8] See also Chapter 3 on bluffing by prosecutors.

---

[9] Of the various factors used to evaluate cases only the estimate of case strength can be validated by an independent event, namely, what actually happens at trial. For all the other factors the only question is whether attorneys agree among themselves as to their importance—although conceivably their judgments could be compared to those of the general public using survey research methodology.

[10] For assault they predicted 69 percent. The actual was 65 percent. For robbery, predicted 71 percent; actual, 78 percent. For larceny, predicted 73 percent; actual, 66 percent. For burglary, predicted 73 percent; actual, 67 percent.

Perspective: prosecution vs. defense. There has been somewhat more research on whether cases are evaluated differently depending upon whether one is looking at them from the point of view of the prosecutor or the defense counsel. Some studies (Mather, 1974; Neubauer, 1974) and our own interview data indicate that prosecutors and defense attorneys evaluate cases the same way—at least up to a point. Both types of attorneys agree on the importance of the big three factors: seriousness of the offense, seriousness of the offender, and strength of the case. Beyond that, little is known about whether they continue to look at cases in the same way. On this point the literature contains only a few somewhat inconsistent hints. Three hypotheses can be identified.

Both Neubauer (1974) and Mather (1974) mention that defense counsel look for mitigating circumstances. But, they seem to differ on how this is done and hence whether this distinguishes defense counsel from prosecutors. Neubauer hints that the evaluation of mitigating circumstances is something which is done after and in addition to the basic assessment of the value of the case in terms of the big three factors. He describes defense counsel as making "particularistic appeals" in an attempt to persuade prosecutors that in this particular case for some special reason the terms of the bargain should be even less severe than the normal discount for such a case. The notion of a two-stage bargaining process is also hinted at by Alschuler's (1975) observation that defense attorneys try to improve upon standard or "normal" deals in a jurisdiction.

In contrast, Mather describes plea bargaining decisionmaking as a one-stage phenomenon in which the defense counsel's assessment of mitigating circumstances is part and parcel of the calculation of the big three factors. Her description implies that there is no difference between prosecutors and defense counsel in their respective evaluations of a case (assuming they both consider the big three factors). A third view is implied by those researchers (e.g., Alschuler, 1968; Newman, 1966; Rosett and Cressey, 1976) who have reported that one of the functions which prosecutors consciously perform at plea bargaining is to mitigate any undue harshness of the law (to tailor the punishment to the unique circumstances of the case and thereby assure that substantive justice is done). This view says nothing about whether there is a one-stage or a two-stage process in plea bargaining, but it strongly implies that prosecutors are as concerned as defense counsel about mitigating circumstances.

Horney (1980) found that prosecutors and defense counsel differ substantially on how valuable certain types of deals are [11] and they differed significantly in their ratings of 6 of 11 factors affecting their evaluations of the cases they had jointly negotiated. Prosecutors rated the seriousness of the crime and the degree of punishment deserved higher than did defense counsel. But, defense counsel thought the likelihood of conviction was higher. They also thought that the present workload was higher and that it would take longer to try the case (2.8 days compared to 2.0 days). In addition they regarded the deal they worked out as worth more than what the prosecutor assessed it to be. These findings suggest that the structural differences between the two parties to the negotiation affect their perceptions of case worth.

Evenhandedness. One of the major concerns about criminal justice decisionmaking is that it be fair, meaning consistent. In practical terms this concerns whether the same case would be evaluated differently if it were handled by different attorneys. Horney suggests this would be true if the two attorneys were on opposite sides of the case. The next question is whether it would be true among attorneys on the same side. Would prosecutors as a group and defense counsel as a group be consistent in evaluating the same case? The evidence on this is ambiguous. Mather suggests that among public defenders there is not a high degree of agreement about how to evaluate any particular case. She (1974:272) writes:

> Certainly, PD's varied in their judgments and their predictions, so that one attorney might evaluate his client's chances differently than another would have. Or, what is a 'good' bargain for one PD might not be to his colleague. But, in general there was a consensus on how to evaluate cases and choose the best method for disposition.

Similarly, Carter (1974) emphasizes the general uncertainty in prosecutorial decisionmaking. In contrast, however, Jacoby (1980b:22) reports that "[t]he resounding conclusion [of her simulations with 855 prosecutors] is that prosecutors are rational and consistent in making decisions." In each of nine jurisdictions the "majority" of prosecutors evaluated each of 30 cases virtually the same with regard to the probability the case would be accepted for prosecution; what the likely disposition

---

[11] On a 100 point scale with 100=most valuable to defendant, defense attorneys rated four types of deals substantially higher than prosecutors (felony to misdemeanor, 82 units of value as seen by defense counsel compared to 66 for prosecutors; dropping of felonies, 65 compared to 49; lesser felony, 81 to 64; dropping counts, 42 to 34). Defense counsel agreed with prosecutors, on the high value of not filing habitual offender accusations (77 for both); and were close to an agreement on the comparatively low value of not having other charges filed. However, they rated this deal lower than prosecutors (38 to 42).

would be; and what the appropriate sentence (release, conditional release, or incarceration) should be if the defendant were convicted. However, she does not say what the degree of agreement among prosecutors is with regard to specific cases. She only reports that the "majority" agreed—which could mean that only 51 percent agreed and the other 49 percent disagreed.

In contrast, Horney (1980) analyzed the variance in the values of deals offered in real cases and found that the most powerful factor explaining 16 percent of the variance was the identity of the prosecutor. The second most powerful factor (accounting for 15 percent of the variance) was the identity of the defense attorney. Each of these factors alone explained more of the variance than all the "case factors" combined (including the probability of conviction, the seriousness of the crime, and the seriousness of the prior record).

Rhodes (1978) also partially confirms the hypothesis that plea bargaining varies depending upon who is involved. Focusing on the decision as to whether a case is bargained or set for trial (as distinct from the value of the deal offered) he found that the willingness to go to trial varied significantly among prosecutors but not among defense counsel and not between types of defense counsel (when counsel were grouped into "public defender" and "other"). But, Rhodes adds the caveat that his findings do not mean that who defense counsel is does not matter. It only means that differences in the pleading proclivities of individual counsel are not so strong that taking them into account in a statistical analysis improves one's ability to predict whether a case will be pleaded or go to trial.

Personal attributes of attorneys. The anecdotal evidence that the identity of the individual attorneys in plea negotiations makes a difference is considerable. Several researchers (Alschuler, 1975; Mather, 1974; Neubauer, 1974; and Newman, 1966) have found, and our own interview data confirm, that certain attributes of attorneys (both prosecutors and defense counsel) can influence both the decision to plead as well as the terms of the plea agreement. One attribute is the attorney's reputation. A second is the personal relationship between the opposing attorneys.[12]

---

[12] Horney's (1980) findings are curious on this point. Prosecutors and defense counsel were asked to rate each other in terms of "ability at trial" and "relationship with other attorney." On both dimensions they rated each other *equally* (i.e., there were no statistically significant differences). Yet, as noted earlier, the identities of the individual attorneys are the most powerful factors explaining the value of the deals offered.

An attorney's reputation is based on several things, including his honesty, his willingness to go to trial, and his ability at trial. Trying cases is hard work which prosecutors and defense counsel try to minimize to some extent. Some attorneys are known for never going to trial. Alschuler (1975) refers to defense attorneys who never take a case to trial as the "plead them guilty bar." We found a similar tendency among some prosecutors. They prefer to negotiate cases rather than try them. These attorneys who never take cases to trial are believed to negotiate from a position of weakness. Hence, they either get less or give away more in their bargaining.

A second aspect of attorney reputation has to do with skills. Attorneys willing to go to trial vary in their skill at trying cases. Again it is believed that this difference affects their bargaining. Supposedly, the skilled trial lawyer gets better bargains. However, Alschuler (1975) points out that an attorney can become so famous that he or she cannot get opposing attorneys to plea bargain with him or her. They would prefer to try to beat him or her at trial in order to establish their own reputations. We uncovered no instances of this. But we did occasionally hear of a related matter. Attorneys do develop personal animosities or "score cards" with each other. Some attorneys reported that they believe certain other attorneys wanted to take them to trial to try to beat them because the last time the two went to trial the opposing attorney had lost. It was never suggested, however, that this was the overriding consideration in the decision about whether to plea bargain or go to trial. With regard to honesty, we heard in several jurisdictions that some attorneys have such a reputation for dishonesty that other attorneys refuse to negotiate with them (although they may make a flat, take-it-or-leave-it offer).

The victim. There is little known about how often the victim has any input into plea bargaining or what influence that input has. An experiment in Dade County, Florida, found that when victims were allowed to participate in plea bargaining they rarely were vengeful and generally approved the plea agreements reached by the attorneys (Heinz and Kerstetter, 1980). What is more, the presence of victims at the plea negotiation (apparently) did not affect the severity of the sentences (Kerstetter and Heinz, 1979). The Connecticut Justice Commission (1980:55) found that the victim's attitude toward the case was one of the most frequently cited aspects of cases evaluated by prosecutors and defense counsel. Prosecutors tended to be more influenced by victims whose attitudes were favorable to the defense whereas defense counsel were more sensitive to victims whose attitudes were more favorable to the state. In assault and sex assault cases prosecutors tended to place "pivotal" importance on the attitudes of the victims.

After our initial survey, we concluded (McDonald, 1977) that the victim's wishes were rarely considered in the plea bargaining decisionmaking except for particularly notorious cases and in some jurisdictions regularly in cases of rape. The latter conclusion is supported by the findings of Lagoy et al. (1976). In our indepth study of the six jurisdictions we found 52 percent of 50 judges said they ask for victims' opinions of plea agreements before finally accepting them. But this varied widely by jurisdiction.[13] We also found that 49 percent of 43 prosecutors rarely hear from victims about their views on what the appropriate plea agreement should be. However, 28 percent said they routinely get this information and 23 percent more said they get it in special cases—typically ones involving special violence to the victim or crimes between family members. However, again there were major differences among jurisdictions on this score. Also, 44 percent of 32 prosecutors said that when they do hear from victims regarding plea bargaining they give the victims' wishes very little or no weight. But 28 percent said they give the victims' wishes some or a lot of weight and 28 percent more said it depends on the case. Again, the victims' wishes were usually weighed heavily in cases of violent crimes such as rape and in crimes between people who know each other.

The police. The nature of the police participation in and influence on plea bargaining has also been largely neglected (but see Kerstetter and Heinz, 1979; Kerstetter 1979a and 1979b; McDonald et al. 1981; and also Chapter 2 of this report). We found that in some jurisdictions in the lower courts the police either conduct the plea negotiations themselves or they represent the main power behind the negotiation. Typically, inexperienced prosecutors will be assigned to these courts and they generally will not approve plea bargains unless the police officer involved indicates he has no objection to the deal.

In felony-level courts the situation is usually different but it depends on the jurisdiction, the individual judge and the particular police department. In Detroit the professional association of police detectives prevailed upon the judges to require that prosecutors check with the police before completing any plea negotiations. In Norfolk, Virginia, defense attorneys say that the real key to successful plea negotiations is getting the police approval of the deal.

In our six jurisdictions [14] we found that 51 percent of 51 judges seek the police opinions of plea bargains before accepting the agreements. This varied dramatically by jurisdictions.[15] We also found that 25 percent of 55 prosecutors said they rarely or never get police opinions as to what the appropriate terms of the plea bargain should be. But, 54 percent said they get such input routinely and 20 percent more said they get it in special cases.[16]

The importance of police opinion to plea negotiations is indicated by the finding that 77 percent of 31 prosecutors reported that it made a "substantial difference" to them to "know that the police officer had no objection to the terms of the deal." This was true for most prosecutors in three of the four jurisdictions where the question was asked.[17]

We also found that the majority of prosecutors (73 percent of 52) determine how much weight they are willing to give a police officer's wishes at plea bargaining depending upon who the officer is. They know whether the officer is credible and has reasonable grounds for his or her position. Officers who are known to perjure themselves or who have a past pattern of questionable arrests or who seem to have insubstantial or vindictive reasons for wanting a particular disposition will not have their opinions considered.

Mitigating and aggravating attributes and circumstances. Various attributes of the defendant or the victim or other special circumstances relating to the crime are believed to influence the decision to plea bargain and the terms of the deal. A list of potential special attributes and circumstances is lengthy. A partial listing of those identified by others (Alschuler, 1968; Horney, 1980; Jacoby, 1980b; Lagoy et al., 1976; Mather, 1974; McDonald, 1976; Neubauer, 1974; Newman, 1966; Williams, 1976) and our interview findings are as follows:

(1) attributes of the defendant, such as age, sex, race, marital status, social class, political or family connections, demeanor, history of employment, drug use, alcohol use, psychiatric problems, physical

---

[13] Percentages of judges who do seek victims' opinions of plea agreements are: El Paso (misdemeanor courts), 0 percent; New Orleans, 86 percent; Seattle, 40 percent; Tucson, 0 percent; Delaware County, 92 percent; Norfolk, 72 percent.

[14] In El Paso only the lower court judges were asked.

[15] El Paso, 0 percent; New Orleans, 0 percent; Seattle, 100 percent; Tucson, 27 percent; Delaware County, 83 percent; Norfolk, 50 percent.

[16] The variation among jurisdictions was not as dramatic on this matter (at the felony level).

[17] Percent saying police opinion mattered: New Orleans, 100 percent; Seattle, 57 percent; Delaware County, 100 percent; Norfolk, 77 percent. In El Paso where the question was asked only of prosecutors handling misdemeanors none of four prosecutors answered affirmatively. This is surprising in light of our findings that in misdemeanor courts elsewhere the police have virtual veto power.

health problems, military service, and length of local residence;

(2) the defendant's relationship with the victim;

(3) attributes of the victim including things which could appear in the eyes of decisionmakers to make the victim "blameworthy" (in a more general sense than the legal notion of provocation) such as the victim's age, sex, race, social class, prior record of criminal deviant behavior, and also victim's willingness to testify and ability to establish a linkage between the defendant and the crime. (Of course, this latter item is usually considered in connection with evaluating case strength.); and,

(4) publicity.

Findings from the decision simulation

There is no concise way to convey our data regarding the items of information chosen in the plea bargaining simulation. The two tables presented below provide complementary, partial perspectives on the data. Both compare the decisionmaking of prosecutors and defense counsel. Table 4.2 indicates for each item of information contained in the simulation the respective proportions of prosecutors and defense counsel who consulted the item before deciding the case. To highlight the comparison between the type of attorney, two additional calculations are provided. Column 3 indicates the differences in percentage points between the respective proportions of prosecutors and defense counsel consulting each item of information. Column 4 presents the difference between prosecutors and defense counsel in the form of a ratio of their respective proportions. The ratio was used to rank all items presented in the table in order of decreasing ratios of agreement between prosecutors and defense counsel. Neither measure adequately conveys the many-sided notion of "agreement" between attorneys. But taken together, these two measures give some perspective on the topic. For instance, 54 percent of both prosecutors and defense counsel consulted the card entitled "defendant's age." On the one hand, this means that there is no disagreement *between* prosecutors and defense counsel as aggregates in the importance of this item of information; on the other hand, there is substantial disagreement *within* both of those groups of attorneys over this item of information.

Table 4.2 Comparison between prosecutors and defense counsel on items of information selected in burglary plea bargaining simulation in decreasing order of agreement*

Item	1 % of Prosecutors choosing item (N=134)	2 % of Defense counsel choosing item (N=102)	3 Column 2 minus column 1	4 Column 2 divided by column 1
1. Defendant's age	54	54	0	1.0
2. Defendant's prior record & police reputation	92	93	1	1.0
3. Evidence—substance of available	91	94	3	1.0
4. Ability of defendant to pay restitution	13	13	0	1.0
5. Basic facts of the case	97	94	−3	0.9
6. Codefendants	39	43	4	1.1
7. Propriety of police conduct after arrest	38	35	−3	0.9
8. Effectiveness of witnesses at trial	69	65	−4	1.1
9. Aggravating and mitigating circumstances	86	76	−10	0.9
10. Defendant's aliases	15	13	−2	0.9
11. Detainers on defendant	43	37	−6	0.9
12. Criminal history of defendant's family	8	10	2	1.2
13. Defendant's account of incident	73	87	14	1.2
14. Victim's attitude toward bargain	41	30	−11	0.7
15. Pretrial release, probation/parole status at time of offense	39	54	15	1.4
16. Record of alcohol use by defendant	26	37	11	1.4
17. Police attitude toward proposed bargain	38	23	−15	0.6
18. Defendant's intelligence and education	29	44	15	1.5
19. Defendant's employment status	43	63	20	1.5
20. Defendant's psychological problems	32	47	15	1.5
21. Record of drug use by defendant	36	54	18	1.5
22. Length of local residence of defendant	16	24	8	1.5
23. Defendant's interests and activities	10	15	5	1.5

Continued

Table 4.2 Comparison between prosecutors and defense counsel on items of information selected in burglary plea bargaining simulation in decreasing order of agreement*—Continued

Item	1 % of Prosecutors choosing item (N=134)	2 % of Defense counsel choosing item (N=102)	3 Column 2 minus column 1	4 Column 2 divided by column 1
24. Publicity/community sentiment	13	21	8	1.6
25. Length of time since arrest in instant offense	22	35	13	1.6
26. Victim's race, age, sex	10	17	7	1.7
27. Alternatives to incarceration	22	45	23	2.0
28. Defendant's pretrial release status for this burglary	25	52	27	2.0
29. Defendant's marital status	16	39	23	2.4
30. Trial judge's reputation for leniency	33	75	42	2.3
31. Reputation of prosecutor or defense attorney	19	54	35	2.8
32. Defendant's sex	12	36	24	3.0
33. Defendant's military record	9	27	18	3.0
34. Physical health of defendant	7	22	15	3.1
35. Backlog of docket of judge to whom case is assigned	7	26	19	3.7
36. Defendant's religious affiliation	1	8	7	8.0
37. Defendant's race/ethnicity/nationality	4	35	31	8.7
38. Relationship between prosecutor and defense attorney	5	45	40	9.0
39. Defendant's sexual orientation	1	9	8	9.0

*Source: Georgetown Plea Bargaining Decision Simulation.

Table 4.3 presents a portion of the same data arrayed differently. It shows which items of information were chosen by attorneys for each of their first 12 choices. Because of the length of this table, only the first 12 choices are presented; and items chosen by very small proportions were combined into a miscellaneous category.

Table 4.3 Rank order of the first 12 items of information consulted before deciding whether to plea bargain in simulated burglary case by type of attorney

(In percentages)

Prosecutors (N=134)	Rank order of item		Defense counsel (N=102)
	% of Prosecutors/ defense counsel choosing items		
	Items chosen first		
Basic facts	79	73	Basic facts
Evidence	7	9	Evidence
Prior record	6	5	Judge's reputation for sentencing
Aggravating/mitigating circumstances	2	3	Prior record
Misc. 6 items	6	10	Misc. 7 items
	100%	100%	Continued

Table 4.3   Rank order of the first 12 items of information consulted before deciding whether to plea bargain in simulated burglary case by type of attorney—Continued

(In percentages)

Prosecutors (N = 134)	Rank order of item		Defense counsel (N = 102)
	% of Prosecutors/ defense counsel choosing items		

Items chosen second

Prosecutors (N = 134)			Defense counsel (N = 102)
Evidence	45	40	Evidence
Prior record	19	23	Defendant's account
Basic facts	10	12	Basic facts
Defendant's account	5	3	Defendant's race and ethnicity
Effectiveness of witnesses	4	22	Misc. 13 items
Aggravating/mitigating circumstances	4		
Misc. 11 items	13		
	100%	100%	

Items chosen third

Prosecutors (N = 134)			Defense counsel (N = 102)
Prior record	17	29	Defendant's account
Defendant's account	16	17	Evidence
Aggravating/mitigating circumstances	14	14	Prior record
Evidence	10	9	Defendant's age
Effectiveness of witnesses	10	5	Effectiveness of witnesses
Defendant's age	5	4	Aggravating/mitigating circumstances
Misc. 17 items	28	22	Misc. 14 items
	100%	100%	

Items chosen fourth

Prosecutors (N = 134)			Defense counsel (N = 102)
Defendant account	15	18	Prior record
Prior record	13	14	Defendant's account
Aggravating/mitigating circumstances	11	9	Effectiveness of witnesses
Effectiveness of witnesses	10	7	Codefendants
Police conduct	5	7	Aggravating/mitigating circumstances
None, decision already made	4	5	Defendant's age
Misc. 19 items	42	5	None, decision already made
		4	Defendant's sex
		31	Misc. 13 items
	100%	100%	

Items chosen fifth

Prosecutors (N = 134)			Defense counsel (N = 102)
Effectiveness of witnesses	15	11	Prior record
Aggravating/mitigating circumstances	13	11	Effectiveness of witnesses
Prior record	11	8	Pretrial release status at time of offense
Defendant's account	20	8	Judge's reputation for leniency
Defendant's age	9	6	Codefendants
Codefendants	6	6	Aggravating/mitigating circumstances
None, decision already made	6	6	None, decision already made
Misc. 20 items	30	4	Defendant's age
		4	Defendant's employment record
		4	Pretrial release status for this offense
		32	Misc. 19 items
	100%	100%	

Continued

Table 4.3   Rank order of the first 12 items of information consulted before deciding whether to plea bargain in simulated burglary case by type of attorney—Continued

(In percentages)

Prosecutors (N=134)	Rank order of item		Defense counsel (N=102)
	% of Prosecutors/ defense counsel choosing items		

Items chosen sixth

Prosecutors (N=134)			Defense counsel (N=102)
None, decision already made	13	17	Prior record
Aggravating/mitigating circumstances	10	9	None, decision already made
Prior record	9	8	Judge's reputation for leniency
Defendant's age	7	8	Aggravating/mitigating circumstances
Defendant's account	7	6	Defendant's race and ethnicity
Effectiveness of witnesses	6	6	Effectiveness of witnesses
Evidence	5	6	Pretrial release status at time of offense
Detainers	4	4	Defendant's age
Police conduct	4	4	Defendant's account
Victim's attitude toward plea	4	4	Relationship between prosecutor and defense counsel
Misc. 16 items	31	28	Misc. 17 items
	100%	100%	

Items chosen seventh

Prosecutors (N=134)			Defense counsel (N=102)
None, decision already made	18	12	None, decision already made
Aggravating/mitigating circumstances	10	9	Defendant's age
Defendant's age	6	9	Aggravating/mitigating circumstances
Effectiveness of witnesses	6	6	Prior record
Prior record	5	6	Pretrial release status for instant offense
Evidence	5	6	Pretrial release status at time of offense
Police attitude toward plea	5	6	Detainers
Pretrial release status at time of offense	5	5	Judge's reputation for leniency
Pretrial release status for this offense	4	4	Codefendants
Victim's attitude toward plea	4	4	Reputation of prosecutor as trial lawyer
Codefendants	4	33	Misc. 22 items
Detainers	4		
Misc. 17 items	24		
	100%	100%	

Items chosen eighth

Prosecutors (N=134)			Defense counsel (N=102)
None, decision already made	26	16	None, decision already made
Defendant's age	4	7	Codefendants
Codefendants	4	6	Aggravating/mitigating circumstances
Victim's attitude toward plea	4	6	Reputation of prosecutor as trial lawyer
Pretrial release status for this offense	4	5	Defendant's sex
Police conduct	4	5	Prior record
Time since arrest for this offense	4	5	Defendant's account
Defendant's drug history	4	5	Pretrial release status for this offense
Aggravating/mitigating circumstances	4	4	Defendant's employment history
Misc. 22 items	42	4	Police conduct
		4	Pretrial release status at time of this offense
		33	Misc. 19 items
	100%	100%	

Continued

Table 4.3   Rank order of the first 12 items of information consulted before deciding whether to plea bargain in simulated burglary case by type of attorney—Continued

(In percentages)

Prosecutors (N = 134)	Rank order of item		Defense counsel (N = 102)
	% of Prosecutors/ defense counsel choosing items		

Items chosen ninth

Prosecutors (N = 134)			Defense counsel (N = 102)
None, decision already made	30	20	None, decision already made
Police attitude toward plea	6	6	Defendant's employment history
Defendant's account	6	5	Defendant's age
Prior record	5	5	Police conduct
Defendant's age	4	5	Effectiveness of witnesses
Defendant's employment record	4	5	Relationship between prosecutor and defense counsel
Defendant's education	3	5	Pretrial release status for this crime
Victim's attitude toward plea	3	4	Defendant's marital status
Defendant's alcoholic history	3	4	Judge's reputation for leniency
Detainers	3	3	Docket backlog
Aggravating/mitigating circumstances	3	3	Defendant's account
Misc. 21 items	30	3	Prior record
		3	Detainers
		29	Misc. 20 items
	100%	100%	

Items chosen 10th

Prosecutors (N = 134)			Defense counsel (N = 102)
None, decision already made	37	21	None, decision already made
Pretrial release status at time of offense	7	9	Defendant's employment history
Defendant's drug history	5	7	Aggravating mitigating circumstances
Defendant's education	5	5	Reputation of prosecutor as trial attorney
Defendant's employment history	4	5	Defendant's psychological history
Defendant's psychological history	4	5	Defendant's race and ethnicity
Effectiveness of witnesses	4	4	Defendant's education
Police conduct	3	4	Judge's reputation for leniency
Misc. 22 items	31	3	Defendant's age
		3	Police conduct
		3	Effectiveness of witnesses
		31	Misc. 22 items
	100%	100%	

Continued

Table 4.3   Rank order of the first 12 items of information consulted before deciding whether to plea bargain in simulated burglary case by type of attorney—Continued

(In percentages)

Prosecutors (N=134)	Rank order of item		Defense counsel (N=102)
	% of Prosecutors/ defense counsel choosing items		
Items chosen 11th			
None, decision already made	45	25	None, decision already made
Defendant's psychological history	6	5	Defendant's age
Defendant's age	4	5	Police conduct
Judge's reputation for leniency	4	5	Reputation of prosecutor as trial attorney
Detainers	4	4	Aggravating/mitigating circumstances
Aggravating/mitigating circumstances	3	4	Relationship between prosecutor and defense counsel
Local residency	3	4	Defendant's employment record
Defendant's alcoholic history	3	4	Defendant's marital status
Police attitude toward plea	3	3	Defendant's psychological history
Police conduct	3	3	Judge's reputation for leniency
Misc. 21 items	22	3	Evidence
		3	Available alternatives to incarceration
		3	Victim's attitude toward plea
		3	Pretrial release status for this offense
		3	Pretrial release status at time of this offense
		3	Defendant's drug history
		20	Misc. 10 items
	100%	100%	
Items chosen 12th			
None, decision already made	50	28	None, decision already made
Judge's reputation for leniency	4	7	Defendant's sex
Defendant's employment history	3	7	Defendant's education
Defendant's psychological history	3	7	Defendant's employment history
Codefendants	3	5	Defendant's psychological history
Pretrial release status for this offense	3	4	Judge's reputation for leniency
Defendant's alcoholic history	3	3	Victim's attitude toward plea
Misc. 21 items	31	3	Pretrial release status for this offense
		3	Pretrial release status at time of this offense
		3	Defendant's drug history
		30	Misc. 30 items
	100%	100%	

Case Strength. There is substantial agreement among all attorneys with regard to the primary importance of case strength (see Table 4.2). The concept of case strength could not be reduced to any one card (item of information) in the simulation. The two cards which are most obviously related to it are: "Basic facts of the case" and "Evidence—substance of available." Ninety-one percent or more of each type of attorney consulted these two cards before making their decisions. What is more, these two cards were usually the first cards chosen by both types of attorney (see Table 4.3). Another item of information also related to case strength is "Effectiveness of witnesses at trial." It was chosen by two-thirds of each type of attorney and was usually an early choice. Also consulted by the great majority of both types of attorneys was the "Defendant's account of the incident." The defendant may have an alibi or a defense or a plausible alternative version of what happened. Another item of information related to case strength is "Propriety of police conduct after arrest." Improper police conduct could lose or weaken a case. The literature and our interviews have suggested that plea bargaining is the way prosecutors salvage cases in which the police have acted improperly. Thus, it is somewhat surprising that only 38 percent of the prosecutors and 35 percent of the defense counsel consulted this item. Perhaps this represents a vote of confidence in the lawfulness of the police in handling this type of crime. On the other hand, it may suggest that the local courts are not sympathetic to motions to suppress evidence due to blunders by the constable.

Still another item related to case strength is whether there are codefendants. About 40 percent of both types of attorneys consulted this card. A codefendant changes the nature of a case. The presence of a codefendant does not in itself make the case stronger or weaker, but it does make the case more complicated. Each codefendant will have his own attorney and his own account of the incident. Multiple defendants provide the opportunity for bargaining one defendant against the other.

Still other factors less obviously related to case strength were consulted by some attorneys. Several items of information about the defendant are of this kind. If the defendant had been under the influence of alcohol or drugs, it may have been difficult to establish the requisite criminal intent. The case may not have been burglary but unlawful entry. Some of the prosecutors who consulted these cards later explained that they were concerned with the matter of intent. The fact that so few prosecutors (about one-third) checked these cards might be regarded as indirect evidence of the lack of prosecutorial concern for accurate charging. But we feel that such an interpretation would be stretching the limitations of the simulation. Had these cards been labeled differently, more prosecutors might have consulted them. For instance, if the label had been "Defendant's state of intoxication at time of offense," more prosecutors might have checked the card.

In addition to his records of drug and alcohol use, some attorneys checked other defendant attributes for the purpose of checking case strength. (Asking attorneys why they chose certain cards was not part of the original design of the research; but some attorneys volunteered explanations.) For instance, some prosecutors checked the defendant's race and then somewhat apologetically explained they were just making sure that he matched the description given by the witness. Some prosecutors checked the defendant's psychological history to make sure that the issue of an insanity defense would not come up.

Seriousness of the criminal. There was almost unanimous agreement among both prosecutors (92 percent) and de-fense attorneys (93 percent) that the seriousness of the defendant ("Defendant's prior record and police reputation") must be consulted before the plea bargaining decision could be made (Table 4.2). Also remarkable is the fact that by the end of the third item of information chosen, 42 percent of the prosecutors and 18 percent of the defense counsel had consulted the item (Table 4.3).

In addition, other cards relating to the defendant's seriousness were consulted. The defendant's age, for instance, is relevant to his or her dangerousness because it establishes the rate of criminal activity over time and his or her progress in a criminal career. Other indicators of defendant's seriousness include such things as whether the defendant has outstanding detainers; whether he or she was on some form of release at the time of the instant offense; his military record; and whether he or she comes from a family that is involved in criminal behavior. Even the defendant's employment status can be used as a measure of his or her dangerousness. The defendant with a long history of unemployment readily fits the image of the criminal who will have to make a living through crime if he or she is on the street.

Seriousness of the crime. The general level of seriousness of the crime is established by the nature of the charge—in this case, burglary. But there are variations in the seriousness of burglaries, depending upon the circumstances of the offense. The law, itself, captures these variations (but only crudely) with its distinctions between degrees of burglary. Experienced attorneys make finer distinctions. The law in some places distinguishes between day and night burglaries and between commercial and residential burglaries. Experienced attorneys go further. They distinguish between whether a residence is being lived in at the time of the offense; whether it was actually occupied at the time; and whether the trespasser was breaking in merely to get out of the cold or to find a place to stay while intoxicated on drugs or alcohol or to steal or do violence. It is not surprising that the great majority of prosecutors and defense counsel (86 percent and 76 percent respectively) consulted the card "Aggravating and mitigating circumstances of the offense," or that this card was usually consulted early in the decision making.

Caseload. Our earlier conclusion that caseload pressures act at a distance and are not a major factor in deciding what to do with individual cases is supported by the finding that only 7 percent of the prosecutors and 25 percent of the defense attorneys consulted the card entitled "Backlog of docket of judge to whom case is assigned." Moreover, this card was not consulted by a substantial number of attorneys within the first 12 choices.

Differences in information processing between prosecutors and defense counsel. The most noticeable difference between defense attorneys and prosecutors is that the defense attorneys consulted more information than prosecutors (Table 4.2). In 29 out of the 39 items of information in the table, a greater proportion of defense attorneys than prosecutors consulted the item. For 22 of the items the proportion of defense attorneys was one and a half items or more as great as that of the prosecutors. For only eight items were prosecutors more likely than defense attorneys to consult the items; and for only two of these was the difference substantial. These two items are: the attitudes of the victim and the police toward the plea bargain. The fact that 41 percent of the prosecutors were concerned for the victim's opinion of the plea bargain reveals a much higher degree of prosecutorial concern for victim opinion than was believed to have existed (McDonald, 1977). The fact that 38 percent of the prosecutors were concerned with the police attitude toward the plea bargain suggests that prosecutors are more concerned about police opinion than the police would lead you to believe (McDonald et al., 1981). Also noteworthy about the prosecutors' concern for the police and the victim is the fact it occurs earlier in their decision making than in that of defense counsel.

The distinctive approach of defense counsel to the evaluation of cases for plea bargaining can be further appreciated by reviewing those items of information that defense attorneys consult substantially more often and/or substantially earlier than prosecutors. There are three broad classes of such items: defendant's attributes; personal matters relating to criminal justice actors; and other things. Defense attorneys are consistently more interested in personal attributes of the defendant including his or her sex; race and ethnicity; intelligence and education; employment; marital status; history of drug and alcohol use; psychological problems; sexual orientation; physical health; and whether the instant crime was committed while on some form of release for another crime. The defense attorneys' interest in these matters was unlike the prosecutors' concern that criminal intent might not be provable. Rather, it reflects their special role in plea bargaining, the job of mitigating the case. That role was identified by an experienced public defender, quoted by Mather (1974:278) as follows:

> Let me put it to you this way: What is our job as a criminal lawyer in most instances: No. 1 is . . . no kidding, we know the man's done it, or we feel he's done it, he may deny it, but the question is, *Can they prove it?* The next thing is: *Can we mitigate it?* Of course you can always find something good to say about the guy—to mitigate it. Those are the two things that are important and that's what you do [emphasis in the original].

Assessing case strength is something both prosecutors and defense attorneys do. But, the job of "mitigating" the case is primarily that of defense counsel. Mitigation can be construed narrowly in a legal sense or broadly. Both prosecutors and defense attorneys are concerned with aggravating and mitigating circumstances in the narrow sense, such as whether a weapon was used, whether there was a provocation by the victim, or whether the victim was threatened. But the defense counsel's job of "mitigating" a case means more than merely consulting the card. "Aggravating and mitigating circumstances." It refers to the overall strategy and purpose of the defense counsel in plea bargaining. It means playing down the defendant's worst features and playing up his or her best. Thus, when it comes to the seriousness of the crime and the criminal, the defense counsel's job is to reinterpret reality so his or her client will appear in the best possible light. For instance, a defense attorney from Norfolk, Virginia, told us how he was able to get an "excellent" deal in a murder case by pointing out to the police and prosecutors that the victim was a well-known drug pusher whom everyone was delighted to be rid of. The attorney felt he could have gotten an even better deal but for the fact that his client "had shown bad form" in the killing. His client had confronted the victim over an alleged mistreatment of the client's sister. The victim had pleaded for mercy and then turned and ran. The client gave chase and shot the victim in the back. The defense attorney felt that if his client had shot the victim when they were face to face it would have been easier to portray him as simply an outraged brother. The shooting in the back after the pleas for mercy could not be easily "mitigated." It conveyed the image of a person who was heartless, hence, more dangerous, and, hence, deserving of a more severe plea bargain.

The job of mitigation begins with playing down the seriousness of the offense and the seriousness of the offender but does not end there. It involves looking "for something good to say about the guy." Neubauer (1974:219) was correct in saying that defense counsel evaluate cases the same as prosecutors do as far as the big three factors are concerned but then go on to make "particularistic appeals." The idea of a two-stage model of plea bargaining, the first stage dealing with a general discount usually given to a general category of cases and the second stage wherein improvements upon that general discount are sought, seems to be supported by our simulation data. It is at this second stage of plea bargaining where the defense counsel plays his or her unique role.[18] Here

---

[18] Although we have described plea bargaining as a "two-stage model," we don't mean to imply that defense counsel consciously divide their

is where he or she looks for *any* reason that his or her client should get an additional break. This accounts for the fact that defense attorneys consistently consulted more information. Several of them desperately flipped through our array of cards commenting, "Doesn't this guy have *anything* going for him?"

The second broad class of items which defense counsel consulted substantially more often than and earlier than prosecutors involved personal characteristics of criminal justice actors. More specifically, defense counsel were more concerned than prosecutors with: (1) the trial judge's reputation for leniency (75 percent compared to 33 percent); (2) the reputation of the opposing attorney (54 percent compared to 19 percent); and (3) the relationship between the prosecutor and the defense attorney (45 percent compared to 5 percent).

By the end of the ninth card chosen, at least 30 percent of the defense attorneys (compared to 9 percent of the prosecutors) had consulted the "Judge's reputation for leniency" card. This suggests that the judge has a much more influential role in setting the limits of plea bargains than was evident before. Our interview findings were ambiguous on this point. On the one hand, it was clear that some judges establish the upper limits of bargained-for terms by their sentencing tendencies. Prosecutors had to offer the judge's known sentence limit or something better in order to get a defendant to plead. In several jurisdictions, judges would not tolerate prosecutors "embarrassing" them or "putting the heat on them" by recommending sentences more severe than the judge's usual standards. It is not uncommon for judges to reprimand assistant prosecutors or call their supervisors and have them moved to a different courtroom if prosecutors persist in recommending sentences that are higher than what the judge cares to impose. Thus, it is somewhat surprising to find in the decision simulation that relatively few prosecutors (33 percent) showed concern for the judge's sentencing practice.

On the other hand, we also found that some judges seem to follow what the prosecutor recommends. (Of course, these prosecutors might recommend what they know the judges want to hear.) Other judges state that they take the prosecutor's recommendation as the upper limit on the terms of any deal and then usually settle on something less than that or split the difference between what the prosecutor and the defense want. In short, our interviews left us in a quandary about whether the judge's personal sentencing preferences played a decisive role in setting the limits of plea bargaining. Although the deci-

sion simulation does not fully resolve that quandary, it does suggest that in the minds of defense counsel the judge's preferences are decisive.

Return now to the other two "personal" items that defense attorneys consulted more frequently than prosecutors, namely, reputation of the opposing attorney and the professional relationship between the two attorneys. Although the literature and our own interviews had indicated that the reputation of an attorney has a bearing in some pleas bargains, there was nothing to indicate that this factor would be three times more important to defense counsel than to prosecutors. Nor was there anything to explain why defense attorneys would consult this item much earlier than prosecutors. If anything, reports about the "plead them guilty bar" would lead one to predict that prosecutors would be more concerned than defense attorneys regarding the reputation of the opposing counsel. Nor can we offer any convincing explanations for why defense counsel were nine times more likely to want to know about the professional relationship between the hypothetical prosecutor and themselves.

Finally, we turn to the "all other" category. We cannot convincingly explain why defense counsel should be 3.7 times more interested in the state of the judge's docket. Perhaps it is because of the defense tactic of seeking continuances in order to delay a case in the hopes of weakening the case. Defense counsel's greater interest in "alternatives to incarceration" is for obvious reasons. The only surprising thing may be that only 45 percent of them consulted this card. As to why defense counsel should have a greater interest than prosecutors in the victim's age, sex, and race, we have no convincing explanation. In the basic facts of the case it was clear that the victim had not been personally confronted by the burglar. Also unclear is why defense counsel are more concerned than prosecutors with publicity. However, all of these differences might be explained as part of defense counsel's desperate search for any grounds for particularistic appeals.

Consistency of estimates of case strength. The question of whether given the same case different attorneys would agree in their estimates of its chance of conviction at trial is addressed by the data in Table 4.4. Two cases, a robbery and a burglary, each with strong and weak versions of case strength, were presented to attorneys. As Table 4.4 indicated, the attorneys were willing to give estimates of case strength in finer categories than the simple dichotomy of "deadbang" or "reasonable doubt." They gave specific probabilities of conviction. Their answers have been grouped into seven categories to show the considerable disagreement that occurred in some cat-

---

thinking into two parts. We are making such division only for analytic purposes.

egories. However, if one collapses these categories into three broader categories (namely, 40 percent probability of conviction or less, 41 to 70 percent; and 71 percent or greater), then one can more easily see the degree of consistency with regard to these estimates. On the one hand, there is remarkably strong agreement among both prosecutors and defense attorneys in their conviction estimates for the strong versions of both cases. From 82 percent to 94 percent of these attorneys felt that these cases had a 71 percent or better chance of conviction. What is more, there is no statistically significant difference between prosecutors or defense counsel in their estimates in these strong cases. These findings are all the more remarkable when one recalls the terms of the simulation. That is, these attorneys had been instructed to give their estimates of the probability of conviction on the assumptions that (1) they would be the attorney at trial and (2) their trial would be before a jury like the ones with which they were familiar in their own respective jurisdictions. Given the pervasive courthouse folklore about the importance of differences in the trial ability of attorneys and differences in the preferences of local juries, one would expect much greater disagreement in these estimates of the probability of conviction. Recall that our attorneys were from many different jurisdictions.

Table 4.4 Attorneys' estimates or probability of conviction by type of attorney, strength of case, and type of crime*

Type of crime and probability of conviction	Strong case		Weak case	
	Prosecutors	Defense attorneys	Prosecutors	Defense attorneys
Estimated probability of conviction in **Robbery** case was:	(N=69)	(N=54)	(N=69)	(N=51)
Less than 20%	0.0	0.0	17.4	13.7
21–40%	0.0	1.9	8.7	11.8
41–60%	0.0	3.7	24.6	15.7
61–70%	5.8	5.6	5.8	3.9
71–80%	14.5	16.7	10.0	0.0
81–90%	29.0	22.2	0.0	0.0
91–100%	50.7	50.0	33.3	54.9
	100.0%	100.1%**	100.0%	100.0%
	$x^2=4.464$		$x^2=10.2431$	
	d.f=5		d.f=5	
	P=.49 n.s.		P=0.7 n.s.	
Estimated probability of conviction in **Burglary** case was:	(N=66)	(N=52)	(N=68)	(N=50)
Less than 20%	0.0	0.0	4.4	4.0
21–40%	4.5	3.8	7.4	14.0
41–60%	7.6	1.9	19.1	6.0
61–70%	4.5	11.5	4.4	12.0
71–80%	22.7	11.5	22.1	4.0
81–90%	24.2	13.5	10.3	0.0
91–100%	36.4	57.7	32.4	60.0
	100.0%	100.0%	100.0%	100.0%
	$x^2=10.404$		$x^2=23.846$	
	d.f=6		d.f=6	
	P=0.7 n.s.		P<.001	

*Source: Georgetown Plea Bargaining Simulation.
**Percentages not summing to 100.0 are due to rounding errors.

The surprising amount of agreement suggests that (at least under certain circumstances) the estimation of case strength can be done with a good deal of reliability. That is, when cases approach being "deadbang" and when the estimates of case strength are given in broad categories (such as "71 percent or better"), there will be considerable agreement among different attorneys about the probability of conviction, no matter who the attorney is and no matter what the vagaries of local juries may be.

On the other hand, looking at the two weak cases in Table 4.4, one notices considerably less agreement in the estimates of case strength. A striking disagreement occurs in the weak robbery case. Also noteworthy is that the same split occurs among both prosecutors and defense attorneys. The difference by type of attorney is not statistically significant.

In the weak case, however, there is both a split among attorneys of the same type and between the two types of attorney. The latter split is statistically significant. More defense attorneys than prosecutors see this case as a very strong case (91 percent or stronger). But also more defense attorneys than prosecutors (18 percent compared with 11.8 percent) see it as a weaker case (40 percent or less chance of conviction)!

In sum, the findings suggest that when cases are strong different attorneys regardless of whether they are prosecutors or defense counsel will agree on the estimates of case strength. But, when cases are weak there will be moderate to substantial disagreement among attorneys and between attorneys of different types. Perhaps strong cases "try themselves" whereas the skills of an attorney and the vagaries of local juries make a greater difference in the weaker cases.

The prosecutor's choice of disposition. The question of what factors influence the prosecutor's decision to (1) take a case to trial, (2) dismiss it, or (3) plea bargain it was the subject of several analyses performed on the decision simulation data. Particular attention was given to the influence of prior record and case strength. Previous research and our own interview data gave us conflicting expectations about what relationships would occur between each of these two factors and the prosecutor's choice of disposition route.[19] Experience and the litera-

ture suggest that prosecutors would be less likely to dismiss defendants with serious prior records. As to the effect of case strength, it was hard to know what to predict. There were some grounds to believe that each of the three options might be increased when a case is weak. Some prosecutors feel weak cases do not belong in the system. Hence, weak cases might be nollied more often. Alternatively, some prosecutors feel that weak cases are precisely the ones whose outcomes should be determined by the trial process. Hence, weak cases might be taken to trial more often. Finally, there is the "half-a-loaf" hypothesis first noted in the 1920's by Moley (1929) and reconfirmed by Alschuler (1968) and our own interview data. Prosecutors feel it is their duty to try to get a conviction for something rather than dismiss a case or take the risk of losing it at trial (see Chapter 3). Hence the weaker the case the more likely the prosecutor is to plea bargain it.

Of the three hypotheses, the half-a-loaf hypothesis is the one that most practitioners and researchers would probably expect to be supported by our simulation data. But surprisingly, it was not. No matter how the data were analyzed (including an analysis of variance not presented here), the half-a-loaf hypothesis was consistently *not* supported. Prosecutors were *not* more likely to plea bargain the weaker version of the cases. Prior record and strength of case did have a significant impact on the prosecutor's choice of disposition routes but not in a simple, straightforward way. Their greater impact occurred when the two factors were taken together.

Table 4.5 illustrates this joint effect and also shows that the half-a-loaf hypothesis was not supported. The data indicate that when a defendant with a serious prior record is involved, differences in case strength do not produce statistically significant differences in the prosecutor's choice between dropping the case, taking it to trial, or plea bargaining it. But, when a minor prior record is involved, then prosecutors are more likely to either go to trial or to drop the case than negotiate it.

This finding suggests that prosecutors are more consistent and rational in their decisionmaking than their critics believe. The data indicate that there is a logic to prosecutor's decisionmaking. This fact alone should provide some comfort to those critics who fear that prosecutors exercise their discretion haphazardly. But whether or not the particular logic revealed by the data is regarded as desirable depends on one's perspective.

There are two critical perspectives from which prosecutorial decisionmaking is usually judged: (1) from a concern for the safety of the community; and (2) from a concern for the fairness and propriety of procedures

---

[19] American defendants today are not required by law to go to trial. They may plead guilty. Thus, when we speak of prosecutors "choosing" to go to trial, we only mean they are refusing to offer a plea bargain. The defendants might still plead guilty as charged.

Table 4.5   Prosecutor's disposition decision by strength of case controlling for prior record and type of crime*

Type of crime and disposition decision	Strong case Serious prior record	Weak case Serious prior record	Strong case Minor prior record	Weak case Minor prior record
Robbery:	(N=35)	(N=38)	(N=34)	(N=29)
Nolle prosequi	0	5	3	21
Go to trial	6	8	12	4
Plea bargain	94	87	85	75
	100%	100%	100%	100%
	$x^2 = 1.9459$ d.f.$=2$ P(x^2)$=.37$ n.s.		$x^2 = 5.9730$ d.f.$=2$ P(x^2)$=.05$ gamma$=.35$	
Burglary:	(N=29)	(N=35)	(N=35)	(N=28)
Nolle prosequi	3	3	0	14
Go to trial	10	6	11	11
Plea bargain	87	91	97	75
	100%	100%	100%	100%
	$x^2 = .50155$ d.f.$=^2$ P(x^2)$=.66$ n.s.		$x^2 = 7.3861$ d.f.$=2$ P(x^2)$=.02$ gamma$=.84$	

*Source: Georgetown University Plea Bargain Simulation.

used in administering criminal justice. Both types of critics will find things to comfort and distress them in Table 4.5; but what is a comfort to one will be a distress to the other. Some persons concerned for the public's safety worry that prosecutors for reasons of laziness, ineptness, or political ambition prefer to get rid of (dismiss) weak cases and thereby put the community safety at risk. Such people should be reassured by the finding that prosecutors are more likely to dismiss weak cases only if the defendant has a minor prior record. But while this may reassure people concerned for community safety, it worries persons concerned about due process and the principle of legality. From the latter perspective if cases are weak enough to dismiss, then prior record should not have any effect. Such cases should be dismissed regardless of whether the defendant has a serious prior record.

Another matter addressed by the data in Table 4.5 is the concern of the due process critics is that plea bargaining is used by prosecutors to "get" serious defendants in weak cases that might be lost at trial. To these critics the findings should be of some comfort. They suggest that prosecutors are not trying to defeat the principle of le-

gality through plea bargaining. Among cases with serious prior records there was no significant increase in plea bargaining among the weak compared with the strong version of the case. This same finding, however, may be distressing to the persons concerned about community safety. Less troubled by the possible coerciveness of plea bargaining, these people may feel that the fact that prosecutors did *not* resort to plea bargaining significantly more often when serious criminals were involved represents a critical neglect of the public interest.

The Prosecutor's Sentencing Decision. In this analysis we present two sentencing decisions. The first is the prosecutor's choice between type of sentence, i.e., probation, jail time, or prison time. The second is the length of the sentence. The focus of our analyses is on the influence of prior record and case strength on these two decisions. An analysis not presented here found that differences in the seriousness of prior record by itself did not significantly affect any of the four decisions analyzed here, i.e., the type of sentence and length of sentence decisions for the burglary and the robbery cases. As for the influence of case strength, it by itself did have a significant effect on the prosecutor's two sentencing decisions (type and length of sentence) with respect to the burglary case but not to the robbery case.

The analyses presented in Tables 4.6, 4.7, 4.8, and 4.9 examine the influence of case strength and prior record taken together. Five of the sixteen comparisons were significant. That is, five combinations of case strength and prior record but not all combinations made a difference in the sentencing decisions of prosecutors. When one looks at just cases involving minor prior records, then differences in case strength do have a significant impact on the prosecutor's decision about type of sentence in both robbery and burglary (Table 4.6). As expected, prosecutors are more likely to seek a lenient type of sentence in a weak case.

Table 4.7 indicates that when dealing with just weak cases and only with burglaries a difference in the seriousness of the prior record has a significant impact on the type of sentence sought by the prosecutor. As expected (logically and from the literature), prosecutors seek a more lenient type of sentence for the defendant with the minor prior record.

Table 4.8 indicates that only when one is dealing with cases that are burglaries and that involve minor prior records does the difference in the strength of the case make a significant difference in the length of sentence sought by the prosecutor in plea bargaining. Finally, Table 4.9 indicates that only in robbery cases that are weak does a difference in the seriousness of the prior record make a significant difference in the length of sentence sought by the prosecutor. As expected, prosecutors seek more lenient sentences for defendants with minor prior records.

In summary, differences in case strength and seriousness of prior record do not by themselves or acting together consistently influence the prosecutor's sentencing decisions. But when they do have significant impacts either alone or conjointly, the impacts are in the expected directions. That is, prosecutors are more likely to give more lenient deals in weaker cases and in cases with minor prior records. Generally, it seems that the influence of these factors tends to be significant only in "marginal" circumstances, situations that present the greatest opportunity for dissent over disposition and sentence. No one thing identifies these situations; but they can be thought of as the opposite of those cases that "try themselves." They are the cases that "do not dispose of themselves." They tend to be the ones with the less extreme circumstances, e.g., the crimes of medium seriousness; the cases that are neither terribly strong nor completely nonexistent; the ones involving defendants with some prior record but not a life of crime.

Table 4.6   Type of sentence sought by prosecutor in plea bargaining by case strength controlling for prior record and type of crime*

Type of crime—Type of sentence	Strong case Serious prior record	Weak case Serious prior record	Strong case Minor prior record	Weak case Minor prior record
Robbery:	(N=26)	(N=26)	(N=21)	(N=18)
Time in prison	81	77	81	50
Time in jail	11	15	19	28
Probation	8	8	0	22
	100%	100%	100%	100%
	$x^2=1.672$		$x^2=6.3032$	
	d.f.=2		d.f.=2	
	$P(x^2)=.91$ n.s.		$P(x^2)=.04$	
			gamma=†.65	
				Continued

Table 4.6 Type of sentence sought by prosecutor in plea bargaining by case strength controlling for prior record and type of crime*—Continued

Type of crime—Type of sentence	Strong case Serious prior record	Weak case Serious prior record	Strong case Minor prior record	Weak case Minor prior record
Burglary:	(N=17)	(N=22)	(N=22)	(N=21)
Time in prison	59	41	46	21
Time in jail	29	18	27	5
Probation	12	41	27	74
	100%	100%	100%	100%
	$x^2=5.5864$		$x^2=9.1724$	
	d.f.= 2		d.f.=2	
	$P(x^2)=.06$ n.s.		$P(x^2)=.01$	
			gamma=.72	

*Source: Georgetown University Plea Bargain Simulation.

Table 4.7 Types of sentence sought by prosecutor in plea bargaining by seriousness of prior record controlling for strength of case and type of crime*

Type of crime—Type of sentence	Strong case Serious prior record	Strong case Minor prior record	Weak case Serious prior record	Weak case Minor prior record
Robbery:	(N=26)	(N=21)	(N=26)	(N=18)
Time in prison	81	81	77	50
Time in jail	11	19	15	28
Probation	8	0	8	22
	100%	100%	100%	100%
	$x^2=2.0522$		$x^2=3.6151$	
	d.f.=2		d.f.=2	
	$P(x^2)=.36$ n.s.		$P(x^2)=.16$	
Burglary:	(N=17)	(N=22)	(N=22)	(N=19)
Time in prison	59	46	41	21
Time in jail	29	27	18	5
Probation	12	27	41	74
	100%	100%	100%	100%
	$x^2=4.0437$		$x^2=7.6936$	
	d.f.=2		d.f.=2	
	$P(x^2)=.13$ n.s.		$P(x^2)=.02$	
			gamma= +.62	

*Source: Georgetown University Plea Bargain Simulation.

Table 4.8 Length of sentence sought by prosecutor in plea bargaining by strength of case controlling for prior record and type of crime*

Type of crime—length of sentence sought	Strong case Serious prior record	Weak case Serious prior record	Strong case Minor prior record	Weak case Minor prior record
Robbery:	(N=35)	(N=38)	(N=34)	(N=31)
5 years or more	46	45	47	35
2–5 years	23	26	12	10
1–2 years	11	10	12	3
6 mos.–1 year	8	8	17	10
0–6 mos.	3	3	9	10
Probation	9	8	3	32
	100%	100%	100%	100%
	$x^2=1.6525$		$x^2=1.5428$	
	d.f.=5		d.f.=5	
	$P(x^2)=.89$ n.s.		$P(x^2)=.91$ n.s.	
Burglary:	(N=31)	(N=35)	(N=35)	(N=33)
5 years or more	29	29	14	24
2–5 years	23	14	11	6
1–2 years	5	11	11	3
6 mos.–1 year	13	6	11	12
0–6 mos.	23	11	34	9
Probation	5	29	17	45
	**98%	100%	**98%	**99%
	$x^2=7.6565$		$x^2=12.3679$	
	d.f.=5		d.f.=5	
	$P(x^2)=.17$ n.s.		$P(x^2)=.03$	
			gamma=+.14	

*Source: Georgetown University Plea Bargain Simulation.
**Due to rounding error.

Table 4.9 Length of sentence sought by prosecutor in plea bargaining by prior record controlling for strength of case and type of crime*

Type of crime—length of sentence sought	Strong case Serious prior record	Strong case Minor prior record	Weak case Serious prior record	Weak case Minor prior record
Robbery:	(N=35)	(N=34)	(N=38)	(N=31)
5 years or more	46	47	45	35
2–5 years	23	12	26	10
1–2 years	11	12	10	3
6 mos.–1 year	7	18	8	10
0–6 mos.	3	9	3	10
Probation	9	3	8	32
	**99%	**101%	100%	100%
	$x^2=4.3197$		$x^2=11.0275$	
	d.f.=5		d.f.=5	
	$P(x^2)=.50$ n.s.		$P(x^2)=.05$ n.s.	
			gamma=+.35	

Continued

Table 4.9   Length of sentence sought by prosecutor in plea bargaining by prior record controlling for strength of case and type of crime*—Continued

Type of crime—length of sentence sought	Strong case Serious prior record	Strong case Minor prior record	Weak case Serious prior record	Weak case Minor prior record
Burglary:	(N=31)	(N=35)	(N=35)	(N=33)
5 years or more	29	14	29	24
2–5 years	23	11	14	6
1–2 years	6	11	11	3
6 mos.–1 year	13	11	6	12
0–6 mos.	23	34	11	9
Probation	6	17	29	45
	**98%	100%	100%	**99%
	$x^2=5.7220$		$x^2=5.630$	
	d.f.=5		d.f.=5	
	$P(x^2)=.33$	n.s.	$P(x^2)=.34$ n.s.	

*Source: Georgetown University Plea Bargain Simulation.
**Due to rounding error.

The presence of one or more of these circumstances makes the calculation of what the just disposition and sentence should be much more difficult. Reasonable people are more likely to differ over these cases than over the cases with the more extreme circumstances. It is here apparently that differences in case strength and prior record can make the difference in what decisions are made about the case. This is not altogether surprising. We had chosen burglary because we regarded it as a "marginal" crime. In our early field work it seemed that the greatest amount of consensus among the various actors in the courthouse occurred in the more extreme cases. Burglary was one of those crimes that could go either way depending upon differences in philosophy of the lawyers involved and differences in the crime problem facing the jurisdiction. Some suburban jurisdictions regarded burglary as an extremely serious offense, while neighboring urban jurisdictions with high burglary rates treated it less seriously. Even within jurisdictions there was considerable variation between judges and other actors in their view of the seriousness of burglary. There was greater consensus about robbery.

Similarly, there seemed to be greater consensus about what to do with strong cases than weak cases and with defendants with serious prior records than defendants with minor prior records. Thus, in retrospect we are not surprised to find that the influence of prior record and case strength appear to be significant only in those situations where agreement among actors in the system seems to be at its lowest.

Also, it is not surprising to find that when case strength did have an effect, it was in the direction of a more lenient sentence for weaker cases. This is part of what is implied by the half-a-loaf hypothesis. But, it is remarkable that the *sentencing* implications of the half-a-loaf hypothesis *are* borne out by the data when earlier we saw that the half-a-loaf hypothesis' implication regarding the *prosecutor's choice of dispositions* (i.e., that he would be more likely to plea bargain than to go to trial or dismiss weak cases) *are not* supported by the data. Also remarkable is the fact that prior record and case strength did not significantly affect the sentencing decisions more often than they did. Our conclusion that they seem to make significant differences only in marginal circumstances is an *ex post facto* attempt to make some sense of the data. But, as an explanation it is something less than compelling. For us the data raise more questions than they answer.

Differences in outcome choices between prosecutors and defense counsel. In addition to the question of whether prosecutors and defense attorneys consult the same items of information, there is the question of whether they agree on what should be done with the case once they have learned the facts. We noted earlier that in estimating the probability of conviction there was not statistically significant difference between prosecutors and defense attorneys in three of the four comparisons. It was only in the weak burglary case that the two groups differed.

We turn now to the three subsequent decisions analyzed in this chapter: the choice as to whether to plea bargain or go to trial;[20] the choice of type of sentence sought, i.e., prison time, jail time, or probation; and finally, the choice as to length of sentence.

With regard of all three decisions we were uncertain about what, if any, differences to expect between prosecutors and defense counsel. The literature (Alschuler, 1975; Blumberg, 1967; Cole, 1975; Grossman, 1969; Skolnick, 1967) has emphasized that the adversary system exists in theory only. In practice, the informal social relationships that develop among defense attorneys, prosecutors, judges, and other courthouse actors compromise the adversarial nature of the relationship. Defense attorneys have been described as coopted double-agents who sacrifice their clients' interests in the interests of court efficiency, the maintaining of good relations with judges and prosecutors, and the making of a faster buck. Plea bargaining has been condemned as "an inherently irrational method of administering justice" because, among other things, it "subjects defense attorneys to serious

temptations to disregard their clients' interest" (Alschuler, 1975:1180).

Our interviews and observations confirmed that informal social relationships among courthouse actors do develop and in limited ways do influence their decisions and actions. It is undeniable that plea bargaining offers defense counsel numerous temptations to sacrifice their client's interest. But when we asked defense counsel, prosecutors, and judges how often defense counsel succumb to these temptations, the answers were not unanimous. Yes, a few defense attorneys are notoriously unethical. Yes, a few defense attorneys will do anything to avoid taking a case to trial. Yes, some defense attorneys reveal confidential information obtained from their clients to prosecutors in the course of plea bargaining. But, whether these and other facts mean that the adversarial system is dead is another matter. We concluded that the existing literature had overstated the nonadversarial nature of plea negotiations. While it is true that defense attorneys act cooperatively with prosecutors in plea bargaining and do lean on their clients to plea bargain when the client would prefer to go to trial, it was not our impression that this was usually done with improper motives or that this usually involved a sacrifice of the client's interests. We do not feel that cooperation between defense attorneys and prosecutors precludes an adversarial relationship. It may just make the adversarial characteristics of the interaction more difficult to see.

---

[20] We have deleted the option of nolle prosequi from this part of the analysis because it is only relevant to prosecutors.

Table 4.10   Comparison between prosecutors and defense counsel in their decisions to go to trial or plea bargain by type of crime*

	Prosecutors	Defense counsel
Robbery:	(N=127)	(N=102)
Go to trial	8	31
Plea bargain	92	69
	100%	100%
	$x^2 = 20.8559$	
	d.f. = 1	
	$P(x^2) = <.0001$	
	gamma = $-.80$	
Burglary:	(N=120)	(N=98)
Go to trial	7	32
Plea bargain	93	78
	100%	100%
	$x^2 = 10.1926$	
	d.f. = 1	
	$P(x^2) = <.001$	
	gamma = $-.58$	

*Source: Georgetown Plea Bargain Simulation.

86

Turning now to our first comparison, we have two alternative hypotheses about what the relationship might be between type of attorney and the decision to plea bargain or go to trial. The literature suggests that either there would be no difference between defense attorneys and prosecutors (because defense attorneys have been coopted and nonadversarial) or that there may be a difference in the direction of defense counsel being more likely to decide to plea bargain than to go to trial (because plea bargaining is easier, faster, and more convenient for defense attorneys). The results of our comparison are presented in Table 4.10. Once again the data are surprising. Neither of the two hypotheses is supported.

There is a significant difference between prosecutors and defense counsel in whether they would plea bargain or go to trial. Contrary to expectations it is the defense attorneys and not the prosecutors who are more likely to go to trial! This is true both in the robbery and the burglary case. In both cases the relationship is quite strong.

When interpreting Table 4.10 and the other tables in this section, it is important to remember that all attorneys were clearly instructed to give their "bottom-line" recommendations, not their "opening offers." Thus, differences in their offers do not represent the distance between artificially inflated opening offers between two seasoned negotiators.[21] Defense counsel (in Table 4.10) who recommended that the case should go to trial were not engaging in a ploy to get a better plea bargain out of the prosecutor. Going to trial was their bottom-line decision.

Having excluded the possibility that the relationship described in Table 4.10 is due to negotiation tactics, it remains to explain what does account for the relationship. We are again forced to engage in a retrospective interpretation. Although we felt that the literature had overstated the nonadversary nature of plea negotiations, we had not been prepared for these findings. However, it is possible to construct a rationale explaining why defense attorneys were more likely to go to trial. Earlier we noted that 75 percent of the defense counsel compared with only 33 percent of the prosecutors consulted the card entitled "Judge's reputation for leniency." The data presented earlier (Table 4.2) were only for the burglary case, but the same proportions were true of the robbery case as well. In both cases the description of the judge was the same. It read: "The trial judge is known to be lenient and considers probation in this type of case. He generally favors rehabilitative alternatives to incarceration."

Having read this card, it seems obvious why defense counsel should take the case to trial. They probably could not have gotten a better deal from a prosecutor than the maximum sentence they might get from this judge. Therefore, the logical thing to do was to take the case to trial and go for an acquittal. If they did lose, they would not "lose big." This particular judge makes plea bargaining with the prosecutor an irrelevant waste of time.[22]

Our second comparison between prosecutors and defense attorneys focuses on their choices of type of sentence and length of sentence. That is, the first choice is among prison time, jail time, or probation. The second choice is among different lengths of sentence. For both these comparisons we were uncertain about what to expect. Several alternative hypotheses could be offered with equal plausibility. One line of reasoning would lead one to expect that the two types of attorneys would not differ in these two choices. It could be reasoned that, assuming attorneys are able to evaluate cases, as they claim, then both types of attorneys should agree on the true value of the case, that is, the type of sentence and the length of sentence it deserves. Prosecutors and defense counsel might differ in their opening offers in plea

---

[21] Of course, it is possible that the attorneys may have ignored our instructions and given bottom lines which were really closer to opening offers. However, we feel this would have to have been done on a less conscious level, because our instructions were clear and unambiguous.

[22] We regret that we did not describe one of the judges as a severe sentencer to see if this would have altered the results of this particular comparison.

bargaining, but the bottom line should be fairly close to agreement.

One could reach the same expectation from alternative starting points. For instance, the claim that defense counsel do not take an adversary posture in negotiations would also lead one to expect no difference between types of attorneys. Alternatively, saying nothing about whether attorneys act in an adversarial posture, one could note the mere fact that in today's administration of justice 90 percent of the time prosecutors and defense counsel are able to reach agreements in plea negotiations. Hence, one could expect that there would be no difference between these types of attorneys in the bottom-lines arrived at in our decision simulation.

On the other hand, given our earlier discussion about the defense attorney's special task of mitigating a case, i.e., trying to get a deal which is below the true market value of the case, one might expect that defense counsel's bottom-line would always be lower (more lenient) than that of prosecutors. Or, one might reach this expectation from the belief that defense attorneys do take an adversarial posture in plea negotiations and consequently their demands will differ from those of prosecutors. Still other plausible hypotheses might be advanced. There is nothing in the existing literature to persuasively support one of these hypotheses over another.

We turn now to the data presented in Tables 4.11 and 4.12. In three of the four comparisons, there is no significant difference between prosecutors and defense. Only in the robbery fact situation in Table 4.11 is there a significant difference by type of attorney. However, contrary to what is indicated in Table 4.12, a separate analysis, not presented here, showed that there was also a significant difference between prosecutors and defense counsel in the choice of length of sentence of the robbery case. Thus, the data show that prosecutors and defense attorneys agree in the burglary case on both the type and the length of sentence, but they disagree in the robbery case on both decisions.

Although we were unable to predict these findings, we can offer some retrospective commentary on them. It should be remembered that these tables are based on the combination of all four versions (the serious and the not-serious versions of prior record as the strong and the weak evidence cases) of the two crimes used in the simulation. Therefore, the discrepancy in recommendations that appears in Tables 4.11 and 4.12 should not be mistaken for an indication of a general inconsistency in sentencing. The disparity is an artifact of this particular analysis. Obviously, with the four different fact patterns presented, one would expect sentencing disparities *within* types of attorneys. The crucial question is whether one could expect these differences to exist *between* types of attorneys.

Also, recall that defense attorneys consulted far more information about defendant's background as well as other miscellaneous attributes of the case. Yet, even after consulting all this information, defense counsel still ended up agreeing with prosecutors in the burglary case. This suggests that whatever else those additional items of information may be used for in defense attorneys' thinking, they do not automatically alter the estimates of the bottom-line value of the case. This does not mean that plea bargaining lacks an adversarial quality. In fact when these data are taken together with the findings in Table 4.2 and 4.3, the opposite conclusion emerges. That is, even in the burglary case where the two types of attorney agree on the bottom-line, the data suggest that there is an adversarial character to the plea negotiations. As indicated in Tables 4.2 and 4.3, prosecutors arrive at the bottom-line after consulting a minimum of information. Defense counsel consult the same information and more. Even after consulting the additional information, however, they arrive at the same bottom line as the prosecutor. Why do they bother to consult the additional items of information? We believe it is because even when attorneys agree on the true value of a case the negotiations take on a subtle but real adversarial quality. Defense counsel may appear to be acting cooperatively; but their special role is to interject information designed to conflict with the prosecutor's assessment of the case.

Table 4.11   Comparison between prosecutors and defense counsel in type of sentence sought in plea bargaining by type of crime*

	Prosecutors	Defense Counsel
Robbery:	(N=91)	(N=62)
Prison Time	74	42
Jail Time	17	26
Probation	9	32
	100%	100%

$$x^2=18.381$$
$$d.f.=2$$
$$P(x^2)=<.001$$
$$gamma=+.57$$

	Prosecutors	Defense Counsel
Burglary:	(N=80)	(N=69)
Prison Time	41	27
Jail Time	20	27
Probation	39	45
	100%	**99%

$$x^2=3.2319$$
$$d.f.=2$$
$$P(x^2)=.20 \text{ n.s.}$$

*Source: Georgetown Plea Bargain Simulation.
**Due to rounding error.

Table 4.12   Comparison between prosecutors and defense counsel in length of sentence sought in plea bargaining by type of crime*

	Prosecutors	Defense Counsel
Robbery	(N=138)	(N=105)
5 years or more	43	46
2–5 years	18	10
1–2 years	9	8
1–12 months	17	17
Probation	12	19
	99%	100%

$$x^2=4.4213$$
$$d.f=4$$
$$P(x^2)=.35 \text{ n.s.}$$

	Prosecutors	Defense Counsel
Burglary:	(N=134)	(N=102)
5 years or more	24	30
2–5 years	13	10
1–2 years	8	4
1–12 months	30	25
Probation	25	30
	100%	**99%

$$x^2=4.3413$$
$$d.f.=4$$
$$P(x^2)=.36 \text{ n.s.}$$

*Source: Georgetown Plea Bargain Simulation
**Due to rounding error.

Of course, this may explain what is happening in the burglary case where the two types of attorneys agree; but it does not account for why the attorneys disagree in the robbery case. For that, we can only speculate. Perhaps because robbery is regarded as a more serious crime and the stakes are usually higher for all parties concerned, a strong adversarial quality emerges. That is, perhaps the adversarial nature of the negotiations changes with the seriousness of the crime. Maybe when more is at stake each type of attorney feels the need to take a stronger position.

Summary

• In evaluating cases of plea bargaining, prosecutors concern themselves with fewer items of information than do defense counsel.

• Prosecutors and defense counsel agree on the importance of case strength, seriousness of the offender, and seriousness of the offense. They also agree on the lack of importance of caseload as a determinant of plea bargaining decisions in an individual case.

• Prosecutors are far more concerned than defense counsel with the attitudes of the police and the victim toward the plea bargain.

• Prosecutors are less concerned than defense counsel with a miscellany of attributes about the defendant and the case that do not bear directly on case strength, offender seriousness, or offense seriousness. They are also less concerned with the trial judge's reputation for leniency, the opposing counsel's reputation, or the nature of the personal relationship between the opposing counsel.

• Estimating the probability of conviction in a case is something which is done with a fair degree of reliability when the cases are strong, but not when the cases are weak. Prosecutors generally agree among themselves and with defense counsel in the estimates of the probability of conviction in strong cases. But prosecutors disagree among themselves and in one instance with defense counsel in the estimates of the probability of conviction in weak cases.

• The half-of-a-loaf hypothesis that prosecutors would be more likely to plea bargain weak cases was contradicted by the data. Prosecutors were consistently more likely to take weak cases to trial or dismiss them rather than to plea bargain them.

• However, the other implication of the half-a-loaf hypothesis, namely, that the weaker the case the more lenient the plea offer will be, was partially (but not consistently) confirmed. Differences in case strength did significantly affect the prosecutors' choices as to type and length of sentence but only under certain conditions (i.e.,

when the crime was less serious and/or when a more serious prior record was involved). Even when one or both of these conditions were present, case strength did not always significantly affect the prosecutor's plea offer.

• Differences in the seriousness of prior record did not by themselves have a significant effect on the prosecutors' two sentencing decisions. But, among weak cases differences in the seriousness of the prior record do have a significant impact on these decisions. As one would expect, the less serious prior record is given the more lenient sentence.

• Prior record and case strength seem to exert significant influences only in "marginal" situations, that is, those fact situations where there is likely to be the greatest lack of consensus among criminal justice actors about what the appropriate disposition and sentence should be, e.g., in "medium" serious crimes, when cases are weak, or when they involve minor prior records.

• Contrary to what literature would lead one to expect, defense counsel were more likely than prosecutors to take a case to trial. However, this may be true only if the trial judge has a reputation for leniency.

• In the robbery case prosecutors and defense counsel disagree in both of the sentencing decisions. But, in the burglary case they did not significantly differ in either of these decisions.

• "Court busting" appears to be a myth. Virtually all defense counsel said they never have threatened and never would threaten to take all their cases to trial as a tactic to get a better deal in a particular case.

Conclusion

Most of what is known about the plea bargaining decisionmaking process has been based on interview and observational data. The findings of the present study, based primarily on a decision simulation with a quasi-experiment, strengthen and refine some previous findings but contradict others and raise several new questions. Contrary to popular belief, prosecutors and defense counsel are not concerned with the question of the court's backlog or caseload when they are attempting to evaluate what to do with specific cases. Contrary to courthouse folklore, defense attorneys do not use the threat of taking their case to trial (i.e., to "courtbust") in order to obtain more favorable terms in plea bargaining. As previously reported, the three big factors of case strength, seriousness of the defendant, and seriousness of the offense are regarded by both prosecutors and defense counsel as important in the evaluation of cases for plea bargaining. Not well understood in the past was whether and how prosecutors and defense attorneys differ in their evaluation of cases for plea bargaining, whether the big three factors had the impact on plea bargaining decisions that they were alleged to have, and whether attorneys presented with the same set of facts would arrive at the same estimates of probability of conviction.

This study indicates that prosecutors and defense attorneys evaluate cases the same way up to a point. After the three big factors are evaluated, defense counsel go on to look for anything that might be said on behalf of their clients in order to improve upon the normal plea bargaining discount arrived at on the basis of the big three factors. In addition, defense counsel are far more interested than prosecutors in information about the personal characteristics of the criminal justice actors. These two differences suggest the defense counsel do play a unique role in plea bargaining. That role seems to consist of three different tasks. First, defense counsel try to assure that the big three factors have been properly evaluated and that the usual discount for the particular type of case has been established. Secondly, defense counsel look for tactical advantages in order to advise their client about which route to take. If the judge is notoriously lenient, then there would be a tactical advantage to go to trial and try to win an acquittal. Even if the defendant is convicted, he will not "lose big," given that the judge is lenient. On the other hand if the judge were more severe, then bargaining with the prosecutor may be the better tactic. The third task is that of "mitigating the case." The job here is to find any reason why the defendant should be given more than the usual discount in the case. This seems to be done by introducing information which is designed to contradict the prosecutor's judgment about what the basic value of the case should be.

Contrary to those analyses which have stressed the non-adversarial nature of plea bargaining, our findings suggest that there is an adversarial component. However, that component is of such a latent quality that it can easily be overlooked. Although it is true that cooperative relationships do develop between criminal justice actors, our analysis of the way in which they process information in connection with reaching their plea bargaining decisions suggests that there is a difference between prosecutors and defense counsel both in the amount and type of information they consult and in the decisions they make on the basis of that information. The nature of the adversary relationship that does exist in plea negotiations lies in the difference in information processing more than in the difference in the outcomes of that decision process.

With regard to the evenhandedness of certain aspects of plea bargaining, we conclude that it is more likely to occur under some conditions than others. With regard to that crucial skill of estimating the probability of conviction, we found that when cases are strong both prosecutors and defense counsel can agree in estimating the probability of conviction. But when cases are weak, there is far less agreement. Similarly, with regard to the impact of differences in case strength and differences in seriousness of prior record, we found that these factors have a significant influence on the prosecutor's sentencing decision only under certain conditions. Once again, those conditions are that cases are weak or that there is a minor prior record or the crime is a less serious crime. Why this should be true is not readily apparent.

The results of our simulation do not answer the policy question of whether the plea bargaining should be eliminated or allowed to continue. However, they do show that some of the arguments in that policy debate are either entirely inaccurate or subject to important modifications. The plea bargaining decisionmaking process is not as haphazard as it may appear. Our nonrandom sample of prosecutors drawn from across the country revealed that there is a logic to prosecutorial decisionmaking and that it is distinct from that of defense attorneys. Whether one agrees with that logic depends on one's policy preferences. Our research will not settle the debate on plea bargaining. That is ultimately a debate over policy choices. However, in clarifying and refining some of the factual bases on which that debate rests, we have altered the terms of the debate.

Chapter Five
Differential Sentencing

Introduction

". . . [I]f in one year, 248 judges are to deal with 35,517 defendants, the district courts must encourage pleas of guilty. One way to encourage pleas of guilty is to establish or announce a policy that, in the ordinary case, leniency will not be granted to a defendant who stands trial" (*United States* v. *Wiley,* 185 F. Supp. 679 (N.D. Ill., 1960).)

The primary force behind plea bargaining is differential sentencing. Defendants plead guilty because they believe that if they stood trial they would be punished more severely. This incentive underlies almost all plea bargains no matter whether they involve charge concessions, explicit sentence concessions, or implicit sentence concessions. Supporters of plea bargaining justify such differentials as the very heart of the system. Without them defendants would go to trial. Knowing they would have nothing to lose and everything to gain defendants would try to "beat the rap" at trial. The demand for trials would exceed court capacity and the system would collapse.

Notwithstanding this grim scenario, critics of plea bargaining object to differential sentencing either in principle or to one or another of its more egregious aspects. One basic concern is its "chilling effect" on the free exercise of the fundamental constitutional right to a jury trial. It is argued that the exercise of a right so basic to a free society should not be discouraged by the threat of a more severe sentence. Moreover, just as confessions induced by promises are of doubtful credibility, so too convictions based on induced admissions of guilt are suspect. Such a system is too vulnerable to the possibility of innocent defendants pleading guilty. It compromises the integrity of the truth-finding process.

Alternatively, some concerns focus on certain aspects of the differentials. The size of the differential in some cases is regarded as being so great as to be overbearing, as for example when the defendant is faced with the choice between life or death. Other concerns are with evenhandedness and the integrity of the sentencing process. The former focuses on the belief that the size of differentials varies widely from case to case, that similar cases are not given similar sentences. The latter focuses on the fact that the differentials are based on a factor irrelevant to the sentencing process. In particular the size of the differential is heavily influenced by the strength of the state's case (Alschuler, 1968). The weaker the case the larger the differential must be in order to assure a plea. Thus the sentence imposed is largely determined by a factor that no theory of sentencing or penology has ever regarded as relevant to the correctional process.

Rationales for differential sentencing

The fundamental rationale for differential sentencing is its practical necessity for preventing the collapse of overburdened court systems. Some judges readily admit this. When asked to justify imposing a more severe sentence on a defendant convicted at trial, one judge put it this way, "He takes some of my time. So I take some of his." Other judges and other defenders of the practice have devised various rationales justifying it in terms other than administrative necessity. Each of the more commonplace of these rationales has some plausibility and in a few cases does indeed provide a sound justification for the differential (or at least part of it) in those cases. But it taxes credibility to believe that those rationales taken either singly or together can justify the differentials in the great majority of cases.

One common rationale is that by admitting his guilt the defendant is taking the first step on the road to rehabilitation. Therefore differential sentencing benefits the correctional process. Adding to the superficial plausibility of this rationale is the rehabilitative literature which emphasizes the importance of having a person accept responsibility for his actions and admit his problem before the rehabilitative process can begin (see, e.g., Menninger, 1964). However, to believe that an admission of guilt by a defendant hoping to thereby secure sentencing leniency represents the kind of genuine initial step into self-recognition and appraisal referred to in the psychotherapeutic literature is a profound misunderstanding of that literature. Therapists who have had patients come to them under coercion can attest that they are no faster and probably a little slower in getting "into" therapy than noncoerced patients.

Experienced attorneys do not take this rationale too seriously. Defense counsel and defendants see the plea of guilty as a business deal, not as a therapeutic threshold. A second rationale, however, is given considerable credit by court personnel, especially the defense bar. It is that in cases which go to trial more adverse information about the defendants comes to light. Therefore they are sentenced more severely than what would have occurred through a guilty plea. Defense counsel frequently mention the importance of not letting the judge hear all the gruesome details which might arouse his or her passion or provoke his or her sympathy for the victim. This is so important in some cases that part of the plea agreement is that when the plea is entered the prosecutor will describe the crime in dry, clinical terms so as not to arouse the judge's antipathy. For example, the victim will be described as having received "some lacerations" rather than being "stabbed repeatedly about the neck and face."

The problem with this rationale is that it explains too much. It may fit some crimes of violence where heinous acts were committed, but it is unlikely to account for the vast majority of differential sentences. Actually, this rationale should be regarded more as an indictment of the presentence investigation process than as a justification for differential sentencing. To the extent that the rationale is true, it means that judges are not being provided with information relevant to their sentencing decision. If defendants who plead guilty are being sentenced leniently because judges are inadequately appraised of their actual criminality, this should not become a justification for the leniency but a springboard for reforming the presentence investigation process.

Another rationale for sentence differentials is that defendants who go to trial may perjure themselves or suborn perjury from others. A few judges explained to us that in such cases they have given one sentence for the original crime plus an additional sentence for "the perjury." When asked how they were sure the defendants had perjured themselves, their evidence was less than compelling. One judge relied on how a defendant's

Adam's apple moved. Another relied on his interpretation of the defendant's body language. Of the several examples given by judges the evidence was convincing in only one. A defendant had maintained he was not the same person as someone who previously had been convicted of another crime. The judge knew he was lying because the judge had convicted him. In none of the examples given by judges were the defendants charged with or tried for their "perjuries."

A final rationale which judges frequently gave us was the one endorsed by the ABA (1968; § 1.8). Defendants convicted at trial are not sentenced more severely but those who plead guilty are sentenced more leniently. The subtle difference between these two positions was captured by one judge who after repeating this formula in robot-like fashion explained it was "the difference between tweedle-dee-dum and tweedle-dee-dee." However, he noted, the rationale does provide judges with a professionally justifiable excuse for their differential sentencing practices.

The legality of sentence differentials

Differential sentencing can result from either the sentencing decisions of individual judges or from differentials built into a state's sentencing structure by law. Differentials resulting from both of these sources have been upheld by the courts. In both the *Brady* and the *Parker* cases, defendants faced statutorily imposed differential sentencing schemes. In *Brady* v. *United States*, 397 U.S. 742 (1970), defendant Brady was charged with kidnapping in violation of 18 U.S.C. § 1201(a), which permitted the jury to recommend death if the victim was not freed unharmed as was alleged in that case. Brady pleaded guilty when the judge refused to try the case without a jury. The Supreme Court ruled that such an arrangement did not invalidate the plea.

In *Parker* v. *North Carolina*, 397 U.S. 790 (1970), the defendant charged with first degree burglary faced a death sentence unless the jury recommended life imprisonment. However, the statute provided that if one pleaded guilty to first degree burglary he would receive life rather than a death sentence. Parker appealed on the ground that the differential sentences authorized by the North Carolina law invalidated his plea. But, the Supreme Court dismissed the claim on the basis of *Brady*:

"... we determined in Brady ... that an otherwise valid plea is not involuntary because induced by the defendant's desire to limit the possible maximum penalty to less than that authorized if there is a trial." (397 U.S. at 795.)

94

More recently the Supreme Court held that a state procedure that requires a life sentence following conviction at trial but permits judges to impose lighter sentences following pleas of non vult or nolo contendere does not impose an unconstitutional burden on the right to trial (*Corbit* v. *New Jersey*, 439 U.S. 212 (1978)).

Appellate court support for sentence differentials imposed by judges in individual cases varies. There is a general recognition that such differentials do exist; that they represent the heart of the guilty plea system; and they cannot be eliminated without eliminating that system. For instance, in *Dewey* v. *United States*, 268 F.2d 124, 128 (8th Cir. 1959), the court took "judicial notice of the fact that trial courts quite generally impose a lighter sentence on pleas of guilty cases than in cases where the accused pleaded not guilty but has been found guilty by a jury." In *State* v. *Rice*, 172 Conn. 94, 103 (1976), the court recognized that "an essential ingredient in any plea bargaining situation is the recognition by both the prosecutor and the defense that a trial may produce a less favorable result for the defendant."

However, some courts have concluded that judicially imposed sentence differentials chill the exercise of fundamental constitutional rights (Bond, 1981:41). Other courts which have found sentence differentials improper appear to object to some aspect of the practice involved in the particular case rather than to the principle itself. Differentials which are set categorically without consideration of the differences between individual cases have been disapproved. In *United States* v. *Wiley*, 267 F.2d 453, 457 (7th Cir. 1959), the court ruled that the judge's policy of not granting probation to anyone who refused to plead guilty was an abuse of discretion.

The extent and magnitude of (objective) differential sentencing

Review of literature. Empirical studies going back to the 1920's have shown that in many jurisdictions defendants convicted after trial are punished more severely than those who plead guilty. Illinois defendants convicted at trial were two and a half times more likely than pleaders to be sentenced to incarceration rather than probation (Illinois Crime Survey, 1929). A survey of 176 state and Federal judges found that 91 percent said that they commonly sentenced pleaders more leniently than tried defendants (U.S. Department of Justice, 1939:425). A more recent survey by the *Yale Law Journal* (1956:206) found that 66 percent of 140 federal district judges agreed that it was "accepted practice to take into consideration the fact that the person to be sentenced pleaded guilty, rather than not guilty." It also found that eight of nine responding Connecticut state judges, reported that it was "accepted practice to give less severe sentences if the person pleaded guilty, rather than not guilty" (Ibid: 207). The Yale survey also asked judges to estimate the extent to which the difference in the sentence was attributable exclusively to the fact of going to trial rather than pleading. Some judges stated that the magnitudes varied from case to case. Others asserted that they could not separate out the effect of the plea from other factors. Still other judges gave estimates of from 10 percent to 95 percent.[1]

More recent studies of actual sentence differentials continue to suggest that pleaders do indeed get more lenient sentences. In Alameda County, California pleaders were three times more likely to get probation and six times less likely to get a prison term (University of California, 1975). In Los Angeles County, California, Rand (Greenwood, et. al., 1973) found that "across all categories of offense and prior record, defendants who plead guilty or SOT[2] are sentenced more leniently than defendants who are convicted at trial. Defendants convicted in jury trials are sentenced much more harshly than any others."

In Philadelphia, it was found that for three offenses (burglary, aggravated robbery, and aggravated assault) defendants convicted at trial are given sentences that are three to seven times longer than pleaders (Constant, 1971). But surprisingly, for three other offenses (narcotics possession, larceny and receiving stolen goods), it was the *pleaders* who received the longer sentences! This was apparently due to differences in their pretrial release status. Defendants incarcerated prior to trial were often sentenced to time served, which in some cases was longer than would have been imposed after trial (Id.). In the Federal courts differential sentencing is strongly indicated by their annual statistical reports. Federal defendants convicted at trial are about twice as likely to be sentenced to imprisonment (rather than probation) and their sentences are about twice as long as those of pleaders (see Table 5.1).

---

[1] One 10 percent; five 20 percent; six 25 percent; one 30 percent; three 33⅓ percent; one 33⅓–50 percent; three 50 percent; one 75 percent; one 80 percent; two 90 percent; one 95 percent (*Yale Law Journal*, 1956:207).

[2] "Submission on the transcript" of the preliminary hearing.

Table 5.1 Differences in type and length of sentences for federal offenders by whether convicted by plea or trial, 1963 and 1971*

	Guilty plea	Trial by	
		Judge	Jury
Type of sentence			
Imprisoned, 1963	43%	53%	72%
Imprisoned, 1971	32%	61%***	
Length of sentence**			
1963	4.9	6.8	11.4
1971	4.7	6.3	13.5

*Sources: Administrative Office of the United States Courts, 1963 and 1977.
**Sentences are in "weighted averages".
***Combined rate for jury and judge trials.

Despite the impressive number of studies indicating that tried defendants are punished more severely than pleaders there continues to be some question as to the extent to which this is due solely to the fact of going to trial. The plausible rival hypothesis which could explain the differentials is that tried cases represent more serious cases and are punished accordingly. Supporting this alternative explanation is Jacob and Eisenstein (1977) who found sentencing differentials but were able to account for them in terms of characteristics of the defendant, the type of offense, and courtroom work group.

Other studies cast doubt on whether differentials even regularly occur. Using data from the District of Columbia, Rhodes (1978) found no differentials for three of four offenses.[3]

In Dade County, Florida, Wildhorn et al. (1976:149) concentrated solely on the impact on sentencing severity of charge concessions in breaking and entering and robbery cases. They found "that tried disposition (as compared to pleas) did not increase sentence outcomes in a statistically significant manner." Concerned that this finding may have been due to the very small number of

trials in their sample, Wildhorn et al. adopted a technique similar to the one Rhodes (1978) used. They matched all those convicted at trial with a group of otherwise similar defendants who entered straight pleas.[4] Amazingly the effect of trial was to *reduce* the sentence by about 13 percent.

Differentials in six jurisdictions. The nature and amount of real differential sentencing in the six study sites was determined through a multivariate analysis of 3,397 robbery and burglary cases. The analysis permitted an examination of the extent to which the mere fact of going to trial rather than pleading guilty affected the severity of the sentence imposed holding other factors constant.[5]

Two distinct aspects of sentence severity were examined, namely, the in-or-out decision and the length-of-time decision.[6] The first question focused on whether defendants convicted at trial were significantly more likely to receive sentences involving some time to serve in incarceration (in-time) as opposed to straight probation or other no-incarcerative sentence. The second question focused on whether tried defendants received significantly longer sentences than the pleaders and how much longer these sentences were.

The analysis revealed the existence of real sentence differentials in each of the six sites although their nature and magnitude varied substantially. In two jurisdictions, going to trial significantly increased the chance that the defendant would receive an in-time sentence; see Table 5.2. In El Paso (where the "no plea bargaining" experiment was in operation), defendants who were convicted at trial experienced a 29 percent increase in the probability of being sentenced to incarceration.[7] In Norfolk, tried

---

[3] Assault, burglary, and larceny had no differentials but robbery did.

[4] Pleas of guilty without any charge or count concessions but frequently with some sentence bargain.

[5] The other factors held constant in this analysis included: offense charged; presence of a weapon; monetary loss; amount of property damage; number of witnesses; physical evidence; charge reduction from information to conviction; positive identification; total charges at conviction; harm to victim; marital status of defendant; number of charges dropped between original filing and formal charging; prior felony convictions; type of counsel; length of time between arrest and disposition; and length of time between filing of formal charging and disposition. Some of these factors were deleted from some of the analyses upon which this composite presentation is based if they were found to have negligible effects.

[6] Dividing the sentencing decision into these two parts follows the work of Wilkins et al. (1978).

[7] Interpreting this finding is difficult for two reasons. Some of these sentences may have been imposed by juries—something which could not be controlled for in our data. Also, the "no plea bargaining" program provided defendants with a point system by which they were supposed to be able to determine whether they would receive probation if they pleaded guilty. Thus, one would expect that this system

defendants were 12 percent more likely to get sentences involving in-time.

Table 5.2 Increase in severity of sentence for robbery and burglary cases convicted at trial compared to those convicted by pleading guilty, by jurisdiction

Jurisdiction	% Increase in probability of incarceration vs. nonincarceration sentence	% Increase in length of incarceration	Actual increase in length of incarceration (in months)
Norfolk	12%	91%	49.7
Seattle	ns [1]	88%	75.1
Tucson	ns	16%	11.1
El Paso	29%	ns	ns
New Orleans	ns	138%	86.6
Delaware Co.	ns	14%	5.7

[1] Not statistically significant.

It was also found that in five of the six sites defendants who went to trial received significantly longer sentences than those who pleaded guilty (holding other factors constant).[8] However, the magnitude of the increase varied widely from a low of 14 percent in Delaware County to a high of 138 percent in New Orleans (where the District Attorney had a restricted plea bargaining policy in effect). Translated into months this means that in Delaware County, a defendant charged with robbery or burglary could expect to get a sentence that was 5.7 months longer after conviction at trial than he would have received for a plea. In New Orleans the increase was an extra 86.6 months. But in El Paso, there was no significant difference in the length of sentence.

---

would encourage defendants who calculated that they were not eligible for probation to go to trial. Once convicted, they supposedly would be sentenced to incarceration as promised by the point system.
[8] *See* fn. 5 above.

Reported and perceived differential sentencing

Review of literature. Previous research has concentrated primarily on establishing whether differentials exist and why. Less attention has been paid to the *perception* of differentials and the relationship between the perception and the reality. It is sometimes assumed that the two are synonymous. For instance, in reporting that they found no (objective) differential sentencing, Wildhorn et al. (1976:148) proceed to a conclusion about whether defendants believe that differentials do exist. "Our statistical analysis [of actual sentencing patterns] did not support the view that the *expectation* of harsher sentences at trial induces many defendants to enter a guilty plea." [9]

The relative inattention to the perception of differentials is a serious weakness in the literature. After all, it is the perception of the actors in the system that govern their decisions. The advice given by attorneys to the defendants, the willingness of defendants to plead, and the relative strengths of the positions of prosecutors and defense attorneys in plea negotiations are all influenced by perceptions about differentials.

A few studies related to selected aspects of the perception of differentials are available. Vetri (1964:896) found that the majority of prosecutors in his sample believe that defendants are punished more severely for going to trial. Kerstetter and Heinz (1979:123) found that 60 percent of the defendants in Dade County, Florida, who pleaded guilty reported that "the fear of a more severe sentence at trial was an important, if not critical, reason for pleading guilty." This fear was not significantly increased by having defendants participate in a plea bargaining conference in which the judge, prosecutor, defense attorney, and victims or police also participated. Horney (1980) found that certain kinds of plea negotiations were believed by the prosecutors and defense attorneys who made them to have greater impacts on the sentence differential than others.

Reported and perceived differentials: judges and attorneys. We approached the perception of sentence differentials in three ways: by asking judges to report on themselves; by asking prosecutors and defense attorneys for their perceptions of the differential sentencing tendencies of individual judges; and by asking defendants for their perceptions.

Our judges were much less willing to admit to punishing defendants for going to trial than those surveyed in 1956 by the *Yale Law Journal* and in 1939 by the Attorney

---

[9] Emphasis added.

General. Only 11 of 49 judges indicated that they do sentence tried cases more severely than pleaders (see Table 5.3). However, comparing the judges' self-reports with the results of our statistical analysis of actual sentence differentials (compare Table 5.2 with Table 5.3), one finds reason to be skeptical about judicial self-reports. In Seattle where all ten judges reported they do not differentially sentence, our statistical analysis found that going to trial adds 75.1 months to the length of the sentence. In Tucson where all 11 judges denied sentencing differentially, our analysis found that going to trial adds 11.1 months to a sentence.

The perceptions of differential sentencing of prosecutors and defense attorneys were obtained by asking each attorney to answer the following question for each local judge with whom he or she was familiar: "As far as you know, does Judge ——— sentence a defendant more severely if he/she goes to trial rather than pleading guilty?" A total of 42 judges in six jurisdictions were rated this way by varying numbers of prosecutors and defense counsel.

Four noteworthy features emerge from the analysis of the data (Table 5.3). First, there is a surprisingly large amount of disagreement among the attorneys as to whether particular judges sentence differentially. This finding conflicts with the ubiquitous courthouse truism that regular practitioners know the sentencing tendencies of local judges. It suggests there is a much greater ambiguity about this essential factor in plea negotiating and sentencing decisionmaking than has been recognized. It

Table 5.3   Self-reported and perceived sentencing differentials for cases convicted at trial rather than by pleading guilty by jurisdiction and by type of attorney

Jurisdiction	Judges' self reports of whether they differentially sentence	Attorneys' perceptions of whether specific judges differentially sentence
Norfolk	Yes, 2 judges No, 4 judges	3 judges were assessed by 13 attorneys who were almost evenly split (6 to 7) over each judge. Prosecutors were far more likely than defense counsel to report that the judges differentially sentence. Five prosecutors reported that all three judges differentially sentence whereas five defense counsel reported that all three judges do not.
Seattle	Yes, 0 judges No, 10 judges	13 judges were assessed by 6 attorneys who were split (3 to 3, or 2 to 4) over each judge. Prosecutors were more likely to answer "yes" (2 of 3 for 12 of the 13 judges) and defense counsel were more likely to answer "no" (2 of 3 for 11 of the 13 judges).
Tucson	Yes, 0 judges No, 7 felony judges 4 misdemeanor judges	10 judges were assessed by between 5 and 7 attorneys. Overall there was general agreement that the judges do not differentially sentence. For 6 of the 10 judges the attorneys were in total agreement; 2 defense attorneys thought two judges do differentially sentence; one defense attorney thought that two other judges differentially sentence.
El Paso	Yes, 1 judge No, 1 judge 1 judge uncertain	6 judges were assessed by 5 attorneys all of whom except one were in agreement that one judge does differentially sentence but the rest do not. The lone dissenter was simply uncertain about two judges.
New Orleans	Yes, 4 judges No, 4 judges	10 judges were assessed by from 4 to 6 attorneys who were largely in agreement among themselves regarding the sentencing practices of specific judges but disagreed with the judges' self-reports in 3 of the 8 comparisons possible.
Delaware Co.	Yes, 4 judges No, 7 judges	14 judges were assessed by between 2 and 6 attorneys who largely agreed among themselves that 7 of the judges do differentially sentence. It is noteworthy that the disagreement among the attorneys was more likely to occur over the assessment of those judges who reported that they do not differentially sentence.

also suggests that, in order to keep plea bargaining operating, it is not necessary for there to be a unanimous or even close to unanimous perception among attorneys that differential sentencing exists or that every judge does it.[10]

Secondly, where disagreements occurred, prosecutors tended to believe that the specific judges do differentially sentence whereas defense counsel perceived the opposite (Norfolk and Seattle).[11] This unanticipated finding is difficult to explain. If anything, one would have expected the reverse, namely that defense counsel would be more likely to believe that judges differentially sentence. Predicting such a finding would have been logical in light of the high rate of guilty pleas and the literature indicating that defense counsel routinely advise clients to plead guilty (Blumberg, 1967; Mather, 1979).

Thirdly, the amount of disagreement among the attorneys differs by jurisdiction. In three jurisdictions (Norfolk, Seattle, and Delaware County) disagreement is high. In contrast the other three jurisdictions (Tucson, El Paso, and New Orleans) show more agreement than disagreement. This finding was also unanticipated and is not convincingly explainable even retrospectively. One might speculate that when the prosecutor reduces or eliminates his office's role in plea bargaining (as in El Paso and New Orleans) this forces a clearer recognition of the importance of differential sentencing. Hence local attorneys pay more careful attention to this practice. However, this does not explain Tucson. Fourthly, the degree of agreement between the judges' self-reports and the attorneys' perceptions is mixed. Sometimes the attorneys perceive what the judges report and other times they disagree. What is more this varies by jurisdiction as well as by individual judge. In Seattle all 10 judges who were questioned denied sentencing differentially; yet, some of the attorneys believed otherwise. In contrast in Tuscon where 11 judges said they do not differentially

sentence, the attorneys' perceptions agreed for the most part with the self reports.

A closer look at the degree of agreement between self-reports and perceptions is available for two jurisdictions (New Orleans and Delaware County). The data from those sites were coded so that direct comparisons between the self-reports of individual judges and the perceptions of local attorneys were possible (see Table 5.4). In New Orleans there is a high degree of consensus among the attorneys in their perceptions of each judge. Moreover, there is more agreement than not with the judge's self-report.[12] In Delaware the attorneys were in substantial agreement in their perceptions for 8 of 14 judges and disagreed on the rest. Comparing their perceptions with judges' self-reports, one finds discrepancies in six instances where judges reported they do not differentially sentence but some or almost all of the attorneys believed otherwise.

In attempting to understand what influences the perceptions of sentencing differentials, one obvious candidate explanation should be addressed. Is the actual size of the differentials imposed by a judge related to the perception attorneys have of his or her practice? Unfortunately, this cannot be directly answered with our data due to its aggregate nature. But it is still of value to compare the average differential for the whole jurisdiction with the perceptions of the attorneys (compare Tables 5.2 with 5.3 and 5.4). This comparison suggests that the degree of agreement in the perception of differential sentencing is not related to the average magnitude of the differential for the jurisdiction. A high degree of agreement in perception occurs both in Tucson with the second lowest differential (16 percent increase in length of sentence) and in New Orleans with the highest differential (138 percent).

One further comparison of Tables 5.2, 5.3 and 5.4 is instructive. In Tucson the judges claim they do not differentially sentence; the attorneys largely agree that the judges do not differentially sentence; and the objective rate of sentence differential is nonexistent (statistically insignificant) for the in-out decision and minimal (16 per-

---

[10] Of course, there is a difference between asking whether judges do differentially sentence under the present way of doing business in a jurisdiction and what they would do if no other way of securing pleas were available. In a jurisdiction where all plea bargaining is done with charge bargaining, there would be no need for any judge to differentially sentence and attorneys may correctly perceive this to be the case as long as there was no need for the judges to assume a direct responsibility for motivating guilty pleas.

[11] There is no way of knowing whether the prosecutors or the defense counsel were correct in their judgments about individual judges. Our *objective* measures of differential sentencing were for the jurisdictions as a whole with cases from different judges pooled together.

However, we are able to compare the attorneys' perceptions of specific judges with the self-reports of those same judges in two jurisdictions (see two paragraphs below). Of course, the judges' self-reports are not the equivalent of objective, statistical measures of the magnitude and frequency of the actual differentials (if any) these judges impose.

[12] The two instances of major disagreement (judges E and I) are in the reverse direction from what one might expect. The judges indicated they *do* sentence differentially and the attorneys believed that they *do not*. This may represent coding error. In answering this question some judges seemed to be overly scrupulous. They answered after searching their souls and thinking that maybe they did differentially sentence. Others were circumspect, using some justification for their differential sentencing that seemed like a hollow excuse. Coding these answers required some judgment as to what the correct meaning of the response was.

cent) for the length-of-time-to-serve decision. Yet, the system is managing to keep a steady stream of guilty pleas flowing. It should also be noted that in Tucson, unlike the other jurisdictions, most of the plea agreements involve only charge modifications.

Table 5.4 Comparison by individual judges of self-reported and perceived differential sentencing

Jurisdiction	Judge	Judge's self-report [1]	For each judge the number of attorneys who believe the judge does/does not differentially sentence [2]	
			Does	Does not
New Orleans	A	no	1	4
	B	yes	5	0
	C	no	2	4
	D	yes	4	2
	E	yes	0	4
	F	NA [3]	6	0
	G	no	0	6
	H	NA	4	0
	I	yes	0	6
	J	yes	5	1
Delaware Co.	A	no	3	3
	B	no	3	2
	C	no	2	4
	D	NA	3	3
	E	no	0	2
	F	no	4	2
	G	no	4	1
	H	yes	3	2
	I	yes	3	1
	J	no	4	1
	K	yes	4	1
	L	NA	3	1
	M	yes	4	1
	N	NA	4	1

1. Based on responses to the question, "Do you sentence those defendants who are convicted at trial differently than those who plead guilty to a given offense?"
2. Based on responses to the question, "As far as you know, does Judge ———— (names of the individual judges were inserted here) sentence a defendant more severely if he/she goes to trial rather than pleading guilty?"
3. No answer.

Defendant perceptions. Among defendants interviewed the perception that they would have been punished more severely if they had gone to trial was almost universal. Many of them said they were told this directly and explicitly by someone. Frequently it was their lawyer who conveyed the message. But police officers and fellow jail inmates also served this function or reinforced the attorney's message. A sample of defendant responses [13] to one of our questions illustrates the point. We asked, "Did anyone at any stage tell you that things would go differently for you if you pleaded guilty as opposed to going to trial on any of the charges?" They responded:

Norfolk: Defendant

A: My lawyer told me that things would go worse for me if I pled not guilty and then being forced into a jury trial I would get more than ten.

Norfolk: Defendant

A: The police told me they would help me as much as they could and they would drop the strong armed robbery charge.

---

[13] Some responses are summaries or paraphrases of actual responses.

El Paso: Defendant
A: The defendant said that his lawyer and county jail inmates told him he would get a harsher sentence if he went to trial. (But, he perceived trial to mean a jury trial with the sentencing done by the jury (possible in Texas) not the judge.)

Some defendants did not need to be told about differential sentencing. For them it was common knowledge.

New Orleans: Defendant
Q: Did anybody tell you what would happen if you went to trial? Whether things would be worse for you?
A: No. I kind of figured that myself. I always heard, you know, if you fight it they're going to give you the maximum sentence and everything but the lawyer didn't tell me.

Q: You just . . . that was the word you got in the parish (Jail)?
A: Well, yeah, out of all the times I've been in jail, and like I say, quite a few times, I always heard if you fight it they really try to hang you.

Tucson: Defendant
A: Public defender told him things would go harder for him if he fought the charges. Would get a longer sentence.

Tucson: Defendant
A: They used threats against my wife. They said "one or both of you is going to prison."

New Orleans: Defendant
Q: Did he (the lawyer) tell you what would happen if you told Judge Shea that you weren't guilty?
A: I knew that then I would have to go to trial and I would really have no case and I guess I . . . another reason I can't say I copped out was because if I would have fought against the law I believe I would have gotten a lot more time than I did.

Q: Is that just what you believe or did the attorney tell you that also?
A: Well, he also told me that, but I knew that beforehand, you know.

Q: How did you know? From the parish (jail mates)?
A: Just from the guys that been to court before, you know, besides me.

New Orleans: Defendant
Q: Did you think you'd get more time if you went to trial on the case?
A: Oh, sure enough——

Q: Did your lawyer tell you you'd get more time?
A: Ah-ah. (Affirmative.)

Q: But you knew it also didn't you?

A: Right.

Almost all defendants reported that an important reason why they pleaded guilty was to avoid the harsher sentence after trial as indicated by the sample of answers to our question, "If you pleaded to any of the charges can you give me all the reasons for doing so? (Probe: Is that all?)"

Norfolk Defendant
A: I did it to keep from getting other charges.

Tucson Defendant
A: Was pregnant at the time and wanted reduced sentence.

Norfolk Defendant
A: I thought I would be helping myself. I thought the judge would go easier.

Norfolk Defendant
A: Back in 1973 a guy got 120 years on narcotics who claimed he was innocent. My maximum was 220 years and . . .

New Orleans Defendant
Q: Ah, so what was, what was the main reason you pleaded guilty—because of the sentence?
A: Well, because of the possibility that I might get the 20 years without the benefit of good time.

For almost all defendants pleading guilty was seen as making the best of a bad situation. It was a rational strategy for minimizing their losses. Many of them felt that the state had a strong case against them. They had been caught in the act, or had already "confessed" to the police; or they "knew" that codefendants would testify against them or that the police would lie about the constitutionality of the search or the arrest or the available evidence. Others felt the cases against them were weak or problematic but they did not want to risk losing at trial. Several maintained that because they were Indian or Negro they thought they could not win their cases at trial. Several emphasized that they pleaded guilty to get the case over. The utter resignation and hopelessness that prompts some pleas is suggested by the following interview.

Q: So, what ultimately decided to make you plead guilty other than the fact that you knew you didn't have a chance in this case? Was that the only factor?
A: I guess well, after I escaped from down there for various reasons and everything, I just wanted to get it all over with, and I knew I was guilty, there wasn't——

Q: They had you, cold.

A: I guess if I could have come up with some money to get a lawyer and everything I might could have got out of it or something, maybe a good deal, or something. But, I just pleaded guilty, and it gets to a point where there ain't nothing you can do about it.

None of the usual official rationales with which judges and the ABA justify sentence differentials were evident in the reasons given by defendants for their pleas with one small possible exception. Two defendants mentioned that they felt "morally guilty" or that the crime "bothered them." This reason was given in addition to the fact that they thought the case against them was strong and that their attorneys had advised them to plead guilty. Thus their motives in pleading were not solely to cleanse their souls. But, nonetheless, the two cases suggest that sometimes the entry of a guilty plea may be accompanied by a genuine sense of regret which might become the basis for a successful rehabilitative program. On the other hand, however, defendants are aware of the importance of appearing contrite and remorseful for the judge in order to assure the acceptance of the plea, as is suggested by the following remarks.

Q: Why did you want to plead guilty?
A: Well, I figured if I went ahead and pled guilty that I would probably get a lesser sentence, you know, in the eyes of the judge by going ahead and making my guilty plea. I talked to this DEA man that was supposed to, you know. Well the last time I talked to him he says, "Don't worry when you go back to court and plead guilty just . . . you're going to get out that way."

Thus, while there may be some defendants who feel some genuine contrition in entering their pleas, there are others who do whatever they think judges want to see. It is doubtful that the two could be distinguished with sufficient accuracy to support a policy of lenient sentencing for the genuinely remorseful defendant. But even if the distinction could be made, the rationale for such a policy needs close examination. It is unclear by what ethical theory genuine remorse merits less punishment. Similarly, if genuine remorse indicates a readiness for rehabilitation, it still does not follow that the sentence should be shorter. Perhaps it should be longer so that a thorough rehabilitation can be achieved. The noncontrite defendant should perhaps be released earlier because there is no hope of rehabilitation and he is just consuming limited rehabilitative resources.

On eliminating plea bargaining

Over the last decade, recommendations to eliminate plea bargaining and claims that it has been eliminated in particular jurisdictions have abounded. As with much of what is said about plea bargaining, these statements typically are misleading because of a failure to specify what is meant by plea bargaining. At least four distinct meanings are useful. The things that might be eliminated are: charge bargaining; explicit sentence bargaining; implicit sentence bargaining; and the general perception that a defendant will receive some special benefit from the state by pleading guilty that he would not receive if he stood trial. If one accepts our definition of a bargained-for guilty plea as a plea entered by a defendant with the reasonable expectation of receiving some consideration from the state, it is evident that eliminating plea bargaining is not synonymous with eliminating charge bargaining or explicit or implicit sentence bargaining. Not until defendants no longer believe on some reasonable basis (such as the opinions of their attorneys or the experience of fellow defendants) that they will be punished more severely for going to trial can it be said that plea bargaining has been genuinely eliminated.

Obviously, this subjective standard is a difficult one to meet. A more feasible test of the elimination of plea bargaining is the objective one of whether criminal justice officials (notably prosecutors and judges) have stopped offering considerations (such as charge or sentence concessions) in exchange for pleas, and stopped fostering or permitting the perception of differential sentencing. In short, if no one in the system is offering considerations directly; or suggesting that there are implicit benefits for pleaders; or allowing others to foster that perception, then on an objective basis the system has achieved a no plea bargaining policy.[14] Any other kind of "no plea bargaining" policy must be understood for what it is. It may mean that one or another criminal justice official (prosecutors and judges) is not plea bargaining. But, it does not mean that plea bargaining has been eliminated. In examining the merits of these "no plea bargaining policies" one is not choosing among different ways of eliminating plea bargaining but rather different ways of allowing the practice to occur. Usually the choice is between having the bargaining done by prosecutors using either or both charge concessions or sentence recom-

---

[14] In such a system it may take a while before defendants come to believe that the no plea bargaining policy is a reality. During that interval the system may continue to benefit from pleas entered by defendants who refuse to believe they will not get some consideration for their pleas. To that extent the system has not completely eliminated plea bargaining.

mendation; or allowing judges to negotiate directly with the defense; or operating a well-known but indefinite implicit system where the defendant does not know exactly what he is getting for his plea but knows he would get something worse after trial.

When prosecutors establish a no plea bargaining policy, this usually means simply that charge bargaining will end (for all crimes or those crimes which fall within some targeted category).[15] This, of course, does not mean that plea bargaining has been eliminated in the jurisdiction. Rather it means that the locus and nature of plea bargaining will shift to the judiciary as occurred in El Paso, Texas; Alaska, and New Orleans. In El Paso when the prosecutor's office refused to plea bargain the judges were left with having to provide the incentive for pleading by offering differentials to pleaders. This exposed them to the risk of public criticism for lenient sentencing. As an alternative, they promulgated a point system by which defendants were supposed to be able to calculate whether they would be sentenced to imprisonment or probation. In theory defendants were then expected to plead guilty, for which they were given no special consideration. Thus, rather than replace the prosecutor's plea bargaining system with one of their own, the judges tried to eliminate explicit and implicit sentence bargaining. Evidently they were partially successful. No explicit sentence bargaining occurred; and all the judges except one did not engage in implicit bargaining. This is confirmed by our statistical analysis of cases (Table 5.2); our interviews with attorneys and the judges (Table 5.3); and, ironically by the fact that the court began to develop backlog problems. Realizing that there was no penalty for going to trial, defendants were reluctant to plead guilty. After two years of the point system, the judges modified it to provide an incentive for pleading guilty.

In Alaska, the Attorney General's office (which controls criminal prosecutions throughout the state), announced a "no plea bargaining policy" for prosecutors (Rubinstein and White, 1979a). They could no longer dismiss, reduce, or alter charges solely to obtain a guilty plea. When prosecutorial bargaining ended, the courts immediately took up the slack by negotiating with the defense themselves. Today the "no plea bargaining" policy is being regarded as a successful instance of the elimination of plea bargaining. Yet, Alaska has a sentencing differential that is almost three times greater than the largest differential in our sample of six sites. Going to trial in Alaska increases the length of one's sentence by 334 percent (Rubinstein and White, 1979a: 266). What is more, judges, defense counsel, and undoubtedly defendants are fully aware of the existence of this implicit sentencing system.

In New Orleans, the prosecutor established a "no plea bargaining" policy that is better thought of as a restricted charge bargaining policy. It involves careful screening and accurate charging together with a prohibition against reducing or dismissing charges solely to secure guilty pleas. Once a case is charged, the assistant prosecutor in the trial division must get a conviction for that charge unless he or she gets special permission from the screening unit or the chief prosecutor to alter the charge. Alterations happened in 29 percent of the burglary and robbery cases in our analysis. The policy, however, does allow prosecutors to make sentence recommendations as part of plea bargains (which they did in 60 percent of our sample of cases). This policy has the effect of reducing the importance of charge bargaining while increasing the importance of sentence bargaining. Not surprisingly, as in Alaska, the sentence differential in New Orleans is substantial and represents the largest differential among our six sites. Defendants convicted after trial can expect a 138 percent increase in length of sentence.[16] In contrast to Alaska and New Orleans where charge bargaining is eliminated or restricted, Tucson and Delaware County are places where charge bargaining represents the most frequently used token of exchange in plea negotiation. In Tucson, among those cases in our sample in which plea bargaining had occurred, 93 percent of the bargains involved charge modifications. Among Delaware County pleaded cases, 98 percent involved charge modifications. In neither jurisdiction were sentence recommendations the sole form of plea negotiation with any frequency. This contrasts sharply with New Orleans where 56 percent of the pleaded cases involved sentence recommendations only. Coincidental with this extensive charge bargaining in Tucson and Delaware County is the fact that these two jurisdictions have the smallest sentencing differentials in our sample.[17] In contrast to Alaska's differential of 334 percent and New Orleans' of 138 percent, Tucson has only 16 percent and Delaware County 14 percent. Figure 5.1 portrays the general relationship between the degree to which a jurisdiction relies on charge bargaining (measured as the percent of guilty pleas in which any charge concessions were given and the size of the

---

[15] Of course, if the prosecutor's office had previously been making sentence recommendations as part of their plea bargains, this will be terminated as well.

[16] However, if the perceptions of local attorneys are correct, only five of the ten judges are contributing to this differential (see Table 5.4).
[17] Excluding El Paso.

sentence differential (measured in terms of the percent increase in the length of sentence for tried defendants compared to pleaders).

In Tucson where the bargaining is largely in terms of charge concessions and where (objective) differential sentencing is nonexistent for the in-out decision and minimal for the length-of-time-to-serve decision, the judges all claim that they do not differentially sentence and most of the attorneys believe that this is true. Thus Tucson might be said to have achieved a no plea bargaining policy that is the inverse of Alaska's policy. Instead of the prosecutor taking himself out of plea bargaining and forcing the judges to provide plea incentives through differential sentencing, the Tucson prosecutor carries the bulk of the responsibility for obtaining pleas through charge concessions and frees the judges from the real or apparent role of penalizing defendants into pleading guilty.

The difference between the two jurisdictions represents an interesting choice for policymakers and reformers interested in abolishing plea bargaining. Neither jurisdiction has actually eliminated plea bargaining altogether; rather, each has eliminated one of the two main forms of plea bargaining (charge or sentence bargaining) by shifting the focus of bargaining to the other form. The choice between the two is whether it is "better" (fairer, more just, more effective, more efficient) for plea bargaining to be done by prosecutors through charge modifications or by judges through implicit but substantial sentencing differentials. The former policy places the responsibility for plea bargaining in the office of the prosecutor, an elected official accountable to the public. The bargaining could be in terms of explicit charge concessions, which in theory could be controlled by one central office policy, recorded in case files, and subject to review and accountability. Defendants could be given specific considerations for their pleas. This policy would not eliminate sentencing differentials but could change their nature, appearance and rationale. Assuming a penal code with graded classes of offenses and no mandatory minimum sentences, charge bargaining could be an orderly process of reducing the range of penalty exposure. Defendants who refused the plea offer would not be punished "more severely" for going to trial. Rather they would be punished for the original charge. The many defendants who plead guilty would not be punished for the crime they appeared to have (or actually) committed but rather something less. This would make clear that under this system the price being extracted by plea bargaining was from the community's safety rather than from the defendant. The reason for the price paid would be the community's unwillingness or inability to bear the cost of providing defendants with trials.

There are dangers in a charge bargaining system. It may encourage inaccurate or maximum charging done solely for the purpose of bargaining. It assumes that the prosecutor's office can and will exercise systematic internal controls over the bargaining practices (not a valid assumption in some places). And it assumes a rational, graded sentencing structure.

In contrast, sentence bargaining leaves plea bargaining in the hands of the judiciary, which in theory is responsible for the sentencing anyhow. However, there are important deficiencies in sentence bargaining. Judges are not privy to the prosecutor's file. They do not know the strength of a case and therefore are unable to consider one of the main factors used in evaluating a case for plea bargaining, namely, case strength. Judges are not subject to the centralized policy control and review that is (potentially) possible within prosecutors' offices. Different judges may or may not agree to plea bargain and may do it directly or indirectly. The size of differentials is likely to vary from judge to judge and even case to case. If the bargaining operates implicitly defendants are less able to know what if anything they will receive for their pleas. They will be more dependent on their attorney's ability to correctly read the judge's differential sentencing tendencies—which we have seen above is a dubious skill.

Recasting the no plea bargaining choice

The debate over eliminating plea bargaining has been cast as a two-value choice: plea bargaining or no plea bargaining. Those choices appear to be unnecessarily stark and unproductive. There are other choices. One set of alternatives has just been described in the foregoing comparison between charge bargaining and sentence bargaining. Additional choices become evident as one sorts through the objections to and defenses of plea bargaining.

Those objections are usually in two categories, those that focus on accidental aspects of plea bargaining and those focusing on the inherent, essential features of plea bargaining. Accidental features are things that might be remedied without changing the essential character of plea bargaining. In some jurisdictions, for example, there are built-in financial incentives for defense counsel to plead cases rather than take them to trial. Such incentive systems add to the general suspicion about plea bargaining. Even if they were remedied, there would still be other objections to plea bargaining.

Two features of plea bargaining which raise fundamental objections are that it is an institutionalized way of disposing of cases without the evidence in the case being subjected to review by an impartial third party (see, e.g., Alschuler, 1976) and that pleas are obtained by "coercing" or inducing defendants. The remedy most relevant to the first objection is the requirement that judges establish a factual basis for a guilty plea before accepting the plea. In practice this remedy has not represented a complete safeguard.[18] But it could be fortified.

The problem of coercing, enticing or inducing defendants to plead guilty is also subject to a partial solution. Assuming that some inducement must be given in order to get defendants to plead, the partial remedy is to keep the inducement as small as possible. The compromise objective should be to determine just how minimal inducements can be and still be enough to keep guilty pleas coming at a rate sufficient to prevent system overload. If this could be determined, then a logical alternative to the abolition-or-not controversy could be advanced. Plea bargaining could be regarded as an acceptable policy if the price for going to trial were no more than the minimum necessary to sustain the plea bargaining system and if it were imposed equally on all similarly-situated defendants. Such a policy would respond to the concerns of those critics of plea bargaining who focus on its excessive coersiveness and its inconsistency. It is to these questions of whether minimal inducements can be determined and what they might be, that we turn now.

There is some reason to believe that the state could operate for an indefinite period of time successfully securing pleas by giving virtually nothing in exchange. In one jurisdiction defendants regularly plead guilty in exchange for promises of concurrent sentencing of multiple offense. Yet, such concurrent sentencing is required by law; so in effect the defendants are getting nothing in the exchange. In Baltimore County, Maryland, a senior prosecutor described five cases of first degree murder in which the defendants pleaded guilty even though no plea bargain was offered and their attorneys evidently tried to convince them that they would get nothing for their pleas.

Deliberately operating a system of bogus plea bargains, however, would raise obvious ethical problems. Thus, the search must be for minimum non-bogus inducements. In order to simplify the discussion of the various types of real inducements which might be offered, it is useful to think in terms of a continuum which can be quantified, such as the length of a sentence. Thus the question becomes, "How much of an increase in the length of sentence is the average minimum sentence discount necessary to keep a plea bargaining system operating? Ten percent? One hundred percent? Five hundred percent?" Our data cannot answer that question directly because it is not possible to translate the value of charge reductions into differences in length of sentence. But our data on sentence differentials in various jurisdictions do suggest that the minimum necessary differential is closer to 14 percent or 16 percent than to 138 percent or 334 percent. That is, it appears that if the state offered defendants a reduction in the length of sentence of about 15 percent to 30 percent, that would be sufficient to keep pleas coming. Perhaps for certain crimes or in some special cases larger or smaller discounts would be needed. But even if our 30 percent discount were doubled, it would still be smaller than the actual differentials found in three of our six jurisdictions.

In summary, then, policymakers concerned with balancing the need for plea incentives while simultaneously minimizing the coerciveness and inconsistency of plea bargaining, would do well to consider a proposal that has been recommended in the past (Yale Law Journal, 1972; Alschuler, 1976). Fixed discounts for pleading guilty could be offered to defendants. The size of the discounts might vary by type of offense and even by stage in the justice process (bigger discounts for earlier pleas). But, our data suggest that the discounts do not need to be large. Possibly they could average as little as 14 percent off the severity of the sentence that the judge would have imposed after trial and a proper presentence investigation. In jurisdictions where the plea bargaining is primarily over charges, the sentence differential could be considerably less and the standard discount could be in terms of graded reduction in charges.

Summary

The analysis of the reality as well as the perceptions and self-reports of differential sentencing produced the following results:

• Defendants almost universally believe that they will be punished more severely for going to trial than pleading guilty. This is frequently conveyed to them by their attorneys but for many it is common knowledge.

• The majority of judges (37 of 49) deny that they punish defendants who are convicted at trial more severely solely because they go to trial.

• Significant increases in the severity of sentence (either in terms of an increased probability of being sentenced to some time in incarceration or an increased length of incarceration or both) for defendants convicted at trial

_____
[18] See Chapter 6.

compared to those pleading guilty occurred in all six jurisdictions.

• The magnitude of the sentence differentials varies enormously among the jurisdictions (from a 14 percent to 138 percent increase in the length of sentence and from a 12 percent to a 29 percent increase in the probability of a sentence with time-to-serve). The largest differential occurred in a jurisdiction where the prosecutor's office has a restricted plea bargaining policy.

• The perceptions by prosecutors and defense counsel of differential sentencing vary in unexpected and unexplainable ways. Surprisingly, there is a substantial amount of disagreement among attorneys in their perceptions of whether specific judges do sentence differentially.

• Defense counsel are more likely than prosecutors to believe judges do not differentially sentence.

• The degree of agreement among all attorneys in their perceptions of the differential sentencing practices of judges varies by jurisdiction but does not vary by the magnitude of the average actual differentials in jurisdictions.

• The judges' denials of differential sentencing are questioned both by the perceptions of attorneys who know their practices and by the existence of actual differentials in sentences after controlling for relevant confounding variables.

• Perceived sentence differentials are an important factor in the decisions of most defendants to plead guilty. But a substantial number of defendants felt that the cases against them were strong.

• Defendants see their decisions to plead guilty as ways of cutting their losses. They do not appear to be taking the first step on the road to rehabilitation although a very few defendants mentioned that in addition to wanting to avoid a harsher sentence they pleaded guilty because they "felt bad" or "morally wrong" about the crime.

Discussion

At the heart of the plea bargaining system is the policy of punishing defendants who are convicted after trial more severely than those convicted by pleading guilty. This policy has been approved by the courts and the ABA has enumerated a set of rationales justifying the practice. Nonetheless, it continues to generate controversy both as to whether the practice actually occurs; whether it is needed; and whether it should be allowed to continue.

Several studies suggest that tried defendants are punished more severely than pleaders but most of these studies have not controlled for variables which might account for both the fact that the case went to trial and the fact that it was sentenced more severely. A few studies which were able to control such confounding variables found that the mere fact of going to trial did not account for the sentence difference. However, our analysis, which also controlled for such variables, came to a different conclusion. The mere fact of going to trial does appear to contribute to the severity of the sentence. But, the nature of the contribution varies considerably by the nature of the plea bargaining system in the jurisdiction. In jurisdictions where the prosecutor's office has restricted its charge bargaining, there is the greatest degree of difference in the length of sentences between pleaders and tried defendants. Where charge bargaining flourishes, the difference in the severity of sentences is smallest. This supports the plastic or hydraulic model of the justice process which holds that if discretion is reduced in one area it will be compensated for elsewhere. It also suggests that programs which purport to have eliminated or reduced plea bargaining such as in Alaska or New Orleans have only shifted the nature of plea bargaining. However, it is in the analysis of the relative merits of these alternative forms of plea bargaining rather than in debates over the absolute abolition of plea bargaining that the most productive course of policy formation lies.

Although many defendants believe the cases against them are strong and are anxious to settle the matters and would probably plead guilty for very little or no consideration, a substantial number of them believe their cases are problematic. Thus, it appears that the offering of some incentives to plead guilty is necessary. The policy questions are about what the incentives should be; who should offer them; and how large a differential between pleaders and tried defendants is necessary to secure enough pleas to keep the court system from overloading. The main choices are between prosecutors offering charge concessions, sentence concessions, or both; or judges offering sentence concessions. If bargaining is done by prosecutors it can take account of case strength in setting the terms of the plea. Whether this is desirable or not depends on one's perspective. As a practical matter most attorneys regard case strength as a critical factor in plea negotiations. To some critics, however, case strength is an inappropriate factor and dilutes the legal standard of proof required by our jurisprudential ideals. In so doing it thereby increases the possibility of wrongful conviction.

Plea bargaining by prosecutors does not have to mean that case strength would necessarily influence dispositions. An aggressive screening program with a high standard of proof for case acceptability could minimize the influence of case strength. Further uniformity among plea offers could be introduced by office policy. Potentially this would allow for greater evenhandedness in plea bargaining than would occur among judges because assistant prosecutors are subject to policy control by one chief executive whereas judges are not.

If the bargaining is done in terms of charge modifications (dismissals or reductions) the integrity of the criminal justice system's record system is compromised. Defendants are not convicted of the crimes they committed. Moreover, the calculation of the value of changes in charges is difficult to interpret meaningfully. It is less clear to both defendants and the public what, if anything, the state is giving the defendant when, for example, it drops charges which may not have affected the sentence anyhow. The opportunity for both bogus as well as overly generous plea considerations to go unrecognized are greater when pleas are in terms of charge modifications than when they are in specific sentence lengths. Thus, both fairness to defendant (in terms of letting them know what they are getting) and meaningful accountability of the prosecutor to the public are less feasible with charge bargaining than with sentence bargaining.

The question of how much of a sentence differential needs to be given in order to secure a guilty plea usually gets answered in practice after an evaluation of the merits of each individual case. But a policy of tailoring plea offers to individual cases fosters unevenness in plea bargaining.[19] Alternatively, plea bargaining could be made more evenhanded and less coercive by establishing set discounts for pleas. Coerciveness could be reduced by holding the size of the discount to the minimum necessary to secure pleas. Evenhandedness would be achieved by offering the same discounts to all defendants (or, if necessary, to vary the discount by type of offense). While this policy would not eliminate plea bargaining it would minimize and control two of its more troublesome aspects. The problem is trying to determine how much of a differential is enough.

Our analysis was unable to answer this precisely; nor was it able to determine whether it would be necessary to vary the size of the discounts by type of offense. However, for the two offenses on which our analysis is based and for cases taken as an aggregate it appears that the threat of as little as about a 14 percent increase in the length of sentence (plus some charging concessions) is enough to obtain a sufficient number of pleas to maintain a system. On the other hand, as charging concessions are increasingly restricted the sentence differentials must be enormously increased—to about 80 percent when charge bargaining is restricted, to as much as 334 percent when it is eliminated. The inequity and coerciveness of the plea bargaining system seems to increase as charge bargaining is minimized, the prosecutor removes himself from the negotiating process, and the system shifts to implicit bargaining by judges.

---

[19] See Chapter 4 for degree of prosecutorial disagreement over plea offers in selected circumstances.

Chapter Six
Judicial Supervision of the Guilty Plea Process

Introduction

Judicial supervision of the guilty plea process is regarded by many as a crucial strategy for bringing fairness and legitimacy to the institution of plea bargaining. Some reformers may have reached this conclusion after deciding that plea bargaining need not be eliminated because judicial supervision could serve as an adequate safeguard. Others may have decided that plea bargaining could not be eliminated; hence, judicial supervision is the best way to make virtuous this necessity. In any event, numerous nationally recognized groups as well as appellate court decisions have identified the trial judge as the key actor in taming the dragon.[1] While these writers are by no means unanimous on all specific points they are in general agreement.

The judge is expected to assure the fairness of the process both to defendants and to the community. For defendants he is to determine that (1) their pleas are "voluntary"—an elusive term which has come to mean not induced by "improper" inducements, such as bribing or physical violence, but not including the inducements normally associated with charge and sentence bargaining (except for inducements involving "overcharging" by prosecutors);[2] (2) their pleas are "intelligent"—also an elusive and open-ended term which has gradually assumed greater specificity including the determination that the defendant knows his rights, the nature of the charge to which he is pleading, and the consequences of his plea; and, (3) the judge is to establish a record of the plea acceptance as well as the terms of any plea agreement that may have been struck. The last procedure has been regarded as not only a protection for defendants by ensuring that they get the deal they thought they had agreed to but also as benefiting the general community by making plea bargaining more visible and efficient (by minimizing appeals on the grounds of broken plea promises).

In addition, the judge is to minimize the possibility of innocent people being convicted by reviewing the evidence and determining that the plea is "accurate," that a "factual basis for the plea" exists—meaning generally that there is reason to believe the defendant committed a crime of equal or greater seriousness than the one to which he is pleading. As for fairness to the community, the judge is expected to check the plea bargaining practices of prosecutors and reject plea agreements that are not appropriate to the total circumstances of the case including such things as the rehabilitative needs of the defendant, the appearance of justice, and the normal sentencing practices that would apply to similarly-situated defendants. The judge is to reject overly-lenient and overly-severe plea bargains alike.

This chapter describes the development of standards relating to the judge's supervisory role in the process and describes how that role is performed in six jurisdictions. The analysis is based on interviews with judges and others plus in-court observations of guilty plea acceptances in a total of 711 felony and misdemeanor cases before 46 felony and misdemeanor courts between July 7, 1977, and August 31, 1977.

---

[1] For a review of the case decisions as well as the legal literature see Bond, 1981. For a review of the recommendations of national standard-setting groups see Epstein and Austern, 1975.

[2] Two commissions (President's Commission on Law Enforcement and Criminal Justice, 1967; and the National Advisory Commission on Criminal Justice Standards and Goals, 1973:57) have specifically identified "overcharging" as "improper" inducements which judges should reject.

The growth of plea acceptance standards

As recently as the early 1960's the process of entering a plea of guilty in court was usually brief. The court would ask a few questions and defendants, often without the advice of counsel, gave one-word answers leading to their convictions—even of serious crimes. The only formal requirement governing the court in accepting guilty pleas in most jurisdictions was that it determine that the plea be voluntarily entered by a competent defendant (Newman, 1966:8; Washington University Law Quarterly, 1966). Many defendants pleaded guilty after negotiating deals with either the judge, the prosecutor, or the police. But this fact was usually not elicited, much less regarded as having rendered the plea involuntary. On the contrary, such defendants were required to engage in the "pious fraud" (Enker, 1967:111) of denying for the record that any promises, threats, or inducements had influenced their pleas.

The brevity of the plea acceptance process belied the seriousness of its consequences, a point stressed by the United States Supreme Court:

> A plea of guilty differs in purpose and effect from a mere admission or an extra-judicial confession; it is itself a conviction. Like a verdict of a jury it is conclusive. More is not required; the court has nothing to do but give judgement and sentence. (*Machibroda* v. *United States,* 368 U.S. 487, 493 (1962), quoting *Kercheval* v. *United States,* 274 U.S. 220, 223 (1927)).

Within a few years the consequences had become even more grave because the plea operated as a waiver of precious constitutional rights newly made applicable to the states including: (1) the Fifth Amendment privilege against self-incrimination; (2) the Sixth Amendment right to confront one's accusers; and (3) the Sixth Amendment right to a trial by jury.[3]

By the mid-sixties reforms of the plea taking process were underway. Trial and appellate courts were beginning to pay more attention to the requirements of the process (Newman, 1966:8); and commentators (e.g., University of Chicago Law Review, 1964) and commissions were recommending changes designed to make the process more visible, uniform, fair to defendants and the community, and to minimize the risk of innocent defendants pleading guilty.

In 1966, Rule 11 of the Federal Rules of Criminal Procedure, which governs the process by which federal courts accept guilty pleas, was amended in a small but important way. The federal courts had formerly been obliged to determine that all guilty pleas were entered "voluntarily with understanding" (Federal Rules of Criminal Procedure, pre-1966). But no specific procedure for taking pleas had been prescribed (Washington University Law Quarterly, 1966:308). The 1966 amendment required that the court personally address the defendant in making its determination that the plea was voluntarily and knowingly made. It also added the requirement that the court satisfy itself that there be a factual basis for the plea (Federal Rules of Criminal Procedure, as amended Feb. 28, 1966, eff. July 1, 1966). Nine years later Rule 11 was amended again, this time substantially expanding its scope.[4]

The 1975 text reflected many of the recommendations that were suggested in the mid-sixties or had already been established by case decisions. In 1967, the President's Crime Commission (President's Commission on Law Enforcement and Administration of Justice, 1967:12) went beyond the requirements of the existing FRCP Rule 11. It recommended that if a plea agreement were involved in the case, its terms should be fully stated for the record and, at least in serious or complicated cases, reduced to writing. Such memoranda should contain "an agreed statement of the facts of the offense, the opening positions of the parties, the terms of the agreement, background information relevant to the correctional disposition, and an explanation of why the negotiated disposition is appropriate" (Id.). This material should be probed by the judge, whose inquiries should be "more precise and detailed than the brief and perfunctory question-and-answer sequence that [had] been common in some courts" (Ibid, 13). In contrast to the 1968 American Bar Association Standards Relating to Guilty Pleas (which were being drafted at the time), the Commission recommended that the judge's guilty plea acceptance decision be simultaneous with his sentencing decision. That is, rather than a procedure by which a judge accepts a plea contingent upon a favorable subsequent presentence investigation report, the Commission recommended that such diagnostic and sentencing information should be made available at the time of the plea. The judge is to use it in deciding whether the agreed upon disposition is fair and appropriate in light of all the circumstances. In particular the judge should "determine that . . . the prosecutor did not agree to an inadequate sentence for a serious offender," and should "guard against overcharging by the prosecutor or an agreed sentence that is inappropriately light in view of the crime

---

[3] See Malloy v. Hogan, 378 U.S. 1 (1964); Pointer v. Texas, 380 U.S. 400 (1965); Duncan v. Louisiana, 391 U.S. 145 (1968).

[4] See Appendix B for a comparison of the 1966 and 1975 texts.

or is lenient as to constitute an irresistible inducement to the defendant to plead guilty" (Id.).

The following year the ABA (1968) issued its *Standards Relating to Pleas of Guilty,* which added a few more requirements to the growing list of things judges were being asked to do. For the most part these requirements represented specifications of the existing general requirements that pleas be knowingly and voluntarily given. The ABA (1968: § 1.4) recommended that:

The court should not accept a plea of guilty or nolo contendere from a defendant without first addressing the defendant personally and

(a) determining that he understands the nature of the charge;

(b) informing him that by his plea of guilty or nolo contendere he waives his right to trial by jury; and

(c) informing him:

(i) of the possible sentence on the charge, including that possible from consecutive sentences;

(ii) of the mandatory minimum sentence, if any, on the charge; and

(iii) when the offense charged is one for which a different or additional punishment is authorized by reason of the fact that the defendant has previously been convicted of an offense, that this fact may be established after his plea in the present action if he has been previously convicted, thereby subjecting him to such different or additional punishment.

The court should not accept a plea of guilty or nolo contendere without first determining that the plea is voluntary. By inquiry of the prosecuting attorney and defense counsel, the court should determine whether the tendered plea is the result of prior plea discussions and a plea agreement, and, if it is, what agreement has been reached. If the prosecuting attorney has agreed to seek charge or sentence concessions which must be approved by the court, the court must advise the defendant personally that the recommendations of the prosecuting attorney are not binding on the court. The court should then address the defendant personally and determine whether any other promises or any force or threats were used to obtain the plea.

The ABA (1968) also recommended that the judge satisfy himself that a factual basis for the plea exists; a record be made of the proceedings; and that a defendant not be called upon to plead until he has had aid of counsel and time for deliberation.

By 1973, when the National Advisory Commission on Criminal Justice Standards and Goals (NACC) issued its

recommended plea taking requirements, the list had become even longer and more specific—reflecting changes in the law. In addition, the American Law Institute (1975) and the National Conference of Commissioners on Uniform State Laws (1974) recommended standards for plea acceptance. Each set of standards varies from the other in a few particulars,[5] but they agree on the need for a substantial judicial role in supervising the guilty plea process and the main dimensions along which that role should be performed.

Judicial supervision in six jurisdictions

Despite the modification of case law and the various recommended standards for accepting guilty pleas, the judge's role in supervising the guilty plea process remains fluid and uncertain. This is for several reasons. The standards are: inherently ambiguous;[6] frequently confused with each other by appellate courts;[7] and subject to differing views as to how far the judge should be required to go in fulfilling them.[8] Moreover, although

---

[5] For an itemized comparison of the 1975 FRCP, 1975 ALI, 1968 ABA, NAC, and the 1974 Uniform Rules of Criminal Procedure see Epstein and Austern, 1975.

[6] For instance, the criterion of voluntariness has chameleon-like properties—taking on whatever definition best suits it (Bond, 1981:75). Professor Enker (1967:108) has explained it as follows:

It should be recognized immediately that the term [voluntariness] is an exceedingly ambiguous term. This stems not only from the difficulties involved in trying to discover a past state of mind but also from the fact that we do not even have a clear idea of what, if any, psychological facts or experience we are looking for. The choice to plead guilty rather than face the rack is voluntary in the sense that the subject did have a choice, albeit between unpleasant alternatives. The defendant who decides to plead guilty and seek judicial mercy also makes a choice between what are to him two unpleasant alternatives. If we call the first choice involuntary and the second voluntary what we are really saying is that we are convinced that in the first case almost all persons so confronted will choose to admit their guilt but that the defendant's decision is based on more personal and subjective factors in the second instance.

[7] Some pleas are invalidated on the grounds of voluntariness when the fact pattern suggests the more appropriate grounds would have been lack of requisite knowledge. See, e.g., Pilkington v. United States, 315 F.2d 204 (4th Cir. 1963) (defendant was not accurately informed of the maximum sentence he might receive).

[8] For instance, in requiring that the judge establish a factual basis for a plea those reformers who would have the judge serve as a protection against pleas in weak cases and as a mechanism by which an impartial third-party who assessed the evidence might like to require that the judge determine whether the evidence meets some standard of proof such as probable cause or beyond a reasonable doubt. But others do not agree that such a standard should be required (Bond, 1981).

the Federal courts developed a set of procedures governing the acceptance of pleas in Federal courts (FRCP Rule 11, 1975), no specific set of procedures has been constitutionally imposed upon the states (Bond 1981:88). The states are only constitutionally obligated to assure that whatever procedures they use satisfy due process. This has meant that state courts may not accept a guilty plea unless defendants enter them knowingly and voluntarily. The court in *Larson* v. *Coiner,* 351 F. Supp. 129, 130 (N.D. W. Va. 1972) summarized the point as follows:

> While state courts are not required to enter into arraignment inquiry to the depth and extent required of United States District Courts under Rule 11, Federal Rules of Criminal Procedures, they must nevertheless determine on the record if the plea was intelligently and voluntarily entered.

However, as the Federal courts continue to interpret the knowing-voluntary standards it has become evident that the minimal plea taking procedures of former times would not meet constitutional requirements. The state courts must establish a record sufficient to establish that the defendant is knowingly and voluntarily pleading and that he knows he is relinquishing his constitutional rights, including his privilege against compulsory self-incrimination, his right to trial by jury and his right to confront his accusers (*Boykin* v. *Alabama,* 395 U.S. 238 (1969)). The court must assure that the defendant receives adequate notice of the nature of the charge(s) to which he is pleading guilty, meaning that not every element but at least "critical" elements of the charge(s) be explained to the defendant by someone (either the court or defense counsel) (*Henderson* v. *Morgan,* 426 U.S. 637 (1976)). The states thus remain free to use different and less stringent procedures for accepting guilty pleas than those required in the Federal courts by virtue of Rule 11 and its interpretation. The variation this has permitted is illustrated by the six states included in this study.

Two states (Arizona and Washington) have revised their rules of criminal procedure modeling them after many of the provisions of the ABA's standards and the (anticipated) 1975 revisions of FRCP Rule 11. Both states published lengthy forms for recording the terms of plea agreements and to serve as checklists for determining that pleas are knowing, voluntary and accurate as required by the U.S. Constitution and their respective state case law.[9] In Washington, judges are required to use the forms (Washington Criminal Rule 4.2(g)). Texas has a somewhat less extensive and different set of required procedures.[10] Similarly, Virginia has even less extensive required guidelines plus a recommended list of questions to guide the judicial inquiry.[11] Pennsylvania's required procedure is minimal but detailed guidelines are recommended in dicta in a leading case.[12] Finally, Louisiana has minimal required guidelines. However, the judges in New Orleans have individually established their own procedures (which vary in certain important respects but generally incorporate many of the guidelines used elsewhere).[13]

How the laws of the six states regarding plea taking operate in action and whether they provide the kind of safeguard against defects and abuses of plea bargaining as envisioned by their advocates are examined below. The analysis is divided into five parts: (1) the quality of the plea acceptance process; (2) the knowing standard; (3) the voluntary standard; (4) the accuracy standard (factual basis); and (5) the effectiveness of the procedures.

Background characteristics of the 711 guilty pleas on which this analysis is primarily based are presented in Table 6.1. Both felony and misdemeanor courts were observed, although the majority of observations (72 percent) were of felony courts (except in El Paso). The majority of cases involved pleas to felony charges (70.8 percent), and in the majority of cases (75.4 percent) counsel was present.

The quality of the process. One of the limits of legally prescribed inquiries is that their purpose can be defeated by the manner in which they are conducted. The most carefully worded, required inquiry can be made into an unintelligible rattle of words when read off like a tobacco auctioneer—as was observed in some courts. Similarly, as Mileski (1971) concludes, if defendants are advised of their rights en masse rather than individually, they are less likely to comprehend either the meaning or gravity of the advice. Moreover, it is believed by several standard-setting groups that the effectiveness of the warnings and explanations given in the plea acceptance process depend in part on who gives them to whom. It is believed that the most effective procedure is to have the judge personally address the defendant.[14] But, of course, there is a tradeoff here. The more painstaking the inquiry, the more time consuming and the less efficient the

---

[9] See Appendixes C and D for their respective rules and forms.

[10] See Appendix E.

[11] See Appendix F.

[12] See Appendix G.

[13] See Appendix H.

[14] FRCP Rule 11 (since 1966) requires the judge to personally address the defendant as does the ABA (1972) and the State of Arizona (Az. R.C.P., Rule 17.2). Pennsylvania law does not require it but does recommend it (Pa. R.C.P. Rule 319).

Table 6.1 Selected background characteristics of the guilty plea acceptances observed by jurisdiction (June–August, 1977)

Characteristic	El Paso [N = 106]	New Orleans [N = 120]	Seattle [N = 138]	Tucson [N = 110]	Delaware Co. [N = 131]	Norfolk [N = 106]	Total* [N = 711]**
Number of judges observed	5	6	8	11	9	7	46
Type of court							
Felony	19.0%	87.3%	72.3%	75.5%	100.0%	69.8%	72.1%
Misdemeanor	81.0%	12.7%	27.7%	24.5%	0.0%	30.2%	28.0%
Type of counsel							
Public defender	0.0%	44.9%	67.4%	68.2%	68.5%	0.0%	43.8%
Court appointed	15.4%	2.5%	2.2%	7.3%	0.0%	26.7%	8.3%
Private	0.0%	51.7%	11.9%	15.5%	30.7%	28.6%	23.3%
None	81.7%	0.0%	2.2%	0.0%	0.8%	17.1%	15.3%
Unknown	2.9%	0.8%	16.2%	9.1%	0.0%	27.6%	9.3%
Type of charge							
Felony	22.6%	55.8%	72.5%	62.7%	59.5%	70.8%	58.1%
Misdemeanor	77.4%	44.2%	27.5%	37.3%	40.5%	29.2%	41.9%

*Percentages that do not total to 100 are due to rounding errors.
**The sizes of the respective N's vary slightly due to item nonresponse.

guilty plea process becomes. This can lead to a search for ways around the new safeguards.[15]

Individualization of the inquiry. Several items in our structured observation of the plea-taking process are related to the quality of the process. As indicated in Table 6.2, the majority (78 percent) of guilty pleas (including both felony and misdemeanor charges and felony and misdemeanor courts) are taken from defendants who are addressed on an individual basis and have the litany of advice and explanations recited to them either in a rote, standardized fashion (20 percent) or a more individualized fashion (29 percent); or who in addition to an individualized inquiry also have signed a corresponding list of rights, warnings, and understandings (26 percent); or some combination of the above. Few defendants (11 percent) have their pleas accepted without any judicial inquiry being made, and most of these are in misdemeanor cases (not shown).

[15] This has happened in Maryland where an alternative to the guilty plea procedure is regularly used in part because it is faster than the regular guilty plea acceptance procedures. The alternative is to plead not guilty and agree to have a statement of facts read into the record. The defendant is then found guilty at what is officially recorded as a "bench trial" but in effect is a second form of plea. It is understood by all parties (except sometimes the defendant) that this is a bargained for

disposition; that the outcome of the "trial" is virtually a foregone conclusion; and that the deal the defendant is getting is predicated upon his willingness to agree to this truncated informal trial.

These informal trials do not completely defeat the guilty plea acceptance procedures that would otherwise have operated. Before accepting a not-guilty-statement-of-facts, the judge warns the defendant in a way similar to the warning given at the taking of guilty pleas. But the litany is not quite as long. In one case a 59-year-old defendant charged with sexually molesting a child was advised by the court as follows: "You give up your right to a jury trial and to having a jury find you guilty beyond a reasonable doubt and to having them do this on a unanimous basis. Do you understand? Do you want a jury trial? Do you understand that you will be bound by the paper (statement of facts); there will be no cross-examination; no live witnesses will take the stand? There will be no confrontation of the witnesses against you?" After the defendant said he understood, there was a reading of the statement of facts. It was also noted that the state had agreed to make no sentence recommendation and not to oppose a presentence investigation in exchange for the defendant's agreement to proceed by the not-guilty-statement-of-facts procedure.

Even with this rather extensive inquiry, it is reported that the not-guilty-statement-of-facts procedure is faster than the full procedure required if the defendant pleads guilty. Local estimates are that the full procedure can take two to four times as long as the "5 minutes" needed for the alternative.

It should be noted, however, that notwithstanding the importance attached to it by local personnel, the time savings may not be the only reason why the not-guilty-statement-of-fact is preferred to the regular guilty plea process. There are other benefits as well including inflating the number of "trials" the system can show it conducted and preserving important rights on appeal that are forfeited by a guilty plea.

Length of the Inquiry: (1) By Type of Charge. One important but not unambiguous indication of the overall quality of the plea-taking process is the length of time it takes. In general, the longer the plea-taking session, the more likely it is to be thorough, individualized and to accomplish its multiple purposes. But this is not necessarily the case, as the appellate courts themselves have recognized. They allow the scope of the inquiry to vary according to the circumstances of the case. The seriousness of the offense, the defendant's answers, the presence of defense counsel and other factors are supposed to determine the length to which the trial judge goes in supervising the plea (Bond, 1981:280.7). The court in *State v. McKee,* 362 N.E.2d 1252 (Ohio, 1976) made this point as follows:

The determination that there has been an intelligent voluntary waiver with understanding of rights is a subjective procedure. It can be accomplished by short interrogation. Each determination must be made on an *ad hoc* basis. The depth and breadth of the interrogation depend upon the totality of circumstances surrounding each case.

Notwithstanding this important qualification, it is still useful to examine the length of time plea acceptances take. This is especially instructive in cross-jurisdictional comparisons. Assuming the mix of cases in the samples are similar, major differences in length of time between jurisdictions cannot be accounted for in terms of the differing needs of individual cases.

The average time for plea acceptance for all crimes (felony and misdemeanor cases combined) in all six jurisdictions is 7.8 minutes (Table 6.3). The time of accepting pleas to felony charges (9.9 minutes) is almost twice that taken for misdemeanor pleas (5.2 minutes). Most interesting but not easily explicable is the significant difference among the jurisdictions in the length of the plea-taking procedures. For instance, why felony pleas should take four times as long in Delaware County compared to Seattle or New Orleans is unclear. It does not appear to be due to differences in legal requirements. (Seattle has the more extensive list of mandatory inquiries.) Nor is it apparently due to the efficiency of using prepared lists of inquiries. (The Delaware County judges all use such a list.)

Table 6.2 Setting and nature of guilty plea acceptances by jurisdiction (June–August 1977)

Setting of proceeding	El Paso [N=106]	New Orleans [N=120]	Seattle [N=138]	Tucson [N=110]	Delaware Co. [N=131]	Norfolk [N=106]	Total* [N=711]**
Defendant(s) were:							
In group, *without* individualized followup	2.9%	0.0%	0.0%	25.5%	0.0%	7.5%	5.5%
In group, *with* individualized follow-up	55.8%	1.7%	2.9%	19.1%	4.6%	5.7%	13.7%
Individually addressed	43.3%	86.7%	97.1%	52.7%	95.4%	85.8%	78.2%
Other	0.0%	11.7%	0.0%	2.7%	0.0%	0.9%	2.5%
Nature of judicial inquiry							
Oral/individualized	77.1%	0.0%	14.5%	91.8%	0.8%	23.6%	32.1%
Oral/standardized	1.9%	5.0%	62.3%	5.5%	6.1%	34.9%	20.5%
Written inquiry *not* read aloud, signed by defendant	0.0%	0.8%	18.1%	0.0%	19.8%	0.0%	7.3%
Oral/plus written inquiry signed by defendant	0.0%	89.1%	0.7%	2.7%	71.7%	18.9%	31.6%
No inquiry	21.0%	5.0%	4.3%	0.0%	1.5%	41.5%	11.3%

*Percentages that do not total to 100 are due to rounding errors.
**The sizes of the respective N's vary slightly due to item nonresponse.

Table 6.3   Length of time of plea taking process by jurisdiction (June–August, 1977)

Time for accepting guilty pleas	El Paso [N=106]	New Orleans [N=120]	Seattle [N=138]	Tucson [N=110]	Delaware Co. [N=131]	Norfolk [N=106]	Total* [N=711]**
By type of charge							
Completed within 5 minutes:							
Felony	12.5%	77.6%	83.0%	21.7%	1.3%	24.0%	41.6%
Misdemeanor	93.9%	84.9%	100.0%	65.8%	3.8%	90.3%	72.8%
All cases	75.4%	80.0%	87.7%	38.2%	2.3%	43.4%	54.7%
Completed within 10 minutes:							
Felony	25.0%	100.0%	96.0%	71.0%	20.5%	50.7%	65.9%
Misdemeanor	96.3%	100.0%	100.0%	95.1%	32.1%	93.7%	85.9%
All cases	80.0%	100.0%	97.1%	80.1%	25.1%	66.2%	74.2%
(Average (mean) time for all cases in minutes (m))							
Felony	17.2m	4.3m	4.2m	10.6m	18.2m	11.0m	9.9m
Misdemeanor	3.4m	3.7m	1.7m	4.9m	14.0m	2.2m	5.2m
All cases	5.9m	4.1m	3.5m	8.5m	16.7m	8.4m	7.8m
By type of court							
(Average (mean) time in minutes (m))							
Felony	8.7m	4.3m	4.1m	8.3m	16.7m	8.8m	8.9m
Misdemeanor	3.3m	2.7m	1.7m	3.0m	NA	1.5m	2.6m

*Percentages that do not total to 100 are due to rounding errors.
**The sizes of the respective N's vary slightly due to item nonresponse.

However, it does appear to be related to the degree of formalization of the prosecutor's office; [16] but why this should be so can only be speculated about. Perhaps there is a compensating mechanism at work. In jurisdictions where the prosecutor's office has extensive policy guidelines and internal managerial controls, judges may come to trust in those procedures and feel less of a need to use the plea acceptance procedure as a major protection against possible miscarriage of justice. On the other hand, equally plausible is an explanation in terms of "local legal culture" (Church, 1981). Prosecutors' offices that are more highly formalized also tend to be more concerned about rapid case disposition. Their sensitivity to speedy disposition may stimulate (or result from) a similar concern among the local judiciary.

It bears noting that the fact that the average felony plea acceptance in Delaware County takes 18.2 minutes means that many acceptances take longer. Six percent of them took a half an hour. How so much time can be consumed in plea-taking is illustrated by the following typical case.

Field Note: Delaware County, Felony Court, Summer 1977.

The next case was a negotiated plea to a charge of possession with intent to deliver heroin. Recommended sentence: 2½ months to Broadmeadow Prison. The judge noted the prior record of defendant; asked if defendant had completed probation; told public defender (PD) to advise his client of his rights; asked defendant his age, can he read and write? PD read the rights: Does defendant understand he is waiving his right to trial by jury; right to

---

[16] This assumes El Paso is deleted from this particular analysis, a reasonable assumption. Given the no plea bargaining policy in El Paso, the courts may have taken greater time in accepting pleas to assure that the Court's "point-system" was not misunderstood. For further details in the El Paso no plea bargaining policy see Chapter 2.

challenge jury; to have a unanimous verdict; or if he chooses trial without jury, he has the right to appeal for a new trial within 30 days; he can stand mute at trial; does not need to testify; can cross-examine witnesses? He also has limited appeal rights if he feels the sentence, or the jurisdiction of court, or the involuntariness of his plea are improper. If he cannot afford an attorney, the county will provide one. By pleading guilty does he realize he is admitting to a crime and he gives up the merits of his case?

The judge was not satisfied with the defendant's response to the last question so he rephrased it three different ways until he was certain the man understood.

The PD then explained that the charge the defendant was pleading guilty to was a felony, and told him the maximum penalty and that a guilty plea was a recorded conviction. Then he went on to explain the kind of voluntariness required of a plea; that the lawyers who agreed to the plea could not promise the sentence to be imposed; that parole or probation on a previous charge could be revoked. The PD then asked if the defendant had discussed the case and his possible defenses with the PD and was satisfied that the PD was willing to try the case; that the burden of proof was on the Commonwealth; that the PD would represent him if he changes his mind. He then asked if the defendant was suffering from the effects of narcotics or mental illness.

As the defendant prepared to sign the affidavit, the judge asked him what grade he had reached in school. Answer: "some college in prison." Judge then asked if he could read, write, and understand "what you're signing?"

The judge requested the clerk to make the guilty plea statement part of the record. He then asked defendant if the plea was voluntary—if it isn't, "I won't accept the plea."

He then asked: "What about probation? Do you know that this plea will be a violation of your probation? Do you know that this plea will be a violation of your probation in Delaware? In all likelihood the judge who sentenced you will revoke it."
PD: "During the negotiation we were attempting to determine if this won't affect his sentence."
J: "I don't want you to enter a plea if you're expecting this. It's entirely up to the judge in Delaware."
PD: "There's no guarantee."
J: "In all probability, the judge will revoke. It's entirely up to him. You understand that?"
Def: "Yes."
J: "You realize the negotiated plea is just a recommendation of the D.A., but if I find it inappropriate

I am not bound by it. Do you understand that the criminal code makes it a crime to have the intent to deliver—the intent to transfer, not necessarily a sale?"
Judge then told the D.A. to go ahead. D.A. called an undercover narcotics agent to the stand who testified that the defendant went with him to find a seller in Upper Chester who would sell him (the agent) some heroin. The defendant obtained the heroin and gave it to the agent. The material was tested and found to be heroin.

The D.A. then asked the agent, who worked for the probation department, if his sentence recommendation was in line with the probation department's policies. The answer was yes. There was no cross-examination and the witness was excused.

The judge asked the defendant if the witness' statement was correct. The defendant attempted to argue that he wasn't guilty but the PD tried to talk to him. The judge asked him to speak up. Def.: "We rode all over looking for one to buy—it's not like I'm a salesman."

A general discussion proceeded. It was obvious that all the actors were upset at this turn of events. Everyone stood very quietly. The rest of the courtroom got very quiet. The judge began and very gingerly they worked around the defendant's statement. The judge wanted to know if he was part of "the organization." The D.A. couldn't be certain but said "his name was well known in Chester." The PD offered, "But I don't believe he's a dealer." Finally the judge said he agreed to the plea and told the defendant "You're getting a break. I sentence you to 2½–12 months in the Delaware County Prison, both counts to run concurrently." There was a long pause till the PD indicated there was some problem with the sentence. The negotiated plea was for less time—to include time served. There was some discussion about how much time he had served. After another pause the judge said, "We'll pass this matter over until we find out what time was served." (Did not hear final outcome.)

In contrast to Delaware County, plea taking in the fastest jurisdiction (Seattle) relies to a great extent on the "Statement of Defendant on Plea of Guilty" (hereinafter, "the statement") required by the Washington Superior Court Criminal Rules (Rule 4.2).[17] Despite the existence

---

[17] See Appendix D.

of the required form, Seattle judges differed considerably in their plea-taking procedures both in terms of the extensiveness of and the elements in the litany that were emphasized or included. All judges used the required statement but varied in the degree to which they relied on the defendant's understanding of the form. Many of the issues addressed in the statement were not pursued orally by the felony courts.

With regard to the difference between felonies and misdemeanors, it is clear that in each jurisdiction considerably less time is devoted to supervising pleas to misdemeanors than pleas to felonies (see Table 6.3). This is not unexpected given that appellate courts have permitted the scope of the inquiry to be less extensive in less serious crimes (Bond, 1978). However, those courts have also held that the requirements of Boykin apply to misdemeanors as well as to felonies (see *Whelan v. State*, 472 S.W.2d 141 (Tex. 1971)); and they do require judges to widen the scope of the inquiry when defendants are not represented by counsel (Florida Law Review, 1970). Therefore, one would expect some minimal level of judicial inquiry in every misdemeanor plea and a greater level in cases of unrepresented defendants.

The differences among the six jurisdictions in the length of plea-taking to misdemeanor charges are not as great as those for felony charges. Most of them average between 2 to 5 minutes. The one exception (Delaware County) with an average of 14 minutes must be regarded as a special case because misdemeanors in Pennsylvania include crimes punishable by up to five years in prison. Thus it is not surprising that they are treated more like felonies.

Notwithstanding this general similarity among the jurisdictions in taking misdemeanor pleas there remains a noteworthy difference in the length of time of this procedure. The longest average misdemeanor plea-taking (4.9 minutes in Tucson) [18] is more than twice as long as the shortest (1.7 minutes in Seattle). What accounts for this difference among the jurisdictions is not clear, but one candidate explanation can be discounted. It is not due to differences in the presence of counsel. In New Orleans, where misdemeanors were typically disposed of within 3.7 minutes, all defendants had counsel, whereas in El Paso none of the defendants (pleading to misdemeanors) had counsel. Yet the pleas took about the same time (3.4 minutes).

(2) Misdemeanor Courts. The discussion above focused on the difference in plea acceptance between pleas to felony and misdemeanor *charges.* The discussion below focuses on the difference between felony and misdemeanor *courts.* The rationale for this additional analysis is that studies (Robertson, 1974) have suggested that the quality of justice is more a function of the level of the court than the level of the charge. Therefore, this analysis will explore the implied hypothesis that the quality of plea-taking will be lower in the lower courts. [19]

It can be seen that plea acceptances in felony courts average over three times as long as in misdemeanor courts (see Table 6.3). The two fastest lower courts (Norfolk at 1.5 minutes and Seattle at 1.7 minutes) are worth describing in greater detail because their contrasting practices illustrate an important point. Plea taking can be swift and yet still have a baseline of consistent warnings and checks built into it. In neither jurisdiction does the plea acceptance represent a major protection against unknowing, involuntary or inaccurate pleas. But, in Seattle the District Courts at least use a standard "Statement of Defendant On Pleading Guilty" form, [20] modeled after the one used in the Superior Courts. By contrast, in the Norfolk District Court, defendants are regularly encouraged to waive all rights (including the right to an attorney) and to plead guilty as charged without any inquiry into the plea.

The following field notes provide more detailed pictures. [21]

Field Notes: Norfolk District (lower) Court (Summer 1977.)
The average number of cases handled per day by the Norfolk District Court varies from 48 to 399. All are handled by one judge yet it is not unusual for the docket to be completed by noon.
The courtroom is noisy. Various people mill around. Police officers waiting for their cases to be heard are laughing and talking to each other. Lawyers, police officers, victims, prosecutors, and defendants are walking around either in the courtroom or in the back hall working out deals. It is so noisy we had to sit in the front row and still had difficulty following the proceedings. The frequent comment of prosecutors, defense attorneys and police officers was that the court is "nothing but a zoo."

---

[18] Delaware County is excluded for reasons mentioned above.

[19] This hypothesis could not be explored in the preceding analysis because not all the pleas to misdemeanor charges were in misdemeanor courts. In the following analysis, all the cases labeled, "misdemeanor courts," are pleas to misdemeanor charges whereas the cases labeled "felony courts" include pleas to felonies as well as to misdemeanor charges.

[20] See Appendix I.

[21] The "Statement referred" to in the Seattle field notes is the Defendant's Statement On Pleading Guilty.

The clerk of the court (referred to jokingly as "Judge") tends to control the proceedings. He often tells the judge which case to hear first. According to one of the prosecutors, if the judge sets a very lenient sentence the clerk might lean over and tell the judge that defendant has a long record on something and the sentence may be increased. Also, the prosecutor reports that at one time the clerk took it upon himself to nol pros (dismiss) cases until the prosecutor told him that by law only the Commonwealth Attorney's Office could do so. Now the clerk says, "We will nol pros this case if the Commonwealth will concur."

The typical procedure in misdemeanor cases is that the defendant's name is called and he approaches the bench. The clerk or bailiff asks him if he wants his case heard today or does he want an attorney? The tone of voice encourages defendant to choose having his case heard without an attorney. The defendant will then be told to sign a piece of paper which happens to be a waiver of attorney form. In many cases, no one will verbally state that the defendant has a right to an attorney. No other rights are mentioned.

Once the waiver is signed the defendant is asked, "How do you plead, guilty or not guilty?" There is no litany or inquiry as to the knowingness or voluntariness of the plea. (I asked the judge about this and he replied, "If he pleads, then I assume that he committed it. I don't have time to do anything else.")

In some cases the judge may ask the arresting officer a question. For example, if the defendant pleads to simple possession, the judge may ask the officer about the amount. In some guilty plea cases, the officer may not be present, and no factual basis is established for the plea. The judge then sentences the defendant. The average time elapsed on a misdemeanor guilty plea is one minute.

I asked the judge about misdemeanor cases in which the police officer brings the charge and also acts as the prosecutor. Since there may or may not be any physical evidence, I asked him how he determined guilt or innocence. He stated, "That's why a lot of people don't survive on the bench in police court. They can't handle the pressure. You tend to go along with the police officer. I go along with the police officer unless there is some question as to whether the act actually falls under the charge."

The following are typical cases observed in District Court:

Case #1: Charge: Soliciting.
Do you want your case heard today? "Yes."
Rights: Signed waiver of attorney form.
Facts: Police stated the facts.
Sentence: $100 fine.
Time elapsed: 1 minute.

Case #2: Charge: Drunk and disorderly.
Do you want your case heard today? "Yes."
Rights: Signed waiver of attorney form.
Facts: None; no police officer present.
Sentence: $10 and 10 days suspended on good behavior.
Time elapsed: 1 minute.

Case #3: Charge: Possession of drugs.
Do you want your case heard today? "Yes."
Rights: Signed waiver of attorney form.
Facts: Police state the amount.
Sentence: $25 fine.
Time elapsed: 1 minute.

Case #4: Charge: Drunk in public (10 defendants brought into court at the same time).
How do you plead? "Guilty."
Rights: None; did not sign waiver of attorney form.
Facts: None.
Sentence: $10.
Note: The judge told this group of defendants that the fine was $10 whether they plead guilty or went to trial.
Time elapsed: 1 minute.

Our observations in Norfolk District Court can be summed up as follows:

1. No constitutional rights are recited to the defendant.

2. The defendant is not asked if he understands the rights that he is giving up. He simply signs the waiver of attorney form. In most cases the defendant doesn't even bother to read the form.

3. The defendant is not asked if he is pleading guilty because he is in fact guilty.

4. In many cases no factual basis for the plea is presented.

5. The defendant was not asked if anyone threatened, coerced or pressured him into pleading.

6. The judge did not specify what maximum sentence was permissible by law.

7. No collateral consequences of the plea were noted.

When the judge was asked about all of these problems he stated, "They are usually so happy that they don't have a felony conviction or that they don't have to go to jail, that they don't care."

In Seattle observations were made in three of the five Seattle District Courts. It should be kept in mind that the workload of the Seattle District judges appears to be considerably less than that of the judge in the Norfolk District Court.[22]

Field Notes: Seattle (King County) District (lower) Courts, (Summer 1977):

The procedures for accepting guilty pleas in the District Court tend to be very informal. Generally, there is no judicial litany. Usually the only question asked by the judge is how the defendant wishes to plead. Quite frequently even that question is not asked. If any of the issues considered to be part of the "litany" are included in the proceeding, they are usually stated either by the prosecutor or defense counsel. A "Statement" is almost always required but is often not submitted, or even filled out, until after the plea has been accepted.

In District Court sentencing frequently occurs immediately following the entry of a guilty plea. It is very difficult to really make a distinction between the two procedures. The judge may ask questions about the facts of the case after the plea has, in effect, already been accepted, in order to determine sentence. Since both the entry of the plea and the determination of the sentence occur in the same few minutes of time, the attempted separation of the two proceedings may be meaningless.

All of the District Court judges observed appeared reluctant to allow defendants to enter a plea *pro se.* Although *pro se* proceedings were occasionally observed, judges almost always require the defendant to get an attorney, or at least talk with a public defender present in court, prior to entering a plea.

The amount of participation by the prosecutor and defense counsel may make fairly extensive comments about their representation of a defendant, but generally their comments are limited to stating that the defendant wishes to enter a guilty plea. Comments by the prosecutor are generally limited to stating the defendant's name and (if the original charge was felony) that the state is moving to reduce the charge. Judicial questioning does not seem to be affected by the extent of prosecution or defense comments.

Observations On Specific Courts

One judge relies almost totally on the "Statement." His questioning prior to accepting a plea is general-ly limited to, "What's your plea?" If a "Statement" has not been handed to the court, the judge will ask if a "Statement" has been filled out. If not, he tells counsel to do so and come back. He generally goes into the facts of the case but not until after the plea has been accepted.

Because the majority of the pleas observed before this judge were entered at arraignment, the defendants were generally informed of the charge and asked by the prosecutor if they understood the nature of the charge prior to the entry of a plea. In addition, the judge usually asks defendants if they have read or have a copy of their rights (meaning the pink sheet entitled "Rights," which is given to each defendant appearing on the district court arraignment calendar). He does not ask if defendants understand those rights.

The judge conducts his court in a very informal manner and is brusque with everyone.

Another *judge* places less reliance on the "Statement." She often does not even require a "Statement" to be submitted until after the plea is accepted. Even then she may require it by saying, "I guess you'd better fill out one of those forms." Judicial questioning prior to accepting a plea is generally limited to "what is your plea to the charge?" and sometimes she does not even ask that question.

The third *judge* is really the only one of the District Court judges observed who conducts a litany at all. This judge relies both on the "Statement" and on defense counsel's representation of their clients.

He requires a "Statement" to be submitted prior to accepting a plea and tries to ascertain whether defendants understand the "Statement." An interesting example of this was his requirement that a defense counsel read everything in the "Statement" to an illiterate defendant before he would accept that defendant's plea. He usually asks defendants if they have read and understood the "Statement," and he also asks if defendants have been fully advised of their rights by counsel.

The knowing/intelligent standard. The knowing/intelligent plea standard has three dimensions to it: (1) the waiver of rights, (2) notification of the charges, and (3) notification of the consequences of the plea. In all six jurisdictions the courts are required by virtue of *Boykin* v. *Alabama,* 395 U.S. 238 (1969), to establish an adequate record showing that the defendant knowingly waived his privilege against self-incrimination; the right to a trial by jury; and the right to confront one's accusers. Only one of the six jurisdictions (Texas) requires the waiver of anything more than the three rights enumerated in *Boykin.* It requires the defendant be notified of his right

[22] In 1976 the five Seattle District Court judges had a total of 35,225 cases (criminal, civil and other) to dispose of among them (State of Washington, 1976:44). In contrast the average number of hearings (preliminary, extraditions, and adjudicatory) for the months of January, March, April, and May 1977 in the Norfolk District Court is 2,712 per month. (Statistics obtained from Courtroom A, Norfolk District Court.)

to be sentenced by a jury (Texas Code of Criminal Procedure, Article 26.14).

Waiver of Rights. Our observations of plea acceptances indicate that in 45 percent of all cases (different types of charges and courts combined) three or more rights were *verbally* mentioned by someone to the defendant (see Table 6.4). The right which is most often mentioned *verbally* in court is the right to trial by jury (70 percent of all cases). The least frequently mentioned of the three rights which constitutionally must be waived is the right to remain silent (37.9 percent).

Table 6.4 Methods of establishing the knowing/intelligent nature of guilty pleas by jurisdiction (June–August 1977)

Method/type of charge	El Paso [N=106]	New Orleans [N=120]	Seattle [N=138]	Tucson [N=110]	Delaware Co. [N=131]	Norfolk [N=106]	Total* [N=711]**
Waiver of rights							
One or more rights mentioned as waived?							
Yes	68.2%	95.8%	46.0%	98.2%	87.8%	67.9%	76.8%
Three or more rights?							
Yes	15.1%	55.0%	29.7%	85.5%	64.1%	16.0%	44.7%
Five or more rights?							
Yes	0.0%	24.2%	8.0%	0.0%	51.1%	0.0%	15.0%
Which rights were verbally specified as being waived?							
Trial by jury	67.9%	94.2%	46.7%	97.3%	67.2%	56.6%	70.0%
Remain silent	12.3%	0.0%	7.2%	0.9%	0.0%	0.0%	37.9%
Confront witnesses	15.1%	50.0%	33.3%	80.9%	64.2%	8.6%	44.4%
Appeal	0.0%	81.8%	37.05%	0.0%	78.6%	60.9%	43.0%
Counsel (at no cost)	10.4%	0.8%	1.4%	40.0%	68.0%	11.3%	22.4%
Who recited rights waived?							
Judge	22.9%	94.1%	30.4%	98.2%	8.5%	66.0%	51.9%
Defense counsel	0.0%	0.0%	12.3%	0.9%	73.6%	0.0%	16.0%
None	30.5%	5.9%	53.6%	0.9%	14.7%	32.1%	23.6%
Other	46.6%	0.0%	3.6%	0.0%	3.1%	1.9%	8.6%
Who asked defendant if he understood rights he was waiving?							
Judge	19.0%	96.7%	56.5%	91.8%	24.8%	65.1%	58.8%
Defense counsel	0.0%	0.0%	0.0%	0.9%	45.7%	0.0%	8.5%
None	47.6%	3.3%	42.0%	7.3%	25.6%	33.0%	26.6%
Other	33.3%	0.0%	1.4%	0.0%	3.9%	0.9%	6.1%
Was it noted that defense counsel had explained the defendant's rights to him?							
Yes	8.6%	95.0%	56.9%	18.2%	91.5%	54.9%	56.3%
Explaining the charges							
Who explained charges?							
Judge with one or more others (prosecutor, defense, clerk)	37.2%	0.0%	0.0%	0.0%	54.1%	0.0%	15.5%
Judge alone, *merely* reads charges	0.0%	28.6%	0.0%	0.0%	0.0%	0.0%	4.8%
Judge alone, *more than mere* reading of charges	52.4%	5.0%	37.0%	66.4%	3.1%	73.6%	37.7%

Continued

120

Table 6.4   Methods of establishing the knowing/intelligent nature of guilty pleas by jurisdiction (June–August, 1977)—Continued

Method/type of charge	El Paso [N = 106]	New Orleans [N = 120]	Seattle [N = 138]	Tucson [N = 110]	Delaware Co. [N = 131]	Norfolk [N = 106]	Total* [N = 711]**
Prosecutor alone	0.0%	0.0%	8.7%	0.0%	30.5%	0.0%	7.3%
Defense counsel	0.0%	0.0%	6.5%	0.0%	8.4%	0.0%	2.8%
Other	7.6%	0.0%	0.0%	0.0%	0.8%	0.0%	1.2%
No one							
Fel. charge	.3%	59.1%	40.0%	15.9%	3.8%	18.7%	26.1%
Misd. charge	2.4%	75.5%	68.4%	63.4%	1.9%	45.2%	36.6%
All cases	2.9%	66.4%	47.8%	33.6%	3.1%	26.4%	36.6%
Who asked if defendant understood the charges?							30.6%
Judge	42.9%	80.7%	36.5%	65.5%	35.4%	63.2%	53.2%
Prosecutor	0.0%	0.0%	9.5%	0.0%	0.0%	0.0%	1.8%
Defense counsel	0.0%	0.0%	2.2%	0.0%	11.5%	0.0%	2.5%
Other	1.0%	0.0%	0.7%	0.0%	7.0%	0.0%	1.5%
No one	56.2%	19.3%	51.1%	34.5%	46.2%	36.8%	40.9%
Was it noted that counsel had explained charges to defendant?							
Yes	10.5%	93.3%	18.7%	9.1%	19.8%	55.8%	34.4%
Explaining the consequences							
Defendant notified of the maximum possible sentence?							
Yes	35.8%	75.8%	56.6%	80.0%	6.1%	39.1%	48.5%
Defendant notified he could be sentenced as habitual offender?							
No	99.0%	91.5%	7.2%	97.3%	99.2%	97.2%	79.3%
Yes	0.0%	8.5%	0.0%	2.7%	1.8%	2.8%	2.4%
Not applicable	1.0%	0.0%	92.8%	0.0%	0.0%	0.0%	18.3%
Any collateral consequences of plea explained?							
No	99.1%	96.7%	100.0%	92.7%	88.1%	100.0%	96.1%

*Percentages that do not total to 100 are due to rounding errors.
**The sizes of the respective N's vary slightly due to item nonresponse.

Again, however, our data are based on what was *said* in court. They do not include what may have appeared on written forms signed by the defendants in connection with the entry of pleas. Thus, defendants may have been notified (in writing) of more of their rights than it appears from our in-court observation data. However, it should also be noted that the use of written forms does not guarantee that all three of the rights that constitutionally must be waived will in fact be covered. Note for example that the "Statement" form used in Washington does not mention the privilege against self-incrimination (see Appendix D). This omission is rarely remedied by the Seattle courts. They verbally mention it in 7 percent of the cases.

As for who recites the rights, it is clear that in all jurisdictions except one the judge is more likely to conduct the recitation, if there is one. (In Delaware defense counsel are relied upon heavily (74 percent)). What is more, in 59 percent of the cases the judge asked the defendant if he understood the rights he was waiving. In addition, in 56.3 percent of the cases it was noted for the record that defense counsel had explained to his client the rights being waived.

Explaining the Charges. With regard to explaining the charges to the defendant, the issue that has been raised in the appellate courts is how detailed an explanation must be given (Bond, 1978). Is a mere notification of the charges enough or must the elements of the crime be explained?

The Supreme Court has specifically declined requiring a complete enumeration of the elements of the offense to which an accused person pleads. Rather it has adopted a "totality of the circumstances" test that permits each case to be judged differently. In the leading case in which the Supreme Court found that the defendant had not been given adequate notice of the charges, the circumstances included a mentally retarded defendant indicted for first degree murder who pleaded guilty to second degree murder and who was not advised by counsel or the court that intent to cause death was an element of second degree murder (*Henderson* v. *Morgan*, 426 U.S. 637 (1976)). The court ruled that "intent is such a critical element of the offense of second-degree murder that notice of [it] is required." Also noteworthy in this case is the court's perception of what typically happens regarding the explanation of charges.

Normally the record contains either an explanation of the charge by the trial judge or at least a representation by defense counsel that the nature of the offense has been explained to the accused. Moreover, even without such an express representation, it may be appropriate to presume that in most cases defense counsel routinely explain the nature of the offense in sufficient detail to give the accused notice of what he is being asked to admit.

We were unable to determine statistically how often defense counsel explain charges to their clients, but our observations provide a more specific and less reassuring view of what "normally" happens regarding the explanation of charges in court. In 31 percent of all cases (and 26 percent of the pleas to felonies) no one in court explained or even read aloud the charges to the defendant. In 41 percent of all cases, no one asked the accused if he understood the charges to which he was pleading; and in 66 percent of all cases no mention was made for the record as to whether counsel explained the charges to his client. Once again there are wide differences among the jurisdictions in each of these respects.

Those differences are not related to differences in law in any consistent way. For instance, the two jurisdictions with the highest rates of not explaining the charges (New Orleans, 66 percent, and Seattle, 48 percent) are also ones with no special legal requirements regarding such explanations. On the other hand two of the jurisdictions with the lowest rates of not explaining charges (Delaware County, 3 percent, and Tucson, 16 percent—for felonies) are ones where such explanations are required. Arizona requires that the defendant be advised of the nature of the charge (Arizona Rules of Criminal Procedures 17.2(a)), but the nature of the explanation is permitted to vary from case to case (*State v. Duran*, 562 P.2d 487 (1973)). As long as the defendant understands

what acts are necessary to commit the crime, it appears that Arizona Rule 17.2(a) will be satisfied.

In contrast, Pennsylvania's requirements are more rigorous. The defendant must understand every element of the offense. This understanding must be established through an on-the-record colloquy in which the basic legal elements of the crime(s) charged must be outlined in terms understandable to the defendant (*Commonwealth* v. *Ingram*, 455 Pa. 198, 316 A.2d 77 (1974)). Merely reading the charges and asking the defendant if he understands them does not meet the requirement (*Commonwealth* v. *Minor*, 467 Pa. 230, 356 A.2d (1976)).

If only New Orleans, Delaware County, and Tucson were involved in this analysis it would appear that the data established a relationship between the law on the books and the law in action, that is, that charges were more likely to be explained where the law required that they be explained. But when the remaining two jurisdictions are added to the analysis the relationship becomes unclear.

Virginia and Texas do not have special requirements regarding explanation of the charges and yet their courts have rates of explaining charges comparable to Arizona and Pennsylvania where such explanations are required. Thus, while the existence of state requirements beyond Federal constitutional requirements does increase concern for this issue, the absence of such requirements does not mean a concomitant lowering of concern.

It is worth noting the difference between what was done in explaining the *charges* compared to how the *rights* were explained. With regard to charges it was noted for the record that counsel had explained the charges in only 34 percent of all cases. Yet for the rights this notation was more likely to be made both for all jurisdictions combined (56 percent) as well as within each separate jurisdiction. This suggests that greater care is taken in assuring the explanation of rights than of charges. Perhaps this reflects the difference between *Boykin*'s requirement that specific rights be enumerated and the more vague, open-ended requirements of the "totality of the circumstances" test of *Henderson* v. *Morgan*.

Explaining the Consequences. The last component of the intelligent/knowing plea standard is the determination of whether the defendant understands the consequences of his plea. Again, the appellate courts have not made it clear what consequences must be explained (Bond, 1978). In three jurisdictions studied the defendant must be advised of one or another aspect of the possible sen-

Table 6.5 Method of establishing the voluntary nature of the plea and the existence of a plea agreement by jurisdiction (June–August 1977)

Method	El Paso [N=106]	New Orleans [N=120]	Seattle [N=138]	Tucson [N=110]	Delaware Co. [N=131]	Norfolk [N=106]	Total* [N=711]**
Who asked if defendant was threatened, coerced, or pressured to plead guilty?							
Judge	21.4%	93.3%	31.9%	77.3%	6.9%	50.0%	45.8%
Defense counsel	0.0%	0.0%	0.0%	0.0%	48.1%	0.0%	8.9%
Other	0.0%	0.0%	0.7%	0.0%	2.3%	0.0%	0.5%
No one	78.6%	6.7%	67.4%	22.7%	42.7%	50.0%	44.7%
Who asked if promises other than plea agreement were made?							
Judge	19.8%	17.5%	24.6%	73.6%	5.3%	7.5%	24.2%
Defense counsel	0.0%	0.0%	1.4%	0.0%	41.2%	0.0%	7.9%
Other	0.0%	0.0%	0.7%	0.0%	0.0%	0.9%	0.1%
No one	80.2%	82.5%	73.2%	26.4%	53.4%	91.5%	67.7%
If plea agreement reached, what record made?							
Only that an agreement (unspecified) had been reached	0.0%	5.8%	0.7%	0.0%	3.8%	3.8%	2.5%
Specific terms of agreement	0.0%	43.3%	98.6%	100.0%	96.2%	53.8%	71.4%
No record made	0.0%	50.0%	0.0%	0.0%	0.0%	0.0%	10.3%
Unknown if agreement reached	86.8%	0.8%	0.7%	0.0%	0.0%	2.8%	9.5%
Other	13.3%	0.0%	0.0%	0.0%	0.0%	31.1%	5.1%

*Percentages that do not total to 100 are due to rounding errors.
**The sizes of the respective N's vary slightly due to item nonresponse.

tence he could receive.[23] In the other three states there is either no rule (Virginia); or it is recommended that the defendant be advised of the range of possible sentence but it is not absolutely required that the defendant be notified of the maximum sentence (Pennsylvania, *Commonwealth* v. *McNeil*, 305 A.2d 51, 54 (173)); or, it is assumed that defense counsel will advise the defendant of the consequences and therefore the court must do so only in cases of uncounselled defendants (Louisiana Code of Criminal Procedure, Article 556).

Notwithstanding these differences in legal requirements, however, the forms and standardized procedures used by the felony courts in the six jurisdictions all include some specification of the possible sentence—usually the maxi-

mum possible (see Appendixes D through H). In addition in 48 percent of all cases, defendants were advised in court of the maximum possible sentence. But defendants were rarely (2 percent) told about the possibility of being sentenced as a habitual offender and rarely (4 percent) told of any collateral consequences of the plea. The jurisdictions varied widely on the notification of maximum possible sentence and again this variation does not show any consistent relationship to differences in law among them.

The voluntary standard. As noted earlier, the concept of voluntariness is exceedingly ambiguous. In defining it as a standard in plea taking, the courts often confuse it with what would be more accurately classified as violations of the knowing standard. Thus, for example, in Arizona if a defendant has been advised of his rights and the consequences of his plea and states that he still wishes to plead guilty, then it is presumed he is pleading voluntarily. Hence, to the extent that voluntariness is established by a showing that the plea was knowing/intelligent, our

[23] Texas, Code of Criminal Procedure Art. 26.13(a) "the range of punishment"; Washington, the maximum sentence (In re Vensel, 564 P.2d 326) and any mandatory minimum sentence (Wood v. Morris, 554 P.2d 1032 (1976); Arizona, Rules of Criminal Procedure 17.2(b) "the nature and range of possible sentence. . . . including special conditions regarding sentence, parole, or commutation imposed by statute."

findings presented above regarding the knowing standard are applicable as well to the voluntary standard.

Beyond this there is the matter of whether pleas are involuntary in the sense of being the result of threats, pressures, or promises. The confusion here is that many kinds of pressures, threats and promises—some with severe consequences—are a regular part of the plea bargaining system and are *not* regarded by the courts as per se grounds for declaring pleas involuntary. A prosecutor's promise to dismiss charges and recommend a sentence in exchange for a guilty plea does not make the plea involuntary (*Shelton* v. *United States*, 356 U.S. 26 (1958)); nor are pleas presumed to be involuntary even if they are induced by the hope of avoiding the use of a coerced confession (*McMann* v. *Richardson*, 397 U.S. 759 (1979)); nor because the prosecutor threatened to invoke a habitual offender statute (*Bordenkircher* v. *Hayes*, 343 U.S. 357 (1978)). Rather the courts have adopted a "totality of the circumstances" rule which requires each case to be examined individually. This, of course, leaves the situation without clear guidance. In the six jurisdictions trial judges are given no further guidance by their respective state laws (excluding the required questions related primarily to whether the plea was knowingly entered).

In the absence of specific direction judges sometimes include one or more questions in their plea taking procedures. In 55 percent of all cases observed the defendant was asked (usually by the judge) if he had been threatened, coerced, or pressured to plead guilty (see Table 6.5). This question, of course, can be confusing to the defendant who is pleading in exchange for some promised deal. It is remarkable that it (as distinct from the second question on Table 6.5) continues to be asked with any frequency. Unless accompanied by other questions it perpetuates the old hypocrisy of denying that the plea of guilty was induced by the plea agreement. The more accurate phraseology would be to ask whether any promises, threats, or pressures *other than* the plea agreement have been made. This was asked in only 32 percent of all cases. (Where this question is used the attorneys felt relieved because they think of this as having eliminated the old hypocrisy.) Where plea agreements were reached, the specific terms of the agreement were usually (71 percent of all cases) read into the record.[24]

In Delaware County an interesting custom has developed that contributes to the appearance, if not the reality, that the plea is voluntary. When it comes to that point in the colloquy where defendants are asked if they are pleading guilty because they are guilty, defense counsel often step back away from the table. The defendant is left there standing alone to admit his guilt. This is especially likely to be done if the defendant "chokes" (is initially unwilling to say he did it).

Accurate pleas: the factual basis standard

Ambiguity of meaning and purpose. Three serious institutional weaknesses of plea bargaining compared to trial as a method of determining guilt are: (1) plea bargaining relies on inducements; (2) in plea bargaining the available evidence may not be assessed against any standard of proof, much less the hallowed legal standard of proof beyond a reasonable doubt; and (3) in plea bargaining the available evidence may not be assessed by an independent, impartial third party. For any or all of these reasons plea bargaining is regarded as posing a threat of convicting the innocent.[25] A fourth weakness of plea bargaining is that it often destroys the integrity of the criminal justice record system by allowing defendants to appear to be convicted of crimes different from the ones they actually committed.

The efficacy of using plea acceptance standards to offset these four weaknesses in the plea bargaining system differs. Eliminating inducements is not possible without eliminating plea bargaining as such. Hence, the courts have allowed inducements to continue and have relied on the standards relating to the knowing and "voluntary" nature of pleas to offset this inherent weakness of plea bargaining. As for the other three weaknesses, reformers have tried to minimize the danger they pose by requiring that a factual basis for pleas be established. Whether this "accuracy" standard represents a safeguard adequate to such a critical task; whether it assures that persons will not be wrongly convicted;[26] and whether it means that evidence will be tested against some standard of proof similar to the trial standards of either a prima facie case or proof beyond a reasonable doubt is problematic. The difficulty with the accuracy standard is its ambiguity both as to meaning and purpose. The evidentiary standards to be used in determining whether a factual basis exists are unclear; the scope of the inquiry and the methods to be used are ill-defined; and the action to

---

[24] Where written forms are used but not read into the record in court, they would become part of the record but would be coded in our observation as "no record verbally made."

[25] See generally, Washington University Law Quarterly, 1966; Alschuler, 1976; Kipnis, 1976.

[26] This latter point is not explicitly made but is implied.

be taken by the judge if it appears that a factual basis does not exist is ambiguous (see generally, Bond, 1978:81).

When the accuracy standard was added to F.R.C.P. Rule 11 in 1966, no probability-of-guilt standard was specified; and the 1974 revision also omitted any such standard. The 1968 ABA standards required a factual basis for pleas but gave no probability-of-guilt standard to be used; nor was one given in the 1980 revised ABA standards. However, two other national groups have specified that certain evidentiary standards be met. The American Law Institute (ALI) (1975:350.4(3)) recommended that pleas not be accepted unless reasonable cause exists. The National Advisory Commission (NAC) went further and recommended that a plea not be accepted if the "admissible evidence is insufficient to support a guilty verdict on the offense" for which the plea is offered, or a related greater offense (1973 c:3.7(8)). This is a higher standard than probable (or reasonable) cause because it requires that the proof be established on *admissible* evidence. Thus hearsay testimony and illegally obtained evidence would be excluded from establishing the factual basis. If this standard were used and if judges were required to reject guilty pleas whose factual basis could not be established, then plea bargaining would have one of its major weaknesses significantly minimized.

In considering evidentiary standards that might be incorporated into the accuracy standard it should be recognized that there is a tension between the "efficiency" of plea bargaining and high evidentiary standards of proof. The reason many cases are plea bargained is precisely that they are weak. The higher one sets the evidentiary standard for acceptable pleas, the more of these pleas are going to be unacceptable. Higher rates of plea rejections would necessitate other adjustments in the system. Either cases would have to be made stronger or more would have to be rejected at screening, dismissed, or set for trial. Thus, the policy choice is between two broad alternatives. If evidentiary standards are set low, plea bargaining will continue to have high "efficiency" (dispose of large caseloads of even poorly prepared cases) but it will also continue to represent a wide departure from the traditional legal protections built into the trial system. If evidentiary standards are set high, plea bargaining will become a closer approximation of the trial system. Innocent defendants will be less likely to be wrongly convicted. But, plea bargaining will no longer be able to serve as the great laundering machine it often is. Shoddy investigation and prosecution practices will no longer come out in the wash. They will either have to be improved, or more cases will have to be rejected or dismissed.[27]

Adding to the confusion as to what shall be regarded as an "accurate" plea are the views of appellate courts concerning several common practices which are deemed beneficial to defendants and, hence, not necessarily in their interest to prohibit. Some pleas are to offenses that were not actually committed but which carry lesser sentences (e.g., pleas to daytime rather than nighttime burglary). Some pleas are to offenses which are either not proven by the facts or do not even exist. Sometimes defendants plead guilty but maintain that they are innocent and are only pleading because it is in their best interest to do so. For each of these situations some appellate courts have ruled that the pleas entered were acceptable (see generally, Bond, 1981:159). Thus, the meaning and purpose of the accuracy standard has been clouded.

One court clarified the standard as follows: ". . . the purpose of the factual basis requirement is to ensure accuracy of the plea, that is, to ensure that the defendant is guilty of a crime at least as serious as that to which he is entering his plea" (*Beaman* v. *State,* 221 N.W. 2d 698, 700 (Minn. 1974)). Under this interpretation of the "accuracy" standard (one with which the NAC's standard quoted above concurs) pleas to inaccurate facts and charges are "accurate" so long as the facts show that some crime of equal or greater seriousness was committed by the defendant. Thus the "accuracy" standard is not to ensure "accuracy" in the literal sense. It is not to guarantee the integrity of criminal justice records so that future users of them will be able to determine accurately what the real crime was. Its purpose (under this interpretation) is to safeguard against two possibilities: convicting completely innocent persons and convicting guilty persons of crimes more serious than the ones they actually committed (e.g., a burglary rather than an attempted burglary).

Beyond evidentiary standards and the meaning of "accuracy," there is the question of how a factual basis should be established. Again there is a tradeoff between efficiency and protection against false conviction. Plea bargaining can be made to more closely approximate a trial disposition by requiring that the factual basis be established in ways approximating a trial procedure, such as requiring that evidence and witnesses be produced in court and testimony be taken as to what could be proven if the case went to trial. One might expect such a procedure to provide courts with a better opportunity to assess case

---

[27] We assume trial capacity could not be expanded to accommodate the additional volume of cases.

strength than less demanding procedures (such as asking defendants if they are pleading guilty because they are in fact guilty). But the former procedure would obviously be less efficient than the latter.

The legal standard in six jurisdictions. Unlike the knowing and voluntary standards, the accuracy standard was not explicitly imposed upon the states by *Boykin* v. *Alabama*, 395 U.S. 238 (1969). Previous studies have reported that very few state court judges inquire into the factual basis for pleas (Washington University Law Quarterly, 1966) and that only a few states require detailed inquiries into the factual basis for pleas (Bond, 1981: 159). However, of the six states included in this study, three (Texas, Arizona, and Pennsylvania) [28] require a factual basis for pleas. Washington seems to require it by virtue of the fact that on the plea-acceptance form that must be used in Washington there is a section where the defendant is to state the facts that led to his being charged (see Appendix D). But case law indicates that the factual basis requirement is recommended but not required (*State* v. *Newton*, 87 Wm. 2d at 369, 552 P.2d at 686). Louisiana has no law on point—which is reflected in the fact that five of the seven versions of the plea-taking forms developed by the local judges in New Orleans do not address this issue (see Appendix H). Virginia does not require courts to establish a factual basis for a plea,[29] but the Virginia Supreme Court suggests that the judges ask defendants, "Are you entering the plea of guilty because you are, in fact, guilty of the crime charged?" [30]

By examining the nature of the proof needed to meet the factual basis standard in the states that require or recommend it, the minimal nature of the protection afforded by this standard becomes apparent. The key to the trial system's protection of liberty is its requirement that evidence in criminal cases meet certain legal tests of reliability, legality and persuasiveness. At the core of the notion of "legal innocence" is *not* whether the accused committed the prohibited act but whether a jury presented with the lawfully obtained, admissible evidence would conclude beyond a reasonable doubt that the defendant was guilty. A substantial approximation of this feature of the trial system would require that evidence used to establish the factual basis be credible; be assessed by an independent third party; and, at least, meet the minimum standard of probable cause, if not a higher standard.

None of the six states studied has used the factual basis standard to achieve such an approximation. None has adopted the high evidentiary standard recommended by the NAC nor for that matter have they even addressed the question of evidentiary standards in familiar legal phrases such as "probable cause" or a "prima facie" case.[31] Rather they have spoken in the ambiguous and undefined language of "sufficient evidence" (Texas Code of Criminal Procedure, Article 1.15; Washington, *State* v. *Newton*, 87 Wm. 2d 363, 372, 1552 p.2d 682, 685 (1976)) or evidence that "negates guilt" (*Commonwealth* v. *Roundtree*, 440 Pa. 199, 202, 269 A.2d 709, 711 (1970)).

The states allow the factual basis to be established by a wide variety of means including police reports, affidavits of witnesses, statements of defendants, and other evidence. For instance, an Arizona court ruled that a factual basis was established by a presentence report which the defendant said was "pretty accurate" (*State* v. *Murib*, 116 Ariz. 441, 569 P.2d 1339 (1977)). The states do not require that the defendant participate except in Texas where his consent must be obtained to use evidence introduced by stipulation (Texas Code of Criminal Procedure, Article 1.15). There is no requirement that the information used be reliable except in Washington (where oddly enough a factual basis, itself, is not required) (Washington, *State* v. *Newton*, 552 P.2d 682 (1976)). There is no requirement that the facts established accurately reflect the crime charged or the crime to which the plea is made (except in the latter case for Arizona (*State* v. *McGee*, 551 P.2d 568 (1976); nor is it required that a factual basis be established for each element of the offense except in Arizona (*State* v. *Davis*, 112 Ariz. 140, 142, 539 P.2d 897 (1975)).

Remarkably, Virginia had what appeared to reformers to be "the greatest protection to defendants pleading guilty" (Washington University Law Quarterly, 1966:311). Virginia required a trial by a constitutional provision (Virginia Constitution Article 1, § 8) which was self-executing and could not be waived by the accused. Thus, Virginia's plea bargaining system seemed to closely resemble the trial process in that pleas could not be accepted without sufficient evidence of guilt being presented to a judge. In practice this provision was followed literally by local justice officials. When felony pleas were taken a witness (usually the principal police officer in the case) would give sworn testimony as to

---

[28] Texas Code of Criminal Procedure, Article 1.15; Arizona Rules of Criminal Procedure Rule 17.3; and Pa., Commonwealth v. Maddox, 450 Pa. 406, 409, 300 A.2d 503, 505 (1973).

[29] Kibert v. Commonwealth, 216 Va. 660, 222 S.E.2d 790 (1976).

[30] See Appendix F.

[31] In most felony cases, by the time a guilty plea is entered a determination that probable cause exists has been made either by a judge at a preliminary hearing or by a grand jury. Thus in such cases at least a threshold level of legal proof has been established even before the factual basis standard is met.

what the state would have proven. [32] However, in 1976 the Virginia Supreme Court transformed this provision from one of the nation's strongest to one of the weakest requirements for a factual basis. The case involved a defendant who pleaded guilty to first degree murder. The Commonwealth had evidence sufficient to support only second degree murder. Citing Article 8 of the Virginia Constitution as well as Section 19–1166 of the Virginia Code (which provides that the court will "try" a case if the accused pleads guilty), the defendant argued there had been insufficient evidence to convict. But the court held that these laws only require that a judge will *preside* in the event that the accused pleads guilty. They do not imply that evidence will be presented or that the case will be "tried." It explained that a voluntary and intelligent guilty plea is a self-supplied conviction which operates as a waiver of all defenses (other than jurisdictional defects). Included in the waiver is the potential defense of lack of evidence or insufficiency of evidence (*Kibert v. Commonwealth*, 216 Va. 6609, 222 S.E.2d 790 (1976)). This decision did not radically change the procedures

for accepting pleas in Norfolk, however, as will be shown below.

The practice in six jurisdictions. The ways in which the factual basis for pleas are established in the six jurisdictions were determined both through interviews and observations. The interviews with judges indicate that no one method is used by a majority of the judges, and substantial variations exist both between and within jurisdictions (see Table 6.6).

The most common method judges (40 percent) said they use is simply to ask the defendant if he committed the offense. In jurisdictions with plea-taking forms with a place for statements by the defendants, some judges said they have the defendant read the statement and tell whether it is true. This is preferred to having the defendant state the facts orally because it avoids the possibility of a discrepancy between the written and the oral statements. Such discrepancies require additional time to resolve and can necessitate rejecting the plea or can lead to reversal on appeal. Other methods used by judges include asking additional questions about the offense (such as what the defendant was thinking); and requiring the state to show some evidence (e.g., the drug analysis) or to produce one witness (e.g., the police officer in the case). But none of these were used by substantial numbers of judges.

---

[32] The existence of this procedure was a major factor in our choice of Norfolk as a study site. We also felt that this procedure may represent a model compromise between plea bargaining and trial. But after observing it in practice, we were less impressed as explained below.

Table 6.6 Methods judges report they use to establish factual bases for pleas by jurisdiction (June–August 1977)

[In percentages]

Methods	El Paso [N=9]	New Orleans [N=11]	Seattle [N=23]	Tucson [N=28]	Delaware County [N=9]	Norfolk [N=8]	Total [N=88]
Asks defendant if he committed the offense							
Yes	33	82	22	50	67	13	40
Asks additional questions about offense							
Yes	33	0	22	36	0	0	20
Requires DA to produce evidence							
Yes	33	9	9	21	0	38	17
Requires DA to produce one witness							
Yes	0	0	4	4	22	25	7
Other							
Yes	0	9	43	0	11	25	15

Our in-court observations generally parallel the interview findings (see Table 6.7). The most common method used (59 percent) was that someone (usually the judge) asked the defendant if he were pleading guilty because he was in fact guilty. But again, there is considerable variation among the jurisdictions. Additionally, in 48 percent of the cases the prosecutor either showed or reported evidence. The variation among the jurisdictions here is interesting. In Texas and Pennsylvania, which require a factual basis and that some evidence be introduced, the rates of introducing evidence are highest. In Arizona, which requires a factual basis but allows it to be established by any part of the record, the rate is lowest. In Virginia, where the formerly high factual basis standard has been emasculated, the former practice of entering some evidence and even having a state witness available continues to operate.

Equivocal ("Alford") pleas. When it came to the matter of "equivocal" pleas (i.e., defendants pleading guilty but continuing to assert their innocence), judges were evenly split. Although such pleas are constitutionally acceptable (*North Carolina v. Alford,* 400 U.S. 25 (1970)), only half the judges said they permit them in their courts—al-

though this position varied among jurisdictions (El Paso, 0 percent; New Orleans, 100 percent; Seattle, 78 percent; Tucson, 44 percent; Delaware County, 9 percent; Norfolk, 83 percent). Judges who refused to accept "Alford" pleas said they distrusted them and worried about the lack of finality. Most of them would agree with the view of the Pennsylvania court which wrote: "Defendant should not be permitted to plead guilty from one side of his mouth and not guilty from the other" (*Commonwealth* v. *Roundtree,* 440 Pa. 199, 202, 269 A.2d 709, 711 (1970)). Our in-court observations indicate that defendants rarely (2 percent) maintain their innocence—although again there are substantial differences among the jurisdictions in this respect (see Table 6.7).

Effectiveness of the plea-taking procedures. Measuring the effectiveness of the plea acceptance procedures can not be done in any simple, unequivocal way. Given the ambiguity of the standards, the differing purposes behind them, and the difficulty of getting valid measures of what defendants actually perceived and believed when they were entering their pleas, it is impossible to obtain anything more than partial and indirect measures.

Table 6.7 Methods of establishing the factual bases for guilty pleas by jurisdiction (June–August 1977)

Method	El Paso [N=106]	New Orleans [N=120]	Seattle [N=138]	Tucson [N=110]	Delaware Co. [N=131]	Norfolk [N=106]	Total* [N=711]**
Who asked if defendant pleading guilty because he was in fact guilty?							
Judge	41.3%	72.5%	47.1%	70.9%	26.9%	53.8%	51.6%
Defense counsel	0.0%	0.0%	2.2%	0.0%	28.5%	0.0%	5.6%
Judge and defense counsel	0.0%	0.0%	0.0%	0.0%	10.0%	0.0%	1.8%
No one	58.7%	27.5%	50.7%	29.1%	34.6%	46.2%	41.0%
Who asked additional questions establishing a factual basis for the plea?							
Judge	42.9%	5.8%	14.6%	75.5%	44.5%	9.4%	31.4%
Defense counsel alone or with judge	0.0%	0.0%	0.0%	0.0%	2.4%	0.0%	0.4%
Judge and court clerk	33.3%	0.0%	0.0%	0.0%	0.0%	0.0%	5.0%
No one	23.8%	94.2%	85.4%	24.5%	53.1%	90.6%	63.6%
Did the prosecutor show or report some evidence?							
Yes	100.0%	19.2%	7.2%	5.5%	96.2%	66.0%	48.0%
Did the state have available at least one witness (sworn or unsworn)?							
Yes	0.0%	2.5%	0.0%	0.0%	13.8%	66.0%	12.8%
Did defendant maintain innocence?							
Yes	0.9%	2.5%	5.8%	0.9%	0.8%	0.0%	2.0%

*Percentages that do not total to 100 are due to rounding errors.
**The sizes of the respective N's vary slightly due to item nonresponse.

Plea rejection rates. One indicator that might be assumed to measure effectiveness is the rate at which pleas are rejected. After all it is through the power to reject pleas that the judge ultimately controls the plea process. If judges were to use that power as the most progressive reformers would have them use it, they would reject pleas whenever the prosecution had "overcharged" or had given away too much or too little or other community interests were not properly served by the disposition. Given the frequency with which "overcharging" and inappropriate plea bargains are alleged to occur, one would anticipate a high rate of rejection from judges who were following such a progressive course. But even if judges were adhering to the minimum requirements imposed by law, one might still expect a substantial rate of plea rejection—assuming that there must be many defendants who either are not able to make a knowing plea, or who have been coerced by improper threats or promises, or for whom there is no adequate factual basis.

In any case, it is initially surprising to find that the actual plea rejection rate was as low as 2 percent overall for all six jurisdictions, with a range from 0 percent in Norfolk to 5 percent in Delaware County. However, this finding cannot be taken to mean that judicial supervision of the plea process has failed. Rejection rates are ambiguous when used either as absolute or comparative measures of the effectiveness of the plea-taking process. Using the rejection rate as a comparative measure, the lack of substantial differences among the six jurisdictions on this measure suggests that the differences in law and practice among them make little difference in the bottom line of plea taking, namely, whether the plea is found acceptable. But, on the other hand, it could be argued that differences in the quality of the plea-taking practices do make a difference. The fact that the highest rate of rejection occurred in the jurisdiction with the longest average time for taking pleas (Delaware County) suggests that differences in the "quality" of the procedures (at least as indicated by length of time consumed) do indeed make a difference in the probability of plea acceptance.

Although both interpretations are supportable, we believe the latter is the more accurate.

As an absolute measure, the 2 percent rejection rate suggests that the tightening of the plea-taking procedures over the last two decades has not met certain goals of some of the reformers. Those who had hoped that the new plea-taking procedures would insert into the guilty plea process a test of evidentiary strength approximating what would occur at trial must conclude that they have not. The 2 percent plea rejection rate does not begin to compare with the 22 percent acquittal rate at bench trials in our sample of robbery and burglary cases from our six jurisdictions or the 16 percent to 48 percent acquittal rates at bench trials for all felonies in the four jurisdictions studied by Brosi (1979:49). Also, those who had hoped that judicial supervision would constitute a check on "overcharging" by prosecution must conclude that it has failed in this regard as well. In five of our six jurisdictions there were still complaints about "overcharging."

As for whether the community's interests in proper sentencing is being safeguarded, the meaning of the 2 percent rejection rate is less clear. It suggests that at least in the minds of the judges that interest is being protected. The majority of judges told us they would reject pleas that they thought were inappropriate. But it is difficult to see how some judges make this determination because they do not use presentence reports or take other steps to independently check the appropriateness of the sentence recommended by the prosecutor.

As for the knowing and voluntary criteria of plea acceptability the 2 percent rejection rate seems to indicate that as far as the judges bothered to determine, most pleas meet these criteria. However, defendants may not really understand and may be subject to threats or promises that do not get reported in court. Pleas may be entered that meet the legal requirements but in reality are not knowing or voluntary. In short, the rejection rate only measures whether the procedure was followed, not whether the reality that the procedure was intended to assure in fact occurred.

Table 6.8   The knowing and voluntary standards from the defendant's perspective by jurisdiction*

(June–August 1977)

Standard/Query	Texas		New Orleans		Tucson		Delaware Co.		Virginia		Total	
	%	[N]	%	[N]	%	[N]	%	[N]	%	[N]	%	[N]
The knowing standard												
"When you actually pleaded guilty in court did you understand the questions you were asked about the nature of your plea and the rights you gave up?"												
Yes	62		71		75		100		91		80	
Not sure; understood somewhat	0		29		10		0		0		7	
No	38	(8)	0	(7)	15	(20)	0	(9)	9	(11)	13	(55)
Did your attorney advise you how to answer these questions?												
Yes	33	(9)	57	(7)	70	(20)	29	(7)	45	(11)	52	(54)
Did anyone tell you the maximum you could have been sentenced to?												
Yes	67	(9)	100	(9)	95	(20)	89	(9)	100	(11)	91	(58)
Did the judge tell you the maximum sentence?												
Yes	0	(6)	**		26	(19)	89	(9)	70	(10)	45	(44)
Did your attorney tell you the maximum sentence?												
Yes	83	(6)	**		74	(19)	89	(9)	80	(10)	79	(44)
The voluntary standard												
Did you feel you had to accept the plea bargain?												
Yes	**		0		78		89		82		77	
No	**		100	(2)	22	(18)	11	(9)	12	(11)	23	(40)

*Interviews were not done at all in Seattle. Interviews were not done in the local jails at El Paso and Norfolk but rather in state facilities; and most of the defendants interviewed were not from El Paso and Norfolk.
**Data not available.

Finally, any use of rejection rates as an indicator of the effectiveness of plea-taking must recognize the powerful incentive among judges to keep rejection rates very low. Substantial numbers of rejections would add to the trial docket. Judges are just as concerned, if not more so, as prosecutors in moving the docket. Such an incentive can cause legal standards to be adjusted in practice so that reality is *found* acceptable rather than being *made* acceptable. Reformers must realize that in asking judges to regulate plea bargaining they are not getting a completely disinterested party. Careful and continual scrutiny by appellate courts of the plea-taking practices of trial courts may be necessary to prevent the pressures of the trial docket from reducing plea-taking procedures into mere legal formalities.

The defendants' perspective. In order to get at the reality behind the plea-taking procedures, we asked defendants who had pleaded guilty to tell us about their decision to plead; why they did it; and what occurred at the plea-taking. The samples are small and nonrandom, so their responses can not be generalized to any known population of defendants. Nonetheless, they are instructive. They suggest that while defendants pleading guilty today get a few extra minutes in court, their pleas are not necessarily knowing; not all the promises made are being fulfilled; factually innocent defendants caught up in cases with circumstantial evidence may be just as likely to be convicted as before; and defendants continue to perceive their decisions to plead as "involuntary" (in the layman's sense).

The majority of the defendants indicated that their pleas were "intelligent" in certain respects. Almost all (90 percent) said they were told by someone—usually their attorney (79 percent)—what the maximum sentence could be (see Table 6.8). Most (80 percent) said they understood the rights they had waived and what the charges were. Several added credibility to their responses by reciting for us parts of the plea-taking litany almost verbatim. These findings, of course, are encouraging. But a substantial minority (20 percent) indicated they did not understand either some or all of what was said. Their limited understanding as well as the difficulty faced by the courts in achieving real understanding with certain defendants are indicated below by selected defendant responses to our questions about whether they understood what was said to them during the taking of their pleas.

Tucson: Defendant #14
A: "I . . . was scared and didn't really understand what was going on."

Tucson: Defendant #1
[Defendant] said he understood rights and such but the judge used a lot of big words that he didn't understand.

Virginia: Defendant #1
A: "On one they had to go get a book and show me because I didn't know what they were talking about."

Virginia: Defendant #6
A: "I understood the sentence part. I was thinking more about the sentence than what the judge said. No one told me the judge did not have to go along."

New Orleans: Defendant #10
Q: Okay. when you pled guilty do you remember the judge asking you some questions? Do you remember him telling you some things?
A: I know, un, some kind of thing about we're not making you plead guilty—
Q: Yeah—Do you remember all that?
A: I can't remember all of it.
Q: But did you understand what he was telling you?
A: I think so.
Q: Okay. Did he ask you if you were pleading guilty because you were guilty?
A: I don't know him asking that.

Q: He didn't ask you whether you were guilty at all? No? Why didn't you tell him that you weren't really guilty?
A: You see what really happened, you see, when I pleaded guilty, they brought me a piece of paper, like a little cop-out paper, and I had to sign my name.
Q: Did you read the cop-out paper?
A: Yes, sir.
Q: Did you understand what was on the paper?
A: I think so.
Q: When you did plead guilty and the judge read some rights to you, uh, did the judge ask you if you were pleading guilty because you were, in fact, guilty? Do you remember that?
A: He asked me if I understood, he asked me if I was forced to plead guilty and everything, yeah—
Q: Did—did he ask you if you were guilty?
A: No—he really didn't actually come out and say, "guilty," or, "Are you guilty." He asked do I understand the paper that I signed and all this, yeah.
Q: On the paper, did it ask whether you were pleading guilty because you were in fact guilty?
A: I can't, I can't read that well—understood before I did it.
Q: Did you read it or did your attorney read it to you?
A: I read, uh, what I could understand, yeah. He told us to read it.
Q: Okay.
A: The court, whatever you call it, told us to read it, uh, and then if we go along with it, well, from what I understood it seemed like, you know, a fair shake. And if you can't, don't read that good—I ain't got but six grade experience—

New Orleans: Defendant #3
Q: Do you remember any of the questions that he asked you when you were pleading?
A: No, not really. At the time I was under the influence of narcotics, you know—
Q: At the time you pled you were under narcotics?
A: Yeah, well, I was, I was a junkie at the time and I was loaded and—
Q: You hadn't dried out in the back while you were waiting in jail—
A: No. I made bond.

Texas: Defendant #5
Researcher's note: On probing I learned the defendant did *not* really feel he *could* plead not guilty. Although I had trouble with his broken English and

he had trouble with my Spanish, it seems as if he was convinced he had no right to plead not guilty.

While pleas today appear to be more likely to be "intelligent" they have not lost their coercive character. The majority (77 percent) of the defendants said they felt they had to accept the plea bargain (see Table 6.8). The sense of coercion is conveyed by some of their responses to our questions about whether they felt they had to accept the plea offer.

Virginia: Defendant #7
"I didn't think I had any choice. I didn't see my lawyer but one time before trial."

Virginia: Defendant #5
"My lawyer insisted that I plead guilty. I tried to argue with him."

Virginia: Defendant #10
"The police forced me into it. They threatened me with more charges."

Tucson: Defendant #15
Defendant felt pressured to take reduced sentence because she was pregnant.

Delaware County: Defendant #2
"My parents wanted me to. My mother was crying. I was too young to take a chance on 20 years."

Delaware County: Defendant #15
"I didn't know much at the time. I was under an emotional strain.
"I figured the guy was a lawyer, he knows what he's doing."

Delaware County: Defendant #9
"The judge told me in front of the jury if I didn't plead guilty, I'd get knocked out of the box.

New Orleans: Defendant #7
Q: What do you think would have happened had you gone to trial on your case?
A: Well, by me being a, uh, colored light—if I had gotten myself fighting and lose, might have even got the whole thing—so now————

Q: Did the attorney tell you that or did you just think that?
A: No. But I thought this all along.

None of the defendants who said they felt they had to accept the plea agreement reported inducements which courts would regard as per se unlawful, namely threats of physical violence. Almost all pleaded for virtually the same reason, namely, to avoid the possibility of a harsh-

er sentence if they went to trial.[33] Some complained about broken promises by the police. In Virginia (where the plea agreement must be set forth in writing) these promises by the police are apparently either not included on the written agreement or ignored by the courts—assuming the following reports by defendants are accurate:

Virginia: Defendant #10
"The police told me that if I plead guilty they would help me out in court but they didn't."

Virginia: defendant #4
"The police told me to cooperate and they would help me. I then made a statement. I thought they would help me at the presentence hearing but they didn't."

In the only jurisdiction where the question was asked, 2 of 10 defendants maintained they were innocent but had pleaded guilty anyhow. Both cases involved fact patterns—as told by the defendants—which make it difficult to know whether the defendants actually committed the crimes or not. One is worth reporting in detail because it not only illustrates the difficulty for the plea-taking standards to separate the guilty from the innocent in circumstances where a factual basis exists, but it also shows the coercion and deceptiveness that continue to characterize the guilty plea process.

New Orleans: Defendant #6
Q: Tell me briefly what happened. . . .
A: [T]here was three of us when they caught us but two of us didn't have anything to do with it, you know. But I went ahead and pleaded guilty and the others doing it pleaded guilty because they would have found us guilty. We would have got 6 months. That would have been as a maximum, but still, 6 months plus a $500 fine, you know.

Q: Well, on the simple robbery charge you could have gotten a lot more than 6 months.
A: You see, you see, what we're saying is before you pleaded guilty they had done dropped it down.

Q: I see. Did the third guy, did he do it?
A: Right. The one doing it, he pleaded guilty to it, admitted he did it, and he admitted we didn't have anything to do with it.

Q: Were you with him at the time?
A: Not when he did it, no sir. We was with him— he had done, you see, he snatched a pocketbook, a lady's pocketbook somewhere in the French Quarter. And they even got the pocketbook back before

---

[33] For further discussion see the analysis of differential sentencing, Chapter 5.

the policemen came, but when we got with him he didn't have no money, or nothing on him, you know, no pocketbook. The lady said he gave it back. The lady even told the police that we wasn't with him at the time that he snatched it. They said that they don't know whether we was in it or what, she said. But we wasn't with him when he snatched it.

Q: Okay, now. If they had already dropped you down to misdemeanor theft before you pleaded guilty, right—why didn't you go to trial on the misdemeanor theft?
A: Because I pleaded guilty . . .

Q: Well, why did you plead guilty?
A: Because the police said that they could have got us for accessory. In other words from what I understood, and I didn't know about the law then, but I understood after then when I found out when I pleaded guilty, that there's no such thing as accessory to that charge, we would have gone to trial. And, with which I didn't know at the moment. Anyway, when they did pick up the dude who did it, we was with him. He didn't have nothing on him, but still, they identified us. He pleaded guilty. And we was with him. So I don't know whether we was guilty or what.

*   *   *   *   *

A: He [the lawyer] explained all that to me—if you beat it, you know, you'll go loose. If you don't they can give you the max which is 6 months plus the $500 fine. But if you plead guilty, you'll get 60 days, you know. He already been with the judge. Sixty days.
Q: He had talked to the judge. . . .
A: Right. . . .

Q: And so, is that the reason you pled guilty?
A: That was one of the reasons, you know. . . .

Q: Okay, you said that that was one of the reasons. Any other reasons why you pled?
A: Well, uh, well, any reason cause I wasn't that sure if, you know, how, you know, I didn't know about the law. I didn't know about accessory. Uh, I told you about they had talked about the accessory.

Q: Well, did you know the guy that had ripped off this purse?
A: No, not until after—after we got picked up with him.

Q: Well, when you got picked up did you ask the cops what you got picked up for?
A: Yeah, and he told us.

Q: What did they tell you?

A: He told us simple robbery. He told me purse snatching. Well, I'm really—I'm learned about accessory and all this and I told the policeman, I said, "It don't take but one person to snatch a pocketbook, you know, and uh, and we wasn't with him. You can ask him." And the dude told him even before he threw us in the car. And he said, "Tell the judge that." The lady—they brought us down by Jackson Square where they paint themselves—it was one of those painted ladies that, uh, he snatched her pocketbook, and, uh—she even told him that she knew that we weren't within the 40 foot of her when he snatched the pocketbook—if we was anywhere, she said. So he still booked us for it, charged with—and I told him my rights about it only takes one person to snatch a pocketbook how could he charge three of us with it. You know. The one pleaded guilty, you know, and the lady identified him, so I asked him how could he charge us with it when we weren't nowhere around.

Q: Okay—
A: So that's when he charged me with resisting arrest.

Q: Let me ask you this—
A: I was just trying to stick up for my rights—

Q: But you thought it was a fair shake?
A: Right. Even though I didn't do it I thought it was a fair shake because if I would have got found guilty for it just for being with him I would have gotten the maximum.

Q: Do you think you would have been found guilty?
A: I don't know, you know, uh. If I could have got a decent lawyer, I doubt that I would—since this was my first offense and all that, you know.

The Achilles heel of plea-taking procedures is the fact that defendants can on their own or as the result of coaching by their attorneys answer all questions in a way that will be acceptable to the judge. In effect, the same desire for leniency that leads them to plead guilty can emasculate the effectiveness of the plea-taking procedures as a protection of defendants' interests. The majority (52 percent) of the defendants in our sample reported that their attorneys had advised them how to answer the plea-taking colloquy. Several defendants indicated that their attorneys had told them exactly what to say, and evidently these defendants did so without question, as illustrated below:

Delaware County:
(My public defender said), "Don't make any hassles. Say 'yes' where it says 'yes.' Whatever the sheet says, say 'yes.'"

New Orleans: Defendant #8
Q: Did he go over a written form with you? Your lawyer? The state lawyer?
A: No. The only thing he went over with me and he had me sign some paper that I'm pleading guilty. Yeah.

Q: Yeah? Did he read what was on that paper?
A: Yeah. He read it to me.

Q: Did you understand what was on the paper? Okay. Did he tell you how to answer those questions when the judge talked to you?
A: Yeah, he said that everything the judge would ask about how I would plead to.

New Orleans: Defendant #5
Q: Did your attorney talk to you about this ahead of time? Did he tell you about the rights the judge was going to read to you?
A: Well, he came, uh, he came to me with a piece of paper concerning my rights after I was sentenced, you know—no—it was before I was sentenced, but, it was more or less a plea bargain because, uh, you know, he said I want you to sign right here. Put your initials right here by each at the end of each question, you know, saying that you understand.

Several defendants said their attorneys stood next to them in court and told them what to say. Occasionally this arrangement went awry, as reported by a Virginia defendant. "On the third charge I pled not guilty because [my lawyer] was talking in my ear and I thought he said to plead not guilty. That blew their minds. Then I changed it to guilty."

While there is no way of completely protecting plea colloquies from ingenuine but acceptable answers, there are ways of reducing this vulnerability. Repeating and rephrasing questions; requiring more than simple "yes" or "no" answers; asking defendants to explain what a jury trial is before waiving their right to one; having the prosecutor read the state's version of the crime and then asking defendants to give their version; and other ways of going beyond a mere recitation of the plea litany prevent today's plea-taking procedure from being an empty legal ritual. On the other hand, the use of the plea-acceptance forms, with minimal additional questioning of the defendant; establishing the factual basis in ways designed to minimize the possibility of a discrepancy between what the defendant believes happened and what the state says happened; and the use of other measures designed to meet the mandate of appellate courts in a streamlined manner bring today's plea-taking close to being a new kind of "pious fraud."

Of course, the more determined the effort to make the plea acceptance meaningful the less efficient the guilty plea becomes. Delaware County's average time for taking felony pleas, for example, is four times that of Seattle, where judges rely more on the use of the plea-taking form. Also, in Delaware County there is an increased risk of having pleas rejected.

The state's perspective. While the expansion of the plea-taking procedures since 1966 has not benefited defendants as much as most reformers had hoped, it has come to be recognized as an important benefit to the state. A thorough colloquy does not necessarily reduce the probability of the defendant's appealing the plea [34] but it does reduce his chance of success. This point has not been lost on either prosecutors or judges. One Pennsylvania prosecutor reported that his office has devised a lengthy colloquy, which prosecutors ask of defense counsel. Motioning his hands as if driving nails into a coffin, he said the colloquy even asks for counsel's opinion as to whether the defendant's plea was knowing and voluntary.[35]

Several judges emphasized the importance they attach to using the colloquy to prevent reversals. Fortunately, for defendants and reformers who would have the plea-acceptance be as thorough as possible, there is here a happy coincidence of method in achieving a difference in goals. The greater the state's concern about making pleas reversal-proof, the more likely the colloquy is to be thorough and meaningful.

Summary of findings

• All felony-level judges in the six jurisdictions studied used some form of checklist to guide them at plea taking. But the checklists do not cover all the same issues among the six jurisdictions or even within them (except in two states where standardized plea taking

---

[34] Pleas to serious crimes are appealed almost routinely in some jurisdictions.

[35] Reacting to our finding that in Delaware County much of the plea-taking colloquy is done by defense counsel, this prosecutor expressed concern for such a practice. For one thing, because plea colloquies serve the function of "burying" the defendant he did not think counsel should be the one to do this. But, more importantly, he believes that counsel are increasingly recognizing the litigation value of being ineffective. In order to give their clients a basis for appeal some attorneys are deliberately being ineffective. Allowing counsel to run the plea colloquy increases their opportunity to build in an appeal on the basis of ineffective assistance.

forms are required) and do not guarantee that even constitutionally required queries will be made.

• The average time for accepting pleas for all cases combined is 7.8 minutes. Pleas to felony *charges* take twice as long as pleas to misdemeanor charges (9.9 minutes compared to 5.2 minutes). Pleas in felony *courts* take over three times longer than pleas in misdemeanor courts (8.9 minutes compared to 2.6 minutes).

• The six jurisdictions varied dramatically in the time spent in accepting pleas to felony charges (from 4.2 minutes to 18.2 minutes) and less dramatically in misdemeanor cases (from 1.7 minutes to 4.9 minutes—Delaware County excluded). No convincing explanation could be found for the dramatic differences among the jurisdictions in time spent in accepting pleas.

• At the time of entering their pleas defendants were usually (78 percent) addressed individually before the bench and the plea acceptance inquiry consisted of an oral colloquy (84 percent) sometimes (32 percent) supplemented by the submission of a written inquiry signed by the defendant.

• The defendants were usually told they had a right to a trial by jury (70 percent) and sometimes told of their rights to confront witnesses (44 percent) and remain silent (38 percent). In many cases (56 percent) it was noted that defense counsel had explained the defendants' rights to them. In most cases (73 percent) the defendants were asked if they understood the rights which they had waived.

• In most cases (69 percent) the defendants had the charges explained to them and were usually (59 percent) asked if they understood the charges. It was sometimes (34 percent) noted that defense counsel had explained the charges to their clients.

• Defendants were not always (48 percent) told of the maximum possible sentence; rarely (2 percent) notified that they were eligible for sentencing as habitual offenders; and rarely (4 percent) notified of any collateral consequences of their pleas.

• Defendants were usually (65 percent) asked if any threats or pressures had caused them to plead guilty. Sometimes (32 percent) they were asked if promises other than the plea agreement had been made. Usually (71 percent) the specific terms of any plea agreement were entered into the record.

• The method for establishing the factual basis that was most frequently reported by judges (40 percent) as the one they use is simply to ask the defendant if he committed the offense. This same method was found to be most frequently used in actual plea-takings observed (59 percent). This inquiry was supplemented in many cases by having the prosecutor show or report some evidence (48 percent) and by asking the defendant additional questions about the crime (36 percent).

• Defendants rarely (2 percent) entered equivocal pleas in which they pleaded guilty while maintaining their innocence. Half the judges said they would not accept such pleas.

• Overall, judges rarely (2 percent) rejected any guilty pleas.

• Interviews with nonrandom samples of defendants who had pleaded guilty suggest that most defendants (91 percent) had been told of the maximum sentence they might have received; and most (80 percent) said they understood what was said about the nature of the charges and the rights they waived. But some (20 percent) indicated they did not understand or only partially understood what was said. Most defendants (77 percent) said they felt they had to accept the plea agreement.

• Half the defendants reported that their attorneys advised them how to answer the questions at plea taking. In several cases the "advice" was to say "yes" to everything.

• A few defendants reported that the police had made promises which apparently did not become part of the required written statement of the plea agreement and were not fulfilled.

Conclusion

The reforms of the guilty plea acceptance procedures of the last decade and a half have succeeded in making pleas more intelligent and in assuring that defendants get the deals they thought they were going to get. Before their pleas are accepted the great majority of felony defendants have their constitutional right to trial by jury explained to them as well as the nature of the charges against them and the maximum possible sentence for which they are eligible. In addition, the terms of the plea agreements are made part of the record. Most defendants appear to understand the explanations of their rights and the charges against them. But a substantial minority of defendants apparently do not understand. Moreover, promises made by the police apparently do not get recorded in plea agreements and are not fulfilled.

The reforms have not made guilty pleas "voluntary" in the sense of being uncoerced or free from pressures or inducements. Virtually all defendants still plead guilty because of the inducements offered by the state. But, the reforms did not try to eliminate all inducements, only improper inducements such as the threat of violence or bribery and, in the hopes of two national commissions, the use of overcharging. The former two kinds of improper inducements do not appear to be a regular part of plea bargaining, but the latter two continue to be.

A factual basis for the guilty pleas is now established in the great majority of cases. But this does not guarantee the "accuracy" of the plea in the literal sense (for defendants are allowed to plead to fact patterns which do not accurately reflect their crimes); nor does it mean that innocent defendants are less likely to be wrongly convicted. Contrary to the hopes of some reformers the factual basis established at plea taking does not constitute a test of evidentiary strength. However, it does reinforce the informed nature of the plea.

In short, the expanded plea-taking procedures have made guilty pleas far more informed than they once were and have minimized the possibility of broken, misleading, or misconstrued promises. But they have left the coercive (induced) character of plea bargaining intact. They have not moved plea bargaining much closer to the trial procedure's determination of legal guilt. They do not constitute a means by which an independent third party weighs the evidence against some standard of legal proof. Reformers who had hoped that requiring judges to establish a factual basis for guilty pleas would make the guilty plea system approximate the more rigorous test of evidence that occurs at trial should take careful note of the only case of "wrongful" conviction *by guilty plea* that we have been able to find. The case serves as a reminder that the beyond-a-reasonable-doubt standard of our trial system is a high standard which is a long way from merely establishing some evidence that the defendant committed the crime.

The case involved five men who pleaded guilty to gang-raping a 42-year-old woman who allegedly was a "happy drunk" and willingly went with the men. The fact that the defendants received suspended sentences provoked a public outcry. This prompted the judge to order the defendants either to serve prison terms or stand trial. They chose the latter and were acquitted by a jury (which was not told of their earlier guilty pleas) (Associated Press, 1983).

The effectiveness of the plea-taking procedures is eroded by three countervailing factors: (1) Defendants are advised by their counsel and willingly agree to give acceptable answers to the litany of queries at plea taking because of their desire to secure the inducement offered by the state. (2) Judges are just as anxious as prosecutors and defense counsel to dispose of cases as quickly as possible. Hence they are subject to strong pressures to find pleas acceptable, which they almost always do. (3) Except in the occasional case of extraordinarily unusual plea agreements, judges are not in the position of second guessing the agreements worked out by prosecutors. To do so on a regular basis would require the judge to assess the evidentiary strength of the case as well as other tactical matters (such as using the defendant as an informer or for state's evidence) that fall within the province of the prosecutor. Hence, the judge's ability to protect the community's interest in seeing defendants sentenced "appropriately" is limited by his not knowing certain information that is a major determinant of what an "appropriate" disposition would be.

If innocent defendants choose to plead guilty today rather than risk a more severe penalty at trial, they will be better informed about their constitutional rights; about the nature of the charges against them; about the consequences of the plea; and about the terms of the agreement. There is a 50-50 chance they will not be allowed to plead guilty unless they stop asserting their innocence or facts at variance with the state's version of the crime. And there is an increasing chance that they will be unable to successfully attack their conviction on appeal. Thus the expanded plea-taking procedures have succeeded in bringing a certain kind of fairness to plea bargaining. But they have not altered the fundamental nature of securing dispositions by inducements nor have they remedied the institutional weakness of plea bargaining, the lack of the weighing of the evidence against a legal standard such as that which would be necessary to get a case to the jury.

Appendixes

Appendix A. Delaware County (Pa.) District Attorney's List of Cases Eligible for Diversion, 1976. NB: Robbery not included; Burglary only for non-dwelling; Also note: there must be no prior convictions for misdemeanors or felonies; no prior diversions; and no "bad" record of juvenile or summary offenses.

OFFENSES	ALWAYS OR NEARLY ALWAYS INCLUDED	INCLUDED ACCORDING TO INDIVIDUAL CASES	COMMENTS
Aiding Consummation of Crime X			
Aggravated A & D		X	Minor injury
A & B, Simple	X		
Attempt	X		
Bad Check	X		
Burglary		X	Only non-dwelling
Business practices, deceptive	X		
Conspiracy	X		When not accompanied by ineligible crime
Credit Cards	X		
Disorderly Conduct	X		
Drunkenness	X		
Endangering Another Person	X		
Exposure, indecent	X		
Failure to disperse	X		
False alarms	X		
False Reports	X		
Firearms, Uniforms Act		X	When not fired at living thing
Forgery		X	When restitution can be made
Harassment by Communication	X		
Hindering apprehension	X		
Impersonating Public Servant	X		
Keys, Master to M.V.	X		
Lewdness, open	X		
Loitering and prowling	X		
Minors, Corrupting		X	When not accompanied by ineligible crime
Misapplication entrusted funds		X	When restitution can be made
Mischief, Criminal	X		
Obscenity	X		
Possession instruments of Crime	X		
Prohibited offensive weapons	X		
Prostitution	X		When not accompanied by ineligible
Receiving stolen property	X		
Resisting Arrest	X		When not accompanied by ineligible crime
Retail Theft	X		
Riot		X	With minor consequence
Sexual Intercourse, vol. dev.	X		Consenting adults
Solicitation	X		
Terroristic Threats	X		
Theft by deception	X		
Theft, failure disposition funds	X		
Theft, unlawful taking	X		
Theft, lost, etc. property	X		
Theft of services	X		
Throwing missile into car	X		
Trespass, criminal, etc.	X		
Unauth. use M.V.	X		
Drugs, poss. marijuana	X		Less than 240 grams

139

Appendix A. Delaware County (Pa.) District Attorney's List of Cases Eligible for Diversion, 1976. NB: Robbery not included; Burglary only for non-dwelling; Also note: there must be no prior convictions for misdemeanors or felonies; no prior diversions; and no "bad" record of juvenile or summary offenses.— Continued

OFFENSES	ALWAYS OR NEARLY ALWAYS INCLUDED	INCLUDED ACCORDING TO INDIVIDUAL CASES	COMMENTS
Poss. hashish	X		Less than 64 grams
Possession	X		Not hard drugs
Public assistance fraud	X		When restitution can be made
Leaving scene accident	X		
Turning off lights	X		
Operating Under Influence		X	When restitution has been made, etc.
Sales tax, non payment, etc.		X	When restitution can be made

Appendix B   Federal Rules of Criminal Procedure: 1966 and 1975 Texts Compared

1966 Text of Rule 11
(as amended Feb. 28, 1966, eff. July 1, 1966)

A defendant may plead not guilty, guilty or, with the consent of the court, *nolo contendere*. The court may refuse to accept a plea of guilty, and shall not accept such plea or plea of *nolo contendere* without first addressing the defendant personally and determining that the plea is made voluntarily with understanding of the nature of the charge and the consequences of the plea. If a defendant refuses to plead or if the court refuses to accept a plea of guilty or if a defendant corporation fails to appear, the court shall enter a plea of not guilty. The court shall not enter a judgment upon a plea of guilty unless it is satisfied that there is a factual basis for the plea.

1975 Text of Rule 11
(as amended Apr. 22, 1974, eff. Dec. 1, 1975; July 31, 1975, eff. Aug. 1 and Dec. 1, 1975)

(a) *Alternatives.* A defendant may plead not guilty, guilty, or nolo contendere. If a defendant refuses to plead or if a defendant corporation fails to appear, the court shall enter a plea of not guilty.

(b) *Nolo contendere.* A defendant may plead nolo contendere only with the consent of the court. Such a plea shall be accepted by the court only after due consideration of the views of the parties and the interest of the public in the effective administration of justice.

(c) *Advice to Defendant.* Before accepting a plea of guilty of nolo contendere, the court must address the defendant personally in open court and inform him of, and determine that he understands, the following:

(1) the nature of the charge to which the plea is offered, the mandatory minimum penalty provided by law, if any, and the maximum possible penalty provided by law; and

(2) if the defendant is not represented by an attorney, that he has the right to be represented by an attorney at every stage of the proceding against him, and if necessary, one will be appointed to represent him; and

(3) that he has the right to plead not guilty or to persist in that plea if it has already been made, and that he has the right to be tried by a jury and at that trial has the right to the assistance of counsel, the right to confront and cross-examine witnesses against him, and the right not to be compelled to incriminate himself; and

(4) that if he pleads guilty or nolo contendere there will not be a further trial of any kind, so that by pleading guilty or nolo contendere he waives the right to a trial; and

(5) that if he pleads guilty or nolo contendere, the court may ask him questions about the offense to which has pleaded, and if he answers these questions under oath, on the record, and in the presence of counsel, his answers may later be used against him in a prosecution for perjury or false statement.

(d) *Insuring that the plea is voluntary.* The court shall not accept a plea of guilty or nolo contendere without first, by addressing the defendant personally in open court, determining that the plea is voluntary and not the result of threats or of promises apart from a plea agreement. The court shall also inquire as to whether the defendant's willingness to plead guilty or nolo contendere results from prior discussions between the attorney for the government and the defendant or his attorney.

(e) *Plea agreement procedure*

(1) *In General.* The attorney for the government and the attorney for the defendant or the defendant when acting pro se may engage in discussions with a view toward reaching an agreement that, upon the entering of a plea of guilty or nolo contendere to a charged offense or to a lesser or related offense, the attorney for the government will do any of the following:

(a) move for dismissal of other charges; or

(b) make a recommendation, or agree not to oppose the defendant's request for a particular sentence, with the understanding the such recommendation or request shall not be binding upon the court; or

(c) agrees that a specific sentence is the appropriate disposition of the case.

The court shall not participate in any such discussions.

(2) *Notice of Such Agreement.* If a plea agreement has been reached by the parties, the court shall, on the record, require the disclosure of the agreement in open court or, on a showing of good cause, in camera, at the time the plea is offered. Thereupon the court may accept or reject the agreement, or may defer its decision as to the acceptance or rejection until there has been an opportunity to consider the presentence report.

(3) *Acceptance of Plea Agreement.* If the court accepts the plea agreement, the court shall inform the defendant that it will embody in the judgment and sentence the disposition provided for in the plea agreement.

(4) *Rejection of a Plea Agreement.* If the court rejects the plea agreement, the court shall, on the record, inform the parties of this fact, advise the defendant personally in open court or, on a showing of good cause, in camera, that the court is not bound by the plea agreement, afford the defendant the opportunity to then withdraw his plea, and advise the defendant that if he persists in his guilty plea or plea of nolo contendere the disposition of the case may be less favorable to the defendant than that contemplated by the plea agreement.

(5) *Time of Plea Agreement Procedure.* Except for good cause shown, notification to the court of the existence of a plea agreement shall be given at the arraignment or at such other time, prior to trial, as may be fixed by the court.

(6) *Inadmissibility of Pleas, Offers, and Related Statements.* Except as otherwise provided in this paragraph, evidence of a plea of guilty, later withdrawn or a plea of nolo contendere, or of an offer to plead guilty or nolo contendereto the crime charged or any other crime, or of statements made in connection with, and relevant to, any of the foregoing pleas or offers, is not admissible in any civil or criminal proceeding against the person who made the plea or offer. However, evidence of a statement made in connection with, and relevant to, a plea of guilty, later withdrawn, a plea of nolo contendere, or an offer to plead guilty or nolo contendere to the crime charged or any other crime, is admissible in a criminal proceeding for perjury or false statement if the statement was made by the defendant under oath, on the record, and in the presence of counsel.

(f) *Determining Accuracy of Plea.* Notwithstanding the acceptance of a plea of guilty, the court should not enter a judgment upon such plea without making such inquiry as shall satisfy it that there is a factual basis for the plea.

(g) *Record of Proceedings.* A verbatim record of the proceedings at which the defendant enters a plea shall be made and, if there is a plea of guilty or nolo contendere, the record shall include, without limitation, the court's advice to the defendant, the inquiry into the voluntariness of the plea including any plea agreement, and the inquiry into the accuracy of a guilty plea.

Appendix C   Arizona Rules of Criminal Procedure

RULE 17.1 RULES OF CRIMINAL PROCEDURE
V. PLEAS OF GUILTY AND NO CONTEST
RULE 17. PLEAS OF GUILTY AND NO CONTEST
Rule 17.1 PLEADING BY DEFENDANT

a. Personal Appearance; Appropriate Court. A plea of guilty or no contest may be accepted by a court having jurisdiction to try the offense. Such plea shall be accepted only when made by the defendant personally in open court, unless the defendant is a corporation, in which case the plea may be entered by counsel or a corporate officer.

b. Voluntary and Intelligent Plea. A plea of guilty or no contest may be accepted only if voluntarily and intelligently made. Except for pleas to minor traffic offenses, the procedures of Rule 17.2, 17.3, and 17.4 shall be utilized by all courts to assure the voluntariness and intelligence of the plea.

c. Pleas of No Contest. A plea of no contest may be accepted only after due consideration of the views of the parties and the interest of the public in the effective administration of justice.

d. Record. A verbatim record shall be made of all plea proceedings occurring in a court of record.

Rule 17.2 Duty of court to advise defendant of his rights and of the consequences of pleading guilty or no contest

Before accepting a plea of guilty or no contest, the court shall address the defendant personally in open court, informing him of and determining that he understands the following:

a. The nature of the charge to which the plea is offered;

b. The nature and reange of possible sentence for the offense to which the plea is offered, including any special conditions regarding sentence, parole, or commutation imposed by statute;

c. The constitutional rights which he forgoes by pleading guilty or no contest, including his right to counsel if he is not represented by counsel; and

d. His right to plead not guilty.

Rule 17.3 Duty of Court to determine voluntariness and intelligence of the plea

Before accepting a plea of guilty or no contest, the court shall address the defendant personally in open court and determine that he wishes to forgo the constitutional rights of which he has been advised, that his plea is voluntary and not the result of force, threats or promises (other than a plea agreement). The trial court may at that time determine that there is a factual basis for the plea or the determination may be deferred to the time for judgment of guilt as provided by Rule 26.2(c).

Amended May 7, 1975, effective Aug. 1, 1975.

Rule 17.4 Plea negotiations and agreements

a. Plea Negotiations. The parties may negotiate concerning, and reach an agreement on, any aspect of the disposition of the case. The court shall not participate in any such negotiation.

b. Plea Agreement. The terms of a plea agreement shall be reduced to writing and signed by the defendant, his counsel, if any, and the prosecutor. An agreement may be revoked by any party prior to its acceptance by the court.

c. Determining the Accuracy of the Agreement and the Voluntariness and Intelligence of the Plea. The parties shall file the agreement with the court, which shall address the defendant personally and determine that he understands and agrees to its terms, that the written document contains all the terms of the agreement, and that the plea is entered in conformance with Rules 17.2 and 17.3.

d. Acceptance of Plea. After making such determinations, the court shall either accept or reject the tendered negotiated plea. The court shall not be bound by any provision in the plea agreement regarding the sentence or the term and conditions of probation to be imposed, if, after accepting the agreement and reviewing a presentence report, it rejects the provision as inappropriate.

e. Rejection of Plea. If an agreement or any provision thereof is rejected by the court, it shall give the defendant an opportunity to withdraw his plea, advising him that if he permits his plea to stand the disposition of the case may be less favorable to him than that contemplated by the agreement.

f. Disclosure and Confidentiality. When a plea agreement or any term thereof is accepted, the agreement or such term shall become part of the record. However, if no agreement is reached, or if the agreement is revoked, rejected by the court, or withdrawn or if the judgment is later vacated or reversed, neither the plea discussion nor any resulting agreement, plea or judgment, nor statements made at a hearing on the plea, shall be admissible against the defendant in any criminal or civil action or administrative procceding.

g. Automatic Change of Judge. If a plea is withdrawn after submission of the pre-sentence report, the judge, upon request of the defendant, shall disqualify himself, but no additional disqualification of judges under this rule shall be permitted.

Form XVIII.   Plea agreement

[CAPTION]

PLEA AGREEMENT

The state of Arizona and the defendant hereby agree to the following disposition of this case:

Plea: The defendant agrees to plead guilty/no contest to:

Terms: On the following understandings, terms and conditions:

1. That the defendant will receive a sentence no greater than —————————————————————— and no less than ————————————— and consistent with the following additional terms: ———————————

2. That the following charges are dismissed, or if not yet filed, shall not be brought against the defendant. ————————————

3. That this agreement, unless rejected or withdrawn, serves to amend the complaint, indictment, or information to charge the offense to which the defendant pleads, without the filing of any additional pleading. If the plea is rejected or withdrawn the original charges are automatically reinstated.

4. If the defendant is charged with a felony, that he hereby gives up his right to a preliminary hearing or other probable cause determination on the charges to which he pleads. In the event the court rejects the plea, or the defendant withdraws the plea, the defendant hereby gives up his right to a preliminary hearing or other probable cause determination on the original charges.

5. Unless this plea is rejected or withdrawn, that the defendant hereby gives up any and all motions, defenses, objections or requests which he has made or raised, or could assert hereafter, to the court's entry of judgment against him and imposition of a sentence upon him consistent with this agreement.

6. That if after accepting this agreement the court concludes that any of its provisions regarding the sentence or the term and conditions of probation are inappropriate, it can reject the plea, giving the defendant an opportunity to withdraw the plea.

I have read and understand the above. I have discussed the case and my constitutional rights with my lawyer. I understand that by pleading (guilty) (no contest) I will be giving up my right to a trial by jury, to confront, cross-examine, and compel the attendance of witnesses, and my privilege against self-incrimination. I agree to enter my plea as indicated above on the terms and conditions set forth herein. I fully understand that if, as part of this plea bargain, I am granted probation by the court, the terms and conditions thereof are subject to modification at any time during the period of probation in the event that I violate any written condition of my probation.

—————————————————   —————————————————
Date   Defendant

I have discussed this case with my client in detail and advised him of his constitutional rights and all possible defenses. I believe that the plea and disposition set forth herein are appropriate under the facts of this case. I concur in the entry of the plea as indicated above and on the terms and conditions set forth herein.

—————————————————   —————————————————
Date   Defense Counsel

I have reviewed this matter and concur that the plea and disposition set forth herein are appropriate and are in the interest of justice.

Appendix C   Arizona Rules of Criminal Procedure (continued)

Date _____   Prosecutor _____

Form XIX. Guilty plea checklist

[CAPTION]
GUILTY PLEA PROCEEDING

The defendant personally appearing before me, I have ascertained the following facts, noting each by initialing it.

Judge's
Initial

_____ 1. That the defendant understands the nature of the charges against him ————————

_____ 2. That the defendant understands the range of possible sentence for the offenses charged, from a suspended sentence to a maximum of ———————— and that the mandatory minimum (if any) is ————

_____ 3. That the defendant understands the following constitutional rights which he gives up by pleading guilty:

_____   (a) His right to trial by jury, if any.

_____   (b) His right to the assistance of an attorney at all stages of the proceeding, and to an appointed attorney, to be furnished free of charge, if he cannot afford one.

_____   (c) His right to confront the witnesses against him and to cross-examine them as to the truthfulness of their testimony.

_____   (d) His right to present evidence on his own behalf, and to have the state compel witnesses of his choosing to appear and testify.

_____   (e) His right to remain silent and to be presumed innocent until proven guilty beyond a reasonable doubt.

_____ 4. That the defendant wishes to give up the constitutional rights of which he has been advised.

_____ 5. That there exists a basis in fact for believing the defendant guilty of the offenses charged.

_____ 6. That the defendant and the prosecutor have entered into a plea agreement and that the defendant understands and consents to its terms.

_____ 7. That the plea is voluntary and not the result of force, threats or promises other than a plea agreement.

On the basis of these findings, I conclude that the defendant knowingly, voluntarily and intelligently pleads guilty to the above charges, and accept his plea.

Date _____   Judge _____

CERTIFICATION BY DEFENDANT

I certify that the judge personally advised me of the matters noted above, that I understand the constitutional rights that I am giving up by pleading guilty, and that I desire to plead guilty to the charges stated.

Defense Counsel, if any _____   Defendant _____

Appendix D Washington Superior Court Criminal Rules

RULE 4.2
PLEAS

(a) Types. A. Defendant may plead not guilty, not guilty by reason of insanity or guilty.

(b) Multiple Offenses. Where the indictment or information charges two or more offenses in separate counts the defendant shall plead separately to each.

(c) Pleading Insanity. When it is desired to interpose the defense of insanity or mental irresponsibility on behalf of one charged with a crime the defendant, his counsel or other person authorized by law to appear and act for him, shall at the time of pleading to the information or indictment file a plea in writing in addition to the plea or pleas required or permitted by other laws than this setting up (1) his insanity or mental irresponsibility at the time of the commission of the crime charged, and (2) whether the insanity or mental irresponsibility still exists, or (3) whether the defendant has become sane or mentally responsible between the time of the commission of the crime and the time of the trial. The plea may be interposed at any time thereafter, before the submission of the cause to the jury if it be proven that the insanity or mental irresponsibility of the defendant at the time of the crime was not before known to any person authorized to interpose a plea.

(d) Voluntariness. The court shall not accept a plea of guilty, without first determining that it is made voluntarily, competently and with an understanding of the nature of the charge and the consequences of the plea. The court shall not enter a judgment upon a plea of guilty unless it is satisfied that there is a factual basis for the plea.

(e) Agreements. If a plea of guilty is based upon an agreement between the defendant and the prosecuting attorney, such agreement must be made a part of the record at the time the plea is entered. No agreement shall be made which specifies what action the judge shall take on or pursuant to the plea or which attempts to control the exercise of his discretion, and the court shall so advise the defendant.

(f) Withdrawal of Plea. The court shall allow a defendant to withdraw his plea of guilty whenever it appears that the withdrawal is necessary to correct a manifest injustice.

(g) Written Statement. A written statement of the defendant in substantially the form set forth below shall be filed on a plea of guilty.

SUPERIOR COURT OF WASHINGTON FOR ——————————— COUNTY

STATE OF WASHINGTON,
Plaintiff,
vs.
————————
Defendant.

No. ————
STATEMENT OF
DEFENDANT ON
PLEA OF GUILTY

1. My true name is ————————————.

2. My age is ————.

3. My lawyer is ————————————.

4. The court has told me that I am charged with the crime of ————————————, the maximum sentence for which is ————.

5. The court has told me that:

(a) I have the right to have counsel (a lawyer), and that if I cannot afford to pay for counsel, one will be provided at no expense to me.

(b) I have the right to a trial by jury.

(c) I have the right to hear and question witnesses who testify against me.

(d) I have the right to have witnesses testify for me. These witnesses can be made to appear at no expense to me.

(e) The charge must be proven beyond a reasonable doubt.

6. I plead ———————— to the crime of ———————— as charged in the information, a copy of which I have received.

7. I make this plea freely and voluntarily.

8. No one has threatened harm of any kind to me or to any other person to cause me to make this plea.

9. No person has made promises of any kind to cause me to enter this plea except as set forth in this statement.

10. I have been told the Prosecuting Attorney will take the following action and make the following recommendation to the court: ————

_____

11. I have been told and fully understand that the court does not have to follow the Prosecuting Attorney's recommendation as to sentence. The court is completely free to give me any sentence it sees fit no matter what the Prosecuting Attorney recommends.

12. The court has told me that if I am sentenced to prison the Judge must sentence me to the maximum term required by the law, which in this case is ————. The minimum term of sentence is set by the Board of Prison Terms and Paroles. The Judge and Prosecuting Attorney may recommend a minimum sentence to the Board but the Board does not have to follow their recommendation. I have been further advised that the crime with which I am charged carries a mandatory minimum of ———— years. (If not applicable, this sentence shall be stricken and initialed by the defendant and the judge.)

13. The court has asked me to state briefly in my own words what I did that resulted in my being charged with the crime in the information. This is my statement: _____

_____

14. I have read or have had read to me all of the numbered sections above (1 through 14) and have received a copy of "Statement of Defendant on Plea of Guilty." I have no further questions to ask of the court.

The above statement was read by or read to the defendant and signed by the defendant in the presence of his attorney, ————————, Prosecuting Attorney ————————, and the undersigned Judge in open court.

DATED THIS ———— day of ————, 19—.

_____
Judge

Appendix E   Texas (Veron's Annotated) Code of Criminal Procedure

Art. 1.13 [10a] Waiver of trial by jury

The defendant in a criminal prosecution for any offense classified as a felony less than capital shall have the right, upon entering a plea, to waive the right of trial by jury, conditioned, however, that such waiver must be made in person by the defendant in writing in open court with the consent and approval of the court, and the attorney representing the State. The consent and approval by the court shall be entered of record on the minutes of the court, and the consent and approval of the attorney representing the State shall be in writing, signed by him, and filed in the papers of the cause before the defendant enters his plea. Before a defendant who has no attorney can agree to waive the jury, the court must appoint an attorney to represent him.

Acts 1965, 59th Leg., vol. 2, p. 317, ch. 722.

Art. 1.15. [12] [21] [22] Jury in felony

No person can be convicted of a felony except upon the verdict of a jury duly rendered and recorded, unless in felony cases less than capital, the defendant, upon entering a plea, has in open court in person waived his right of trial by jury in writing in accordance with Articles 1.13 and 1.14; provided, however, that it shall be necessary for the state to introduce evidence into the record showing the guilt of the defendant and said evidence shall be accepted by the court as the basis for its judgment and in no event shall a person charged be convicted upon his plea without sufficient evidence to support the same. The evidence may be stipulated if the defendant in such case consents in writing, in open court, to waive the appearance, confrontation, and the cross-examination of witnesses, and further consents either to an oral stipulation of the evidence and testimony or to the introduction of testimony by affidavits, written statements of witnesses, and any other documentary evidence in support of the judgment of the court. Such waiver and consent must be approved by the court in writing, and be filed in the file of the papers of the cause.

Acts 1965, 59th Leg., vol. 2, p. 317, ch. 722. Amended by Acts 1967, 60th Leg., p. 1733, ch. 659, § 2, eff. Aug. 28, 1967; Acts 1971, 62nd Leg., p. 3028, ch. 996, § 1, eff. June 15, 1971; Atts 1973, 63rd Leg., p. 1127, ch. 426, art. 3, § 5 eff. June 14, 1973.

Art. 26.13. [501] [565] [554] Plea of guilty

If the defendant pleads guilty, or enters a plea of nolo contendere he shall be admonished by the court of the consequences; and neither of such pleas shall be received unless it plainly appears that he is sane, and is uninfluenced by any consideration of fear, or by any persuasion, or delusive hope of pardon, prompting him to confess his guilt. Acts 1965, 59th Leg., vol. 2, p. 317, ch. 722.

Art. 26.14. [502] [566] [555] Jury on plea of guilty

Where a defendant in a case of felony persists in pleading guilty or in entering a plea of nolo contendere, if the punishment is not absolutely fixed by law, a jury shall be impaneled to assess the punishment and evidence may be heard to enable them to decide thereupon, unless the defendant in accordance with Articles 1.13 or 37.07 shall have waived his right to trial by jury. Acts 1965, 59th Leg., vol. 2, p. 317, ch. 722.

Art. 27.14. [518] [582] [571] Plea of guilty or nolo contendere in misdemeanor

A plea of "guilty" or a plea of "nolo contendere" in a misdemeanor case may be made either by the defendant or his counsel in open court; in such case, the defendant or his counsel may waive a jury, and the punishment may be assessed by the court either upon or without evidence, at the discretion of the defendant. In a misdemeanor case arising out of a moving traffic violation for which the maximum possible punishment is by fine only, payment of a fine, or an amount accepted by the court constitutes a finding of guilty in open court, as though a plea of nolo contendere had been entered by the defendant. Acts 1965, 59th Leg., vol. 2, p. 317, ch. 722.

Appendix F   Virginia Rules of Criminal Procedure and Norfolk Plea Agreement Form

Rule 3A:11. Pleas.

(a) Permissible Pleas. An accused may plead not guilty, guilty, or in a misdemeanor case, *nolo contendere*. The court may refuse to accept a plea of guilty. A plea of *nolo contendere* may be made only with the court's consent.

(b) Entering of pleas. In a felony case a plea of guilty may be entered only by the accused after being advised by counsel, except that a corporation may enter a plea of guilty through its counsel or agent. In a misdemeanor case a plea of guilty or *nolo contendere* may be entered by the accused or his counsel. The court shall enter a plea of guilty if a plea of guilty is not accepted or a plea of *nolo contendere* is not consented to, or if the accused refuses to plead, or if the accused fails to appear for trial of a misdemeanor.

(c) Determining Voluntariness of Pleas of Guilty or Nolo Contendere. A court of record shall not accept a plea of guilty or *nolo contendere* without first determing that the plea is made voluntarily with an understanding of the nature of the charge and the consequences of the plea.

(d) Plea Agreement Procedure.

(1) The attorney for the Commonwealth and the attorney for the defendant or the defendant when acting *pro se* may engage in discussions with a view toward reaching an agreement that, upon entry by the defendant of a plea of guilty, or in a misdemeanor case a plea of *nolo contendere*, to a charged offense, or to a lesser or related offense, the attorney for the Commonwealth will do any of the following:

(A) Move for dismissal of other charges;

(B) Make a recommendation for a particular sentence;

(C) Agree not to oppose the defendant's request for a particular sentence; or

(D) Agree that a specific sentence is the appropriate disposition of the case.

In any such discussions under this Rule, the court shall not participate.

(2) If a plea agreement has been reached by the parties, it shall, in every felony case, be reduced to writing, signed by the attorney for the Commonwealth, the defendant, and his attorney, if any, and, in every case, presented to the court. The court shall require the disclosure of the agreement in open court or, upon a showing of good cause, *in camera*, at the time the plea is offered. The court may accept or reject the agreement, or may defer its decision as to the acceptance or rejection until there has been an opportunity to consider a presentence report.

(3) If the court accepts the plea agreement, the court shall inform the defendant that it will embody in its judgment and sentence the disposition provided for in the agreement.

(4) If the court rejects the plea agreement, the court shall inform the parties of this fact, and advise the defendant personally in open court or, on a showing of good cause, *in camera*, that the court will not accept the plea agreement. Thereupon, neither party shall be bound by the plea agreement. The court shall afford the defendant the opportunity to withdraw his plea of guilty or plea of *nolo contendere* and advise the defendant that, if he persists in his plea, the disposition of the case may be less favorable to the defendant than that contemplated by the plea agreement.

(5) Except as otherwise provided by law, evidence of a plea of guilty later withdrawn, of a plea of *nolo contendere*, or of an offer to plead guilty or *nolo contendere* to the crime charged, or any other crime, or of statements made in connection with and relevant to any of the foregoing pleas or offers, is not admissible in the case-in-chief in any civil or criminal proceeding against the person who made the plea or offer. But evidence of a statement made in connection with and relevant to a plea of guilty, later withdrawn, a plea of *nolo contendere*, or an offer to plead guilty or *nolo contendere* to the crime charged or to any other crime, is admissible in any criminal proceeding for perjury or false statement, if the statement was made by the defendant under oath and on the record.

Virginia Supreme Court, Rules of Court
Form 8. Suggested Questions to Be Put by the Court to an Accused Who Has Pleaded Guilty
(Rule 3A:11)

Before accepting your plea of guilty, I will ask you certain questions. If you do not understand any question, please ask me to explain it to you.

1. What is your full name, and what is your age?

2. Are you the person charged in the indictment [information or warrant] with the commission of an offense?

3. Do you fully understand the charge against you?

4. Are you entering this plea of guilty freely and voluntarily?

5. Are you entering the plea of guilty because you are, in fact, guilty of the crime charged?

6. Do you understand that by pleading guilty, you are *not* entitled to a trial by jury?

7. Has anyone connected with the State, such as the police or the Commonwealth's attorney, or any other official, in any manner threatened you or forced you to enter this plea of guilty?

8. The Commonwealth's attorney may have advised your attorney or you what punishment he will recommend if you plead guilty. Has anyone made you any other promise of leniency?

9. Do you understand that in imposing punishment I am not bound by any agreement between you and your counsel and the Commonwealth's attorney, and I need not follow any recommendation of the Commonwealth's attorney?

10. (a) If I accept your plea of guilty, the punishment could be imprisonment for not more than . . . . . . years, a fine of not more than $. . . . ., or both; that is to say, you may be imprisoned or you may be fined, or you may be imprisoned and fined.* Do you understand the punishment that may be imposed?

(b) If you have been previously sentenced to confinement in a penitentiary, additional punishment can be imposed under the mulitiple offender statutes. Do you understand this?

11. Have you had ample time to discuss with your attorney any possible defense you may have to this charge?

12. Have you discussed with your attorney whether you should plead not guilty or guilty?

13. After the discussion did you decide for yourself that you should plead guilty?

14. Are you entirely satisfied with the services of the attorney who was appointed to represent you in this matter?

15. Do you understand that by pleading guilty you may waive any right to appeal from the decision of this court?

16. Do you understand all the questions I have asked you?

---

* The language should be appropriately changed to describe the maximum sentence that can be imposed.

Note: The court may wish to ask other questions—e.g., a question about the accused's education.

VIRGINIA:

           IN THE CIRCUIT COURT OF THE CITY OF NORFOLK

COMMONWEALTH OF VIRGINIA

VS.

On indictment(s)/warrant(s) charging:

1. _____

2. _____

3. _____

4. _____

5. _____

              PLEA AGREEMENT MEMORANDUM

     Pursuant to the provisions of Rule 3A:11(d), the parties
in interest present this memorandum of their plea agreement.

     Upon the Defendant's plea(s) of guilty to the offense(s) set
forth below, the Commonwealth will recommend the following
dispositions to the Court:

_____

_____

_____

SEEN & AGREED

_____
Defendant

_____
Attorney for the Defendant

_____
Attorney for the Commonwealth

Appendix G Pennsylvania Rules of Criminal Procedure and Delaware County Guilty Plea—Statement of Defendant Form

Rule 819. Pleas and Plea Agreements

(a) Generally. A defendant may plead not guilty, guilty, or with the consent of the court, *nolo contendere*. The judge may refuse to accept a plea of guilty, and shall not accept it unless he determines after inquiry of the defendant that the plea is voluntarily and understandingly made. Such inquiry shall appear on the record.

(b) Plea Agreements.

(1) The trial judge shall not participate in the plea negotiations preceding an agreement.

(2) When counsel for both sides have arrived at a plea agreement they shall state on the record in open court, in the presence of the defendant, the terms of the agreement. Thereupon the judge shall conduct an inquiry of the defendant on the record to determine whether he understands and concurs in the agreement.

(3) If the judge is satisfied that the plea is understandingly and voluntarily tendered, he may accept the plea. If thereafter the judge decides not to concur in the plea agreement, he shall permit the defendant to withdraw his plea.

Comment: The purpose of paragraph (a) is to codify the requirement that the judge, on the record, ascertain from the defendant that the guilty plea is voluntarily and understandingly tendered. Recent court decisions have indicated that this is the preferred practice but have not made the requirement mandatory. See Commonwealth ex rel. West v. Rundle, 237 A.2d 196, 428 Pa. 102 (1968); Commonwealth v. Belgrave, 285 A.2d 448, 445 Pa. 311 (1971).

It is difficult to formulate a comprehensive list of questions a judge must ask of a defendant in determining whether the judge should accept the plea of guilty. Court decisions constantly add areas to be encompassed in determining whether the defendant understands the full impact and consequences of his plea, but is nevertheless willing to enter that plea. It is recommended, however, that at a minmum the judge ask questions to elicit the following information:

(1) Does the defendant understand the nature of the charges to which he is pleading guilty?

(2) Is there a factual basis for the plea?

(3) Does the defendant understand that he has the right to trial by jury?

(4) Does the defendant understand that he is presumed innocent until he is found guilty?

(5) Is the defendant aware of the permissible range of sentence and/or fines for the offenses charged?

(6) Is the defendant aware that the judge is not bound by the terms of any plea agreement tendered unless the judge accepts such agreement? Many, though not all, of the areas to be covered by such questions are set forth in a footnote to the Court's opinion in Commonwealth v. Martin, 445 Pa. 49, 54–56, 282 A.2d 241 (1971), in which the colloquy conducted by the trial judge is cited with approval. As to the requirement that the judge ascertain that there is a factual basis for the plea, see Commonwealth v. Maddox, 450 Pa. 406, 300 A.2d 503 (1973), and Commonwealth v. Bernard Jackson, 450 Pa. 417, 299 A.2d 209 (1973).

It is advisable that the judge should conduct the examination of the defendant. However, paragraph (a) does not prevent defense counsel or the attorney for the Commonwealth from conducting part or all of the examination of the defendant, as permitted by the judge.

Paragraph (b) is intended to alter the process of what is commonly known as "plea bargaining" so as to make it a matter of public record and to insure that it does not involve prejudicing or compromising the independent position of the judge. See Commonwealth v. Alvarado, 442 Pa. 516, 276 A.2d 526 (1971); Santobello v. New York, 404 U.S. 257, 92 S.Ct. 495, 30 L.Ed.2d 427 (1971); Commonwealth v. Wilkins, 277 A2d 341, 442 Pa. 524 (1971); Commonwealth v. Evans, 252 A.2d 689. 434 Pa. 52 (1969); cf. Commonwealth v. Scoleri, 202 A.2d 521, 415 Pa. 218 (1964); A.B.A. Minimum Standards Relating to Pleas of Guilty, § 3.3(a), at 71–74 (Approved Draft 1968); President's Commission on Law Enforcement and the Administration of Justice, "The Challenge of Crime in a Free Society" 134 (1967).

The "terms" of the plea agreement, referred to in subparagraph (b)(2) frequently, involve the attorney for the Commonwealth—in exchange for the defendant's plea of guilty, and perhaps for the defendant's promise to cooperate with law enforcement officials—promising such concessions as a reduction of a charge to a less serious offense, or the dropping of one or more additional charges or a recommendation of a lenient sentence, or a combination of these. In any event, Paragraph (b) is intended to assure that all terms of the quid pro quo are openly acknowledged for the court's assessment.

Paragraph (b)(3) requires the judge to permit the defendant to withdraw a plea the judge has accepted when the judge is unable to comply with a plea agreement on which the plea was based. See Rule 320.

When a plea agreement has been negotiated, there must be an inquiry in order to determine whether the plea is made voluntarily and understandingly. However, the terms of the plea agreement should be stated in the record and it should be made clear that the defendant understands the nature and effect of the agreement.

Adopted June 30, 1964, effective Jan. 1, 1965; amended Nov. 25, 1968, effective Feb. 3, 1969; amended Oct. 3, 1972, effective in 30 days; amended and effective March 28, 1973.

Appendix G   Pennsylvania Rules of Criminal Procedure and Delaware County Guilty Plea— Statement of Defendant Form (continued)

I understand that I could be sentenced to the maximum penalty set forth above for each charge to which I am pleading guilty and that the possible sentence resulting from consecutive sentences on the above charges is

I state that in pleading guilty I am admitting that I committed the crimes charged and admitting my guilt of these charges, that the guilty plea will appear on my record as a conviction, that the above possible penalties and sentences have been explained to me, and I understand them, that I make this statement of my own free will, that it is voluntary, that I have not been threatened, forced or pressured to enter a plea of guilty nor received any promise of the sentence I will receive in return for entering a plea, that I have read this statement and discussed it with my attorney and I fully understand my constitutional rights.

I also understand that if I am on parole or probation that this guilty plea might well result in the revocation of that probation or parole.

I also state that I have fully discussed my case with my attorney, that we have discussed the possible defenses to the charges; that my attorney is fully familiar with the facts of my case. I acknowledge that I have reviewed the factual basis for these crimes with my attorney and that in pleading guilty I admit committing the acts alleged. My attorney has advised me that the law presumes me to be innocent, and that the burden is upon the Commonwealth to prove me guilty beyond a reasonable doubt. I am satisfied that he is fully prepared to represent me and that he has advised me that he is ready to defend me to the above charges if I did not enter a guilty plea.

I further state that I am not now suffering from any mental illness or the effects of any narcotics or drugs or alcoholic beverages.

_____
Defendant

I, _____, Esquire, Attorney for _____, hereby state that I have advised my client of the foregoing rights; that the client has discussed them with me and believe that he understands them; that I am prepared to try this case, and that defendant understands what he is doing in entering the above guilty plea.

_____
Attorney for Defendant

Note: To Assistant District Attorney—have this form filled in and signed by the defendant. If defendant signs it and understands what he is doing, have his attorney sign it before the guilty plea is taken, read this form into record, then enter this statement as an exhibit with record papers.

156

Appendix G Pennsylvania Rules of Criminal Procedure and Delaware County Guilty Plea—
Statement of Defendant Form (continued)

Delware County, Pa.
GUILTY PLEA—STATEMENT OF DEFENDANT (REVISED 2/17/76

COMMONWEALTH OF PENNSYLVANIA VS. ————————————————————

T ————, INFORMATION NO(S). ————, ———————— SESSION 19

CHARGES:

I, ————————, hereby state that I am —— years old, that I have been advised by my Attorney, ————————, Esquire, of all the following rights:

1. My right to have my case tried by a judge and a jury of 12 people from the community and of my right to challenge the jury and/or the jury panel for cause shown and of my right to participate in the selection of those 12 jurors, and that verdict of guilty by said jury would have to be unanimous.

2. My privilege to have my case heard by a judge without a jury by leave of court, wherein the judge would be the sole fact finder.

3. My right to take an appeal, with the assistance of counsel provided free without any cost to myself, from a verdict of the jury, or from a verdict of a Court without a jury.

4. My right to file motions for a new trial and to have an attorney provided free without any cost to myself, to file and argue such motions.

5. My right to refuse to testify and to stand mute, and I have been further advised that if I refuse to testify, such refusal will not prejudice me in any way.

6. My right to confront and hear any witness who will give evidence against me and through counsel to cross-examine all witnesses.

7. My right to waive (i.e. not to have) a trial by a jury and/or by a judge and to enter a plea of guilty. That I have limited appeal rights if the plea is accepted and sentence imposed. That is, I may only appeal the legality of sentence, jurisdiction of this Court and the involuntariness of the plea.

8. My right to take the above limited appeal with the assistance of counsel free, without any cost to myself, from the judgment of sentence.

I further state that I have been advised of the nature of the crime(s) of which I am charged, that

(a) ———————— is a felony/misdemeanor and that the penalty as provided in 18 P.S. —— is ————————

(b) ———————— is a felony/misdemeanor and that the penalty as provided in 18 P.S. —— is ————————

(c) ———————— is a felony/misdemeanor and that the penalty as provided in 18 P.S. —— is ————————

(d) ———————— is a felony/misdemeanor and that the penalty as provided in 18 P.S. —— is ————————

(e) ———————— is a felony/misdemeanor and that the penalty as provided in 18 P.S. —— is ————————

157

CRIMINAL DISTRICT COURT

PARISH OF ORLEANS
STATE OF LOUISIANA
SECTION A

Judge Charles R. Ward

STATE OF LOUISIANA   No. _____
vs

_____   Via. _____

WAIVER OF CONSTITUTIONAL RIGHTS
PLEA OF GUILTY

(1) I,_____ have been informed of and understand the charges against me in this case. I know that I have been charged with the crime of_____
_____ : _____

(2) It is my intention to plead guilty to the crime of_____
_____ : _____

(3) The acts constituting the offense to which I am pleading guilty have been explained to me as well as the fact that for this crime the maximum possible sentence which could be imposed on me is_____
_____ : _____

(4) I understand that by entering this plea of guilty I am waiving my right to trial, and my right to appeal if I were found guilty by trial. I also understand that I am waiving my right to confront witnesses who may appear and testify against me, and my right to cross examine those witnesses. I know that I am waiving the right I have to compulsory process of the court to require witnesses to appear and testify for my defense. I further understand that I am waiving my privilege against self incrimination and by pleading guilty I am in fact incriminating myself.   : _____

(5) I have not been forced, threatened, or intimidated, and I desire to enter this plea of guilty and it is by my own free will and is my voluntary act. I understand that no promises which may have been made to me by anyone, other than as set forth on the reverse of this document in the plea bargain, if any, are binding or enforceable and I rely on no other promise.   : _____

(6) I understand that I have a right to have competent counsel represent me at trial, and if I were unable to pay for Counsel the Court would appoint competent counsel to represent me, both for trial and for appeal, if desired, if I were convicted by trial, but I am fully satisfied with the handling of my case by my attorney and the way in which he has represented me.   : _____

_____   _____
Date   Defendant

                                     _____
                                     Attorney for Defendant

Appendix H   New Orleans, LA.: Seven Alternative Procedures for Accepting Guilty Pleas Used by Local Judges (continued)

PLEA BARGAIN AGREEMENT

If the defendant enters a plea of guilty to _____

_____

_____

_____

_____ ,

The State of Louisiana, acting through its duly authorized representative, the Assistant

District Attorney, will _____

_____

_____

_____

_____

_____

New Orleans, Louisiana, this _____ day of _____, 19_____

_____   _____
Assistant District Attorney   Attorney for Defendant

159

CRIMINAL DISTRICT COURT

PARISH OF ORLEANS

STATE OF LOUISIANA

SECTION C

Judge Jerome M. Winsberg

STATE OF LOUISIANA   No. _____

vs

_____   Vio. _____

PLEA OF GUILTY

I, _____, on my plea of GUILTY

to the crime of _____

have been informed and understand the charge to which I am pleading guilty. _____

I understand that I have a right to trial and if convicted a right to appeal and by entering

a plea of guilty in this case I am waiving my rights to trial and appeal. _____

The acts constituting the offense to which I am pleading guilty have been explained to

me as well as the fact that for this crime I could possibly receive a sentence of _____

_____

_____

_____

I am entering a plea of guilty to this crime because I am, in fact, guilty of this crime. _____

I have not been forced, threatened or intimidated into making this plea, nor has anyone

made me any promises in order that I enter a plea. _____

I understand that my attorney has participated in plea-bargaining on my behalf with my

knowledge and permission. _____

I am fully satisfied with the handling of my case by my attorney and the way in which he

has represented me. _____

_____
Defendant

_____   _____
Judge   Attorney for Defendant

                                                              _____
                                                              Date

160

CRIMINAL DISTRICT COURT
PARISH OF ORLEAN
STATE OF LOUISIANA
SECTION "D"

JUDGE: FRANK A. MARULLO, JR.

STATE OF LOUISIANA
VS

NO. _____

_____

VIO: _____

PLEA OF GUILTY

I, _____, defendant in the above case informed the Court that I wanted to plead guilty and do plead guilty to the crime of _____ and have been informed and understand the charge to which I am pleading guilty.   (_____)

The acts which make up the crime to which I am pleading have been explained to me as well as the fact that for this crime I could possibly receive a sentence of _____ (_____)

I understand that in pleading guilty in this matter I waive the following rights:

(1) To a trial by either a judge or a jury and that further the right to a trial by judge extends until the first witness is sworn, and the right to a trial by a jury extends until the first juror is sworn, and if convicted the right to an appeal.. Please specify: Judge trial or Jury Trial   (_____)

(2) To face and cross-examine the witnesses who accuse me of the crime charged.   (_____)

(3) The privilege against self-incrimination or having to take the stand myself and testify.   (_____)

(4) To have the Court compel my witnesses to appear and testify.   (_____)

I am entering a plea of guilty to this crime because I am, in fact, guilty of this crime. I have not been forced, threatened or intimidated into making this plea, nor has anyone made me any promises in order that I enter a plea. I am fully satisfied with the handling of my case by my attorney and the way in which he has represented me. I am satisfied with the way the Court has handled this matter. (_____)

_____
DEFENDANT

JUDGE _____

_____
ATTORNEY FOR DEFENDANT

DATE: _____

NOTE: Defendant is to place his initials in the blocks provided for same.
Defendant is to block out Judge Trial or Jury Trial as it applies.

161

CRIMINAL DISTRICT COURT
PARISH OF ORLEANS
STATE OF LOUISIANA
SECTION E
Judge Rudolph F. Becker, III

STATE OF LOUISIANA   No. _____
vs

_____   Vio. _____

WAIVER OF CONSTITUTIONAL RIGHTS
PLEA OF GUILTY

I, _____, before my plea of GUILTY
to the crime of _____
have been informed and understand the charge to which I am pleading guilty. _____

I understand that I have a right to trial and if convicted a right to appeal and by entering
a plea of guilty in this case I am waiving my rights to trial and appeal. _____

The acts constituting the offense to which I am pleading guilty have been explained to
me as well as the fact that for this crime I could possibly receive a sentence of _____
_____

I understand that by pleading guilty that I am waiving my rights to confront and cross-
examine the witnesses who accuse me of the crime charged, and to compulsory process
of the court to require witnesses to appear and testify for me.

I am entering a plea of guilty to this crime because I am, in fact, guilty of this crime.

I have not been forced, threatened or intimidated into making this plea.

I am fully satisfied with the handling of my case by my attorney and the way in which
he has represented me.

I further understand that I am waiving my privilege against self incrimination and
by pleading guilty I am in fact incriminating myself.

I understand that if I elected to have a trial I have a right to have competent counsel
to represent me at trial, and if I were unable to pay for Counsel the Court would appoint
competent counsel to represent me, but by entering the plea of guilty I am waiving these
rights.

If a plea bargain agreement has been made I understand that no other promises which
may have been made to me other than as set out hereinabove in this plea bargain are
enforceable or binding.

_____   _____
Date   Defendant

_____   _____
Judge   Attorney for Defendant

The Judge has addressed me personally as to all of these matters and he has given
me the opportunity to make any statement I desire.

                                  _____
                                  Defendant

<u>Judge Shea</u>

1. Right to trial and free appeal if convicted.

2. Waives right to trial and free appeal by entering plea of guilty.

3. By pleading guilty waives right against self incrimination.

4. Waives right to confront and cross-examine witnesses and call witnesses on defendant's behalf.

5. Waives right to object to any evidence offered by the State.

6. (If applicable, withdraw all motions previously filed.)

7. Waives right to object to the composition and the way the jury will be selected to try case.

8. Inform defendant of maximum sentence (Parole - Probation - Hard Labor).

9. Defendant has not been forced, threatened or coerced into entering plea of guilty and states he is voluntarily entering the plea of guilty because he is in fact guilty as charged.

_____
(DEFENDANT'S SIGNATURE)

DATE:_____

WITNESS:_____

163

CRIMINAL DISTRICT COURT
PARISH OF ORLEANS
STATE OF LOUISIANA
SECTION H

Judge Bernard J. Bagert, Sr.

STATE OF LOUISIANA   No. _____

vs

_____   Vio. _____

PLEA OF GUILTY

I, _____, on my plea of GUILTY
to the crime of _____
have been informed and understand the charge to which I am pleading guilty. _____

I understand that I have a right to trial and if convicted a right to appeal and by entering
a plea of guilty in this case I am waiving my rights to trial and appeal. _____

The acts constituting the offense to which I am pleading guilty have been explained to
me as well as the fact that for this crime I could possibly receive a sentence of _____
_____
_____
_____

I am entering a plea of guilty to this crime because I am, in fact, guilty of this crime. _____

I have not been forced, threatened or intimidated into making this plea, nor has anyone
made me any promises in order that I enter a plea. _____

I am fully satisfied with the handling of my case by my attorney and the way in which he
has represented me. _____

_____
Defendant

_____   _____
Judge   Attorney for Defendant

_____
Date

CRIMINAL DISTRICT COURT
PARISH OF ORLEANS
STATE OF LOUISIANA
SECTION J

Judge Alvin V. Oser

STATE OF LOUISIANA   No. _____

vs

_____   Vio. _____

WAIVER OF CONSTITUTIONAL RIGHTS
PLEA OF GUILTY

I, _____, on my plea of GUILTY

to the crime of _____

have been informed and understand the charge to which I am pleading guilty. _____

I understand that I have a right to trial and if convicted a right to appeal and by entering
a plea of guilty in this case I am waiving my rights to trial and appeal. _____

The acts constituting the offense to which I am pleading guilty have been explained to
me as well as the fact that for this crime I could possibly receive a sentence of _____

_____

I understand that by pleading guilty that I am waiving my rights to confront and cross-
examine the witnesses who accuse me of the crime charged, to compulsory process of the
court to require witnesses to appear and testify for me, the privilege against self-incrimination or having to take the stand myself and testify, and to have preliminary pleadings
filed and heard on my behalf. _____

I am entering a plea of guilty to this crime because I am, in fact, guilty of this crime. _____
I have not been forced, threatened or intimidated into making this plea. _____
I am fully satisfied with the handling of my case by my attorney and the way in which he
has represented me. _____

_____   _____
Date   Defendant

_____   _____
Judge   Attorney for Defendant

The Judge has addressed me personally as to all of these matters and he has given me
the opportunity to make any statement I desire.

                                 _____
                                 Defendant

165

Appendix I   Seattle (Washington) District Court: Statement of Defendant on Plea of Guilty

IN THE SEATTLE DISTRICT COURT - KING COUNTY - STATE OF WASHINGTON
* * * * * * * * * * * * * * * *

STATE OF WASHINGTON,   )   NO: _____
                         Plaintiff,
                                (STATEMENT OF DEFENDANT
            vs   on
)   PLEA OF GUILTY.
_____
                        Defendant.
* * * * * * * * * * * * * * * *

1. My true name is _____ 2. Date of Birth:_____

3. My lawyer is _____ 4. The court has told me I am charged by complaint / citation and notice, with the crime of

_____felony / gross misdemeanor / misdemeanor

orally amended to ._____ gross misdemeanor / misdemeanor the maximum sentence for which is:

                        Not more than one year   / 90 days in jail,

Not more than $1000   / $500 fine, or both fine and imprisonment.
5. The court has told me that (a) I have the right to counsel (a lawyer) and that if I cannot afford to pay for counsel, one will be provided at no expense to me. (b) I have the right to trial by jury. (c) I have the right to hear and question witnesses who testify against me. (d) I have the right to have witnesses testify for me. These witnesses can be made to appear at no expense to me. (e) The charge must be proved beyond a reasonable doubt. (f) I have the right to appeal. (g) By entering a plea of Guilty, I give up the rights listed in (b) through (f) and I will be sentenced on the basis of my plea.

6. I plead _____ to the crime of _____ as charged in the complaint - oral complaint - citation and notice, a copy of which I have received. 7. I make this plea freely and voluntarily. 8. No one has threatened harm of any kind to me or to any person to cause me to make this plea. 9. No person has made promises of any kind to cause me to enter this plea except as set forth in this statement. 10. I have been told by my attorney that the prosecuting attorney will take the following action and make the following recommendation to the court
_____.

11. I have been told and fully understand that the court does not have to follow the prosecuting attorney's recommendation as to sentence. The court is completely free to give me any sentence it sees fit no matter what the prosecuting attorney recommends. 12. I understand that if I am on probation or parole, a plea of GUILTY to the present charge will be sufficient grounds for a judge or the parole board to revoke my probation or parole. 13. The court has asked me to state briefly in my own words what I did that resulted in my being charged with the crime in the complaint - oral complaint - citation and notice. This is my statement
.

14. I have read or have had read to me all of the numbered sections above (1 to 13), and have received a copy of this statement entitled "Statement of Defendant on Plea of Guilty". I have no further questions to ask of the court

                    _____
                            Defendant.

The foregoing statement was read by or read to the defendant and signed by the defendant in the presence of his attorney

and the Prosecuting Attorney   _____

and the undersigned Judge in open court. _____
DATED THIS_____ day of _____ 197 .

                        _____
                              JUDGE.

References

Administrative Office of Pennsylvania Courts (1975), *Sixth Annual Report on Judicial Case Volume*. Philadelphia: Author.

Administrative Office of the United States Courts (1963), *Federal Offenders in the United States District Courts*. Washington: Government Printing Office.

Administrative Office of the United States Courts (1973), *Federal Offenders in the United States Courts*. Washington: Government Printing Office.

Alaska Judicial Council (1977), *Interim Report on the Elimination of Plea Bargaining*. Anchorage: Author, mimeo.

Alschuler, Albert W. (1968) "The Prosecutor's Role in Plea Bargaining," 36 *University of Chicago Law Review* 50.

Alschuler, Albert W. (1976) "The Trial Judge's Role in Plea Bargaining, Part I," 76 *Columbia Law Review* 1059.

Alschuler, Albert W. (1979) "Plea Bargaining and Its History," 13 *Law and Society Review* 211.

American Bar Association (1968) *Standards Relating to Pleas of Guilty*. New York: Institute for Judicial Administration.

American Bar Association (1971) *Standards Relating to Prosecution Function and the Defense Function*. New York: Institute for Judicial Administration.

American Bar Association (1972) *Standards Relating to the Function of the Trial Judge*. New York: Institute for Judicial Administration.

American Bar Association (1980) "Pleas of Guilty," In American Bar Association, *Standards for Criminal Justice*. Boston: Little, Brown.

American Law Institute (1975) *A Model Code of Pre-Arrangement Procedure*. Philadelphia: Author.

Arcuri, Alan F. (1973) "Police Perception of Plea Bargaining: A Preliminary Inquiry," 1 *Journal of Police Science and Administration* 93.

Arcuri, Alan F. (1977) "Criminal Justice: A Police Perspective," 2 *Criminal Justice Review* 15.

Associated Press (1983) "5 Cleared Of Rape After Guilty Pleas," *The Washington Post* (June 18) A11.

Baker, Newman (1933) "The Prosecutor-Initial of Prosecution," 23 *Journal of Criminal Law and Criminology* 770.

Baldwin, John and Michael McConville (1977) *Negotiated Justice: Pressures to Plead Guilty*. London: Martin Robinson.

Berger, Moise (1976) "The Case Against *Plea-Bargaining,*" 62 *American Bar Association Journal* 621.

Bernstein, Ilene N., Edward Kick, Jan T. Leung, and Barbara Schulz (1977) "Charge Reduction: An Intermediary Stage in The Process of Labelling Criminal Defendants," 56 *Social Forces* 362.

Blumberg, Abraham S. (1967) "Lawyers with Convictions," in A.S. Blumberg (ed.) *The Scales of Justice*. Aldine.

Bond, James E. (1981) *Plea Bargaining and Guilty Pleas*. New York: Clark Boardman.

Breitel, Charles D. (1960) "Controls in Criminal Law Enforcement," 27 *University of Chicago Law Review* 427.

Britt, David W. and Kinley Larntz (1980) "The Effects of *Plea Bargaining* On the Disposition of Person and Property Crimes: A Research Note," in S.E. Fienberg and A.J. Reiss, Jr. (eds.) *Indications of Crime and Criminal Justice: Quantitative Studies*. Washington: Government Printing Office.

Brosi, Kathleen B. (1979) *A Cross-City Comparison of Felony Case Process*. Washington: Institute for Law and Social Research.

Brunk, Conrad G. (1978) "The Problem of Voluntariness and Coercion In The Negotiated Plea." Presented at the Special National Workshop on *Plea Bargaining,* French Lick, Indiana, June.

Brunk, Conrad G. (1979) "The Problem of Voluntariness and Coercion In The Negotiated Plea," 13 *Law and Society Review* 527.

Burk, Peter J. and Austin T. Turk (1978) "Analyzing Postarrest Dispositions," in N. Johnston and L. D. Savitz *Justice and Conviction*. New York: John Wiley.

California District Attorneys Association (1974) *Uniform Crime Charging Standards*. Los Angeles: Author.

California Legislature, Joint Committee for Revision of the Penal Code (1982) *Plea Bargaining: Final Report*. Sacramento: Author.

Carter, Leif (1972) *The Limits of Order*. Lexington: D. C. Health.

Casper, Jonathan, David Brereton, and David Neal (1982) *The Implementation of the California Determinate Sentence Law*. National Institute of Justice. Washington, D.C.

Chambliss, William J. and Robert B. Seidman (1971) *Law, Order and Power*. Reading: Addison-Wesley.

Church, Thomas W. (1976) "Plea Bargaining, Concessions and the Courts: Analysis of A Quasi-Experiment," 10 *Law and Society Review* 377.

Church, Thomas (1981) *Examining Local Legal Culture*. Washington: Government Printing Office.

Cole, George F. (1975) *The American System of Criminal Justice*. North Scituate: Duxbury Press.

Connecticut Justice Commission (1980) *Plea Negotiation Practices in the Con-*

necticut Judicial District Courts. Hartford: Author.

Constant, A. (1971) "Determination of Sentence in Criminal Cases: The Guilty Plea and Related Factors." Unpublished paper on file in the University of Texas Law School Library.

Davis, Kenneth Culp (1969) *Discretionary Justice: A Preliminary Inquiry.* Baton Rouge: Louisiana State University Press.

Davis, Samuel M. (1972) "The Guilty Plea Process: Exploring the Issues of Voluntariness and Accuracy," 6 *Valparaiso University Law Review* 111.

Emery, L. A. (1913) "The Nolle Prosequi in Criminal Cases," 6 *Maine Law Review* 199.

Enker, Arnold (1967) "Perspectives on Plea Bargaining," in President's Commission on Law Enforcement and Administration of Justice. *The Courts.* Washington: Government Printing Office.

Epstein, David and David T. Austern (1975) *Uniform Rules of Criminal Procedure: Comparison and Analysis.* Washington: American Bar Association.

Farr, Bill (1978) "Van de Kamp Will Not Use Courts' *Plea Bargaining* Rule," in California District Attorney's Association, *Prosecutor's Brief* (Jan.–Feb.) 18.

Feeley, Malcolm M. (1978) "Perspectives on Plea Bargaining," 13 *Law and Society Review* 199.

Florida Law Review (1970) "Accepting the Indigent Defendant's Waiver of Counsel and Plea of Guilty," 22 *Florida Law Review* 453.

Forst, Brian, Judith Lucianovic and Sara J. Cox (1977) *What Happens After Arrest? A Court Perspective of Police Operations in the District of Columbia.* Washington: Institute for Law and Social Research.

Gallagher, Kathleen (1974) "Judicial Participation In Plea Bargaining: A Search for New Standards," 9 *Harvard Civil Rights-Civil Liberties Law Review* 29.

Goldstein, Abrahm S. and Marvin Marcus (1977) "The Myth of Judicial Supervision in Three 'Inquisitorial' Systems: France, Italy, and Germany," 87 *Yale Law Review* 240.

Graham, Kenneth and Leon Letwin (1971), "The Preliminary Hearing in Los Angeles: Some Field Findings and Legal-Policy Observations," 18 *UCLA Law Review* 635.

Greenwood, Peter W., Sorrel Wildhorn, E.C. Poggio, M.J. Strumwasser and P. De Leon (1973), *Prosecution of Adult Felony Defendants In Los Angeles County: A Policy Perspective.* Santa Monica: Rand.

Gross, Avrum M. (1978) "Plea Bargaining: The Alaska Experiment." Presented at the Special National Workshop on *Plea Bargaining,* French Lick, Indiana, June.

Hall, Jerome (1935) *Theft, Law and Society.* Boston: Little, Brown.

Heuman, Milton (1975) "A Note on Plea Bargaining and Case Pressure," 9 *Law and Society Review* 515.

Horney, Julie (1980) "Plea Bargaining Decision Factors," In A.W. Cohen and B. Ward (eds.). *Improving Management In Criminal Justice.* Beverly Hills: Sage.

Illinois Crime Survey (1929) *The Illinois Crime Survey.* Chicago: Illinois Association for Criminal Justice.

Institute of Criminal Law and Procedure (1978) *The Study of Plea Bargaining in Local Jurisdictions: A Self Study Manual.* Washington: U.S. Department of Justice.

Iowa Law Review (1975) "Note: The Elimination of *Plea Bargaining* In Black Hawk County, A Case Study," 60 *Iowa Law Review* 1063.

Jacob, Herbert and James Eisenstein (1977) *Felony Justice.* Waltham: Little Brown.

Jacoby, Joan E. (1975) "Case Evaluation: Quantifying Prosecutorial Policy," 58 *Judicature* 10.

Jacoby, Joan E. (1980a) *The American Prosecutor: A Search for Identity.* Lexington: D.C. Heath.

Jacoby, Joan E. (1980b) "Project on Prosecutorial Decision Making—A National Study," unpublished report to the National Institute of Justice, Washington, D.C.

Jacoby, Joan E. (1980c) *Prosecutorial Decision Making Selected Readings.* Washington: Bureau of Social Science Research.

Katz, Lewis, Laurence B. Litwin and Richard H. Bamberger (1972) *Justice Is The Crime.* Cleveland: Case Western Reserve University Press.

Keppel, William J. (1978) "Plea Bargaining in Hennepin County: Present Practice and a Proposal for Change," *Hennepin Lawyer* (Jan.–Feb.) 8.

Kerstetter, Wayne A. (1979a) "Police Participation in Structured Plea Negotiations," *Law and Policy Quarterly.*

Kerstetter, Wayne A. (1979b) "Police Perceptions of Influence in the Criminal Case Disposition Process," *Journal of Criminal Justice.*

Kerstetter, Wayne and Ann Heinz (1979) *Pretrial Settlement Conference: An Evaluation Report.* Washington: Government Printing Office.

Kiernan, Laura A. (1981) "Judge Finds Key Witness In Contempt: D.C. Man Refuses Order to Testify In Robbery Trial," *The Washington Post (February 10) B1.*

Kipnis, Kenneth (1976) "Criminal Justice and the Negotiated Plea," 86 *Ethics* (2) 93.

Klein, John F. (1976) *Let's Make a Deal.* Lexington: Lexington Books.

La Goy, Stephen P., J.J. Senna and L.J. Siegel (1976) "An Empirical Study of Information Usage for Prosecutorial Decision Making in Plea Negotiations," 13 *American Criminal Law Review* 435.

La Goy, Stephen P., Frederick A. Hussey and John A. Kramer (1979) "The Prosecutorial Function and Its Relation to Determinate Sentencing Structures," in W.F. McDonald (ed.) *The Prosecutor.* Beverly Hills: Sage.

Landis, William M. (1974) "Legality and Reality: Some Evidence on Criminal Procedure," 3 *Journal of Legal Studies* 287.

McDonald, William F. (1977) "Victimless Crimes: A Description of Offenders and Their Prosecution In the District of Columbia," Washington: Institute for Law and Social Research.

McDonald, William F. (1979) "The Prosecutor's Domain," in W.F. McDonald (ed.). *The Prosecutor.* Beverly Hills: Sage.

McDonald, William F., Henry H. Rossman, and James A. Cramer (1979) "The Prosecutor's *Plea Bargaining* Decisions," in *The Prosecutor* W.F. McDonald (ed.) Beverly Hills: Sage.

McDonald, William F., James A. Cramer and Henry H. Rossman (1980) "Prosecutorial Bluffing and the Case Against Plea Bargaining," in W.F. McDonald and James A. Cramer (eds.) *Plea Bargaining.* Lexington: D.C. Heath.

McDonald, William F. with Henry H. Rossman and J.A. Cramer (1981) *Police Prosecutor Relations in the United States.* Washington: National Institute of Justice.

McIntyre, Donald M. (1968) "A Study of Judicial Dominance in the Charging Process," 59 *Journal of Criminal Law Criminology and Police Science* 463.

McIntyre, Donald and Ray Nimmer (1973) "Evaluation of Cook County State's Attorney's Office—Felony Review Project." Report on file with the American Bar Foundation, Chicago, Illinois.

Mather, Lynn M. (1974) "The Outsider In the Courtroom: An Alternative Role for the Defense," in H. Jacob (ed.) *The Potential for Reform of Criminal Justice.* Beverly Hills: Sage.

Mather, Lynn M. (1979) *Plea Bargaining or Trial?* Lexington: D.C. Heath.

Menninger, Karl (1964) *The Theory of Psychoanalytic Technique.* New York: Harper and Row.

Merrill, W. Jay, M.N. Milks and Marr Sendrow (1973) *Case Screening and Selected Case Processing In Prosecutors' Offices.* Washington: Government Printing Office.

Mileski, Maureen (1971) "Courtroom Encounters: An Observation Study of A Lower Criminal Court," 5 *Law and Society Review* 473.

Miller, Frank W. (1969) *Prosecution: The Decision to Charge a Suspect with a Crime.* Boston: Little, Brown.

Miller, Herbert S. (1970) "Criminal Law Reform in Oregon," 6 *Willamette Law Journal* 357.

Miller, Herbert S., William F. McDonald and James A. Cramer (1978) *Plea Bargaining In the United States.* Washington: Government Printing Office.

Miller, Justin (1927) "The Compromise of Criminal Cases," 1 *Southern California Law Review* 1.

Mills, J. (1971) "I Have Nothing To Do With Justice," *Life* (March 12) 56.

Missouri Association for Criminal Justice (1926) *The Missouri Crime Survey.* New York: MacMillan.

Moley, Raymond (1929) *Politics and Criminal Prosecution.* New York: Minton, Balch.

National Advisory Commission on Criminal Justice Standards and Goals (1973) *Courts.* Washington: Government Printing Office.

National Center for Prosecution Management (1972) *First Annual Report of the National Center for Prosecution Management.* Mimeograph, National District Attorneys Association, Chicago, Illinois.

National Conference of Commissioners on Uniform State Laws (1974) *Uniform Rules of Criminal Procedure.* St. Paul: West.

National District Attorneys Association (undated) *Screening of Criminal Cases.* Chicago: Author.

National District Attorneys Association (1977) *National Prosecution Standards.* Chicago: Author.

Newman, Donald J. (1956) "Pleading Guilty for Considerations: A Study of Bargain Justice," 46 *Journal of Criminal Law, Criminology, and Police Science* 780.

Newman, Donald J. (1966) *Conviction: The Determination of Guilt or Innocence Without Trial.* Boston: Little, Brown.

Neubauer, David W. (1974) *Criminal Justice in Middle America.* Morristown: General Learning Corp.

Ohlin, Lloyd E. and Frank J. Remington (1958) "Sentencing Structure: Its Effect Upon Systems for The Administration of Criminal Justice," 23 *Law and Contemporary Problems* 495.

Oklahoma Administrative Office of the Judiciary (1976) *Report on the Judiciary.* Oklahoma City: State of Oklahoma.

Packer, Herbert L. (1968) *The Limits of the Criminal Sanction,* Stanford: Stanford University Press.

Parnas, Raymond I. and Riley J. Atkins (1978) "Abolishing Plea Bargaining: A Proposal," 14 *Criminal Law Bulletin* 101.

President's Commission on Law Enforcement and Administration of Justice (1967a) *The Challenge of Crime in a Free Society.* Washington: Government Printing Office.

President's Commission on Law Enforcement and the Administration of Justice (1967b) *The Courts.* Washington: Government Printing Office.

Pound, Rosoe and Felix Frankfurter (1922) *Criminal Justice in Cleveland.* Cleveland: The Cleveland Foundation.

Robertson, John A. (1974) *Rough Justice: Perspectives on Lower Criminal Courts.* Boston: Little, Brown.

Rhodes, William (1978) *Plea Bargaining: Who Gains? Who Loses?* Washington: Institute for Law and Social Research.

Rosett, Arthur and D.R. Cressey (1976) *Justice by Consent.* Philadelphia: J.B. Lippincott.

Rubinstein, Michael and Terri White (1979a) *"Plea Bargaining:* Can Alaska Live Without It?" 62 *Judicature* 266.

Rubinstein, Michael L. and Teresa J. White (1979b) "Alaska's Ban on *Plea Bargaining,"* 13 *Law and Society Review* 367.

Rubinstein, Michael L. and Teresa J. White (1980) "Alaska's Ban on *Plea Bargaining,"* in W.F. McDonald and J.A. Cramer (eds.) *Plea Bargaining.* Lexington: Lexington Books.

Savitz, Leonard (1975) "Early Rejection of Flawed Arrests From the Criminal Justice System: A Case Study," in E. Viano (ed.) *Criminal Justice Research.* Lexington: Lexington Books.

Skoler, Daniel L. (1978) *Government Structuring of Criminal Justice Services: Organizing the Non-System.* Washington: Government Printing Office.

Skolnick, Jerome (1967) "Social Control in the Adversary System," 11 *Journal of Conflict Resolution* 52.

Sudnow, David (1965) "Normal Crimes: Sociological Features of the Penal Code in a Public Defender's Office," 12 *Social Problems* 255.

Tappan, Paul (1960) *Crime, Justice and Corrections.* New York: McGraw Hill.

Thomssen, Carol L. and P.J. Falowski (1979) "Plea Bargaining in Minnesota." Minnesota Statistical Analysis Center (March).

Times-Picayune (1974) "D.A. Refusal of Charges Said 46 Pct.," cited by Neubauer and Cole, "Court Reform: A Political Analysis," in R. Wheeler and

H. Whitcomb (eds.) *Judicial Administration.* Englewood Cliffs, N.J.: Prentice Hall.

Trammell, George W. III (1969) "Control of System Policy and Practice by the Office of District Attorney in Brooklyn and Los Angeles," 5 *The Prosecutor* 242.

United States Bureau of the Census (1978) *State and Local Prosecution and Civil Attorney Systems.* Washington: Government Printing Office.

United States Department of Justice (1939) *The Attorney General's Survey of Release Procedures.* Washington: Government Printing Office.

United States National Commission on Law Observance and Enforcement (1931) *Report on Prosecution.* Washington: Government Printing Office.

University of California (1975) "Plea Bargaining: Structure and Process." Unpublished report from the College of Engineering, Berkeley, to the Alameda County District Attorney.

University of Chicago Law Review (1964) "Note: Official Inducements to Plead Guilty: Suggested Morals For A Marketplace," 32 *University of Chicago Law Review* 167.

Utz, Pamela J. (1978) *Settling the Facts.* Lexington: Lexington Books.

Utz, Pamela J. (1979) "Two Models of Prosecutorial Professionalism," in W.F. McDonald (ed.) *The Prosecutor.* Beverly Hills: Sage.

Vera Institute of Justice (1977) *Felony Arrests: Their Prosecution and Disposition In New York City's Courts.* New York: Author.

Vetri, Dominick R. (1964) "Guilty Pleas Bargaining: Compromises by Prosecutors to Secure Guilty Pleas," 112 *University of Pennsylvania Law Review* 865.

Washington University Law Quarterly (1966) "The Trial Judge's Satisfaction as to The Factual Basis of Guilty Pleas," *Washington University Law Journal* (June) 306.

Washington, State of (1976) *Judicial Administration In The Courts.* Olympia: Supreme Court, Office of Administration of the Courts.

Weintraub, Lloyd and Tough (1941) "Lesser Pleas Considered," 32 *Journal of Criminal Law and Criminology.* 566.

Wildhorn, Sorrel, Marvin Lavin, Anthony Pascal (1976) *Indicators of Justice: Measuring the Performance of Prosecution, Defense, and Court Agencies Involved In Felony Proceedings.* Santa Monica: Rand.

Wilkins, Leslie T., J.M. Kress, D.M. Gottfredson, J.C. Calpin and A.M. Gelman (1978) *Sentencing Guidelines: Structuring Judicial Discretion.* Washington: Government Printing Office.

Williams, Kristen M. (1976) "The Effects of Victim Characteristics on the Disposition of Violent Crimes," in W.F. McDonald (ed.) *Criminal Justice and the Victim.* Beverly Hills: Sage.

Yale Law Journal (1956) "Note: The Influence of the Defendant's Plea on Judicial Determination of Sentence," 66 *Yale Law Journal* 204.

Yale Law Journal (1972) "Note: Restructuring the Plea Bargain," 82 *Yale Law Journal* 286.

☆ U. S. GOVERNMENT PRINTING OFFICE : 1985 461–539/34515